Markets, Market Culture
and Popular Protest
in Eighteenth-Century
Britain and Ireland

Markets, Market Culture and Popular Protest in Eighteenth-Century Britain and Ireland

edited by

ADRIAN RANDALL

and

ANDREW CHARLESWORTH

LIVERPOOL UNIVERSITY PRESS

Published by
LIVERPOOL UNIVERSITY PRESS
Senate House
Liverpool
L69 3BX

British Library Cataloguing-in-Publication Data
A British Library CIP Record is available
ISBN 0-85323-690-9 (*cased*)
ISBN 0-85323-700-X (*paper*)

Typeset by Wilmaset Limited, Birkenhead, Wirral
Printed and bound in Great Britain by
Page Bros (Norwich) Ltd

CONTENTS

Contributors   vii

Preface   ix

1. Markets, Market Culture and Popular Protest in Eighteenth-
   Century Britain and Ireland
   Adrian Randall, Andrew Charlesworth, Richard Sheldon and
   David Walsh   1

2. Popular Protest and the Persistence of Customary Corn
   Measures: Resistance to the Winchester Bushel in the
   English West
   Richard Sheldon, Adrian Randall, Andrew Charlesworth and
   David Walsh   25

3. The Jack-a-Lent Riots and Opposition to Turnpikes in the
   Bristol Region in 1749
   Andrew Charlesworth, Richard Sheldon, Adrian Randall and
   David Walsh   46

4. The Cider Tax, Popular Symbolism and Opposition in Mid-
   Hanoverian England
   David Walsh, Adrian Randall, Richard Sheldon and
   Andrew Charlesworth   69

5. Scarcity and the Civic Tradition: Market Management in
   Bristol, 1709–1815
   Steve Poole   91

6. The Moral Economy of the English Middling Sort in the
   Eighteenth Century: the Case of Norwich in 1766 and 1767
   Simon Renton   115

7. Oxford Food Riots: a Community and its Markets
   Wendy Thwaites   137

8. The Irish Famine of 1799–1801: Market Culture, Moral
   Economies and Social Protest
   Roger Wells   163

Index   195

CONTRIBUTORS

ANDREW CHARLESWORTH is Reader in Human Geography at Cheltenham and Gloucester College of Higher Education. Before taking up this post, he taught at the University of Liverpool. He edited the *Atlas of Rural Protest in Britain* and has written extensively on social protest in Britain between 1500 and 1900. With David Gilbert, Adrian Randall, Humphrey Southall and Chris Wrigley, he is the author of the *Atlas of Industrial Protest in Britain, 1750–1984*. More recently he has begun to publish on the landscape of Nazi death camps.

STEVE POOLE is a Post-doctoral Fellow of the British Academy at the University of the West of England, Bristol. His forthcoming publications include 'Pitt's Reign of Terror reconsidered', *Southern History*, 1996, and 'To be a Bristolian: civic identity and the social order' in M. Dresser and P. Ollerenshaw, *The Making of a Modern City: Bristol since 1530* (Bristol, Redcliff Press, 1996).

ADRIAN RANDALL is currently Head of the School of Social Sciences and Professor of English Social History in the Department of Economic and Social History at the University of Birmingham. He is the author of *Before the Luddites: Custom, Community and Machinery in the English Woollen Industry, 1776–1809* and has published extensively on labour and social protest in the eighteenth and nineteenth centuries. With Andrew Charlesworth et al., he is the author of the *Atlas of Industrial Protest in Britain, 1750–1984*.

SIMON RENTON teaches at University College London and Buckinghamshire College. His research interests centre on crime and prosecution practice in Norwich during the second half of the eighteenth century, the subject of his PhD research for which he is registered at Middlesex University. He was a research assistant working on 'British Parliament and Legislation 1660–1800' at University College London for two years.

RICHARD SHELDON holds a BA degree in History from Middlesex Polytechnic and an MA in History and Social Anthropology from University College London. He is currently a research student in the Department of Economic and Social History at the University of Birmingham, working on a thesis on 'The Politics of Bread in Eighteenth-Century Britain'. He was the Research Assistant on the ESRC project from which the first four chapters of this volume are drawn.

WENDY THWAITES completed her PhD thesis 'The Marketing of Agricultural Produce in Eighteenth-Century Oxfordshire' (University of Birmingham) in 1980. She has written a number of articles arising from this on topics such as the corn market, the assize of bread and women in marketing.

DAVID WALSH is currently teaching at the University of Liverpool. His doctoral thesis, entitled 'Working Class Political Integration and the Conservative Party, 1800–1870', is to be published by Cambridge University Press. He was the Research Fellow on the ESRC project from which the first four chapters of this volume are drawn.

ROGER WELLS is Reader in History at Canterbury Christ Church College. He is the author of *Insurrection: The British Experience 1795–1803* (1983), *Wretched Faces: Famine in Wartime England 1793–1801* (1988) and numerous articles on modern British social history. He has also edited *Victorian Village* (1992) and—with Mick Reed—*Class, Conflict and Protest in the English Countryside 1770–1880* (1990).

PREFACE

This volume originated in an Economic and Social Research Council sponsored research project on 'Social Protest and Community Change in the West of England, 1750–1850' which ran from December 1991 to November 1993. The members of that project were Andrew Charlesworth and Adrian Randall, the 'principal investigators', and David Walsh and Richard Sheldon who were respectively Research Fellow and Research Assistant. We would all like to acknowledge the support of the ESRC in funding the project.[1]

The objective of this archive-centred project was to examine, within a community context, the character and development of social protest within one region, namely the West of England, historically defined as the counties of Gloucestershire, Somerset and Wiltshire, though, as the reader will note, we strayed further afield when the evidence indicated. We were particularly concerned to view such protest both from the 'top down' and from the 'bottom up' and in particular to focus on the way in which local elites perceived and reacted to different types of protest in different kinds of community. We also set out to investigate connections between different forms of protest and changing economic and community structures and to locate social protest within the wider context of changing industrial relations and community politics. Finally, we aimed as a group project to attempt to break down the compartmentalization which continues to isolate specific forms of protest and assumes that there was no inter-connection between them.

As our research progressed, we were able to ask increasingly informed questions concerning the assumptions about the development of the market, of market culture and of popular protest which inform many recent publications in this field. We also began to note the commonalities in the forms of popular protest across the region over time. In particular, as far as this volume is concerned, we noted a pattern in the response of local communities towards attempts to standardize weights and measures in the market place; patterns of common responses towards the 1763 Cider Excise; and patterns in the response towards turnpikes. Historians before us have noted some of these events, but it was our wider geographical spread and chronological time frame which permitted us to identify the links.

In parallel with this and as part of the project's development, we held a series of informal workshops/seminars in both Liverpool and Birmingham to which we invited a variety of people whom we knew were working or who had worked

1 ESRC Project no. R000233043.

upon aspects of social and popular protest. It was from these sessions that the germ of this volume grew since we found that others had identified similar concerns and explanations. Thus we invited Steve Poole, Simon Renton, Wendy Thwaites and Roger Wells to contribute to this volume and we are delighted they all chose to accept. This is not to say that the 'outside' contributors are part of any 'party line'. Their chapters are self contained in themselves. But the reader will detect many contiguities and parallels. For the same reason, there is no 'Conclusion'. The issues and approaches raised in this volume do have a common trajectory but it is up to the reader to pursue these for him or herself. We are not setting out to redefine but to open up.

This volume is concerned, as its title indicates, with markets, market culture and popular protest in eighteenth-century Britain and Ireland. The chapters focus upon both urban and rural communities in both England and Ireland. Towns and cities, villages and corporations, colliers and tradesmen all feature in these studies since the market was ubiquitous and universal. How it was managed, however, varied from place to place and from time to time. That process of management provides us with a major insight into the social, political and economic relationships of eighteenth-century Britain. Some readers will see in these chapters evidence of the heterogeneity of these relations. Others will recognize that, for all the apparent differences, on basic issues of provisioning there was a remarkable uniformity, rhetoric notwithstanding.

The external authors' work is clearly their own. The chapters from the project team reflect in their authorship order the principal commitments made. Thus Richard Sheldon has, with Adrian Randall, fronted the chapter on Customary Measures; David Walsh, with Adrian Randall, that on the Cider Tax; and Andrew Charlesworth, with Richard Sheldon, the chapter on the Jack-a-Lent Riots and Opposition to Turnpikes. Adrian Randall bears principal responsibility for the introductory chapter on Markets, Market Culture and Popular Protest and he has also acted as the principal editor for the whole book.

Others have played important parts in helping us delineate our ideas and have thereby contributed, perhaps unwittingly, to this book. We would in particular like to thank John Bohstedt, Cindy Bouton, Manfred Gailus, Michael Martin, Edwina Newman, Mike Power and John Rule for coming to our seminars and for sharing their thoughts and sandwiches with us. Special thanks are due to Edwina Newman and Michael Martin who have both very kindly given us access to their own research material, while Michael Martin has also chased up elusive references in Gloucestershire for us. One person who had a significant influence, albeit from afar, on this project is sadly no longer with us to be thanked. Edward Thompson was always unfailingly encouraging and supportive of our early efforts, and the questions all the chapters pose of their subject matter is ample evidence of the impact of his writings and of his critical engagement with the very stuff of the social and economic history of this period.

The issues that the chapters in this volume address – markets, market culture and popular protest – were all themes that Thompson himself addressed in his seminal paper on 'The moral economy of the English crowd in the eighteenth century', published in 1971, a paper which continues to have reverberations everywhere that historians of the eighteenth century gather. That said, none of the chapters in this book can be said to follow a slavish Thompsonian line. Our debt to him is clear but it can be paid only through critical engagement with ideas and evidence. Thompson would have expected nothing less.

AJR and AC

Chapter 1

MARKETS, MARKET CULTURE AND POPULAR PROTEST IN EIGHTEENTH-CENTURY BRITAIN AND IRELAND

ADRIAN RANDALL, ANDREW CHARLESWORTH, RICHARD SHELDON AND DAVID WALSH

INTRODUCTION

Markets of one form or another have occupied a key place in the social, economic and political cultures of all peoples throughout recorded history. Exchange seems to have been known since the late stone age and marketing principles feature in the earliest documents of civilization. Market institutions such as regular fairs and markets have an unbroken continuity stretching back to the middle ages. When Adam Smith wrote *The Wealth of Nations* in 1776, commerce had become so ubiquitous that he saw 'the propensity to truck, barter, and exchange one thing for another' as an elementary psychological trait of the human race.[1]

The writings of Smith, however, did more than just focus attention upon market institutions and market principles. The Classical Economists elevated 'the Market' to totemic status. It alone was the agency by which all in society could advance their material condition, provided that their natural inclination to exchange was unhindered by regulation or restriction. As Smith wrote:

> The natural effort of every individual to better his own condition, when suffered to exert itself with freedom and security, is so powerful a principle, that it is alone, and without any assistance, not only capable of carrying on the society to wealth and prosperity, but of surmounting a hundred impertinent obstructions with which the folly of human laws too often encumbers its operations.[2]

From the late eighteenth century onwards, faith in 'the Market', a belief that the self-regulating market functioned at all times in a natural and benevolent manner whenever permitted the liberty so to do, became a kind of secular orthodoxy, 'Political Economy'. The political message was clear. Restrictions upon the operations of the market, in all its aspects—protectionist legislation,

---

1 A. Smith, *The Wealth of Nations* (1776: 1979 edn, eds R. H. Campbell, A. S. Skinner and W. B. Todd, Oxford, Oxford University Press, 1979), p. 25.
2 Smith, *The Wealth of Nations* (1979 edn), p. 540.

paternalist regulation and restraints upon the rights of capital—must all be swept away. In the first half of the nineteenth century this was a value system which carried all before it.

The 1980s, in Britain and in America at least, witnessed an interesting historical parallel to this late eighteenth- and early nineteenth-century rise of Political Economy with the marked ideological shift towards the concept of 'freedom', above all 'freedom' from those models of governmental control over market forces which had developed since the end of the Second World War. Exemplified, but by no means led, in Britain by the values of 'Thatcherism' and in America by a paralleling 'Reaganism', this restatement of *laissez-faire* was deliberately posed in outright opposition to the 'Butskellism' and 'New Deal' consensus of the previous 30 years which had been characterized by restrictions upon the operations of free market forces, manifested among other ways in prices and incomes policies, control of foreign exchange transactions, curbs upon monopoly suppliers and the growth of welfarism. This emphasis upon 'freedom' brought in its train a new deification of the Market as both solution to and explanation of economic and social problems. There was no such thing as 'society', merely individuals and families who traded and exchanged their goods and services in the sensible pursuit of their own advantage. Alone, it was the power of market forces which could break the trammels of restrictive practices and recreate the supposedly-lost vibrancy and dynamism for sluggish or technologically-backward economies. Economic, social and political transformation followed, though not necessarily in the manner or forms predicted.

It is little wonder, therefore, that historians, reflecting their own age and culture in the questions they ask as well as reflecting upon the ages they research, should, in the last two decades, likewise have become increasingly interested in markets and market mechanisms. This is particularly true of those historians whose work has been focused upon the so-called 'long eighteenth century', the years roughly from 1688 to 1815, the study of which has seen a spectacular recrudescence in recent years.

Sandwiched between the excitements of the Civil War of the seventeenth century and the Industrial Revolution of the nineteenth, eighteenth-century historical studies languished in the middle decades of the twentieth century. However, the fragmentation of old Marxist orthodoxies in the 1970s, the need to account for the prehistory of industrial transformation, the changing cultural interests of new social history and an awakening interest in plebeian political antecedents to the radical movement of the nineteenth century, all reflecting the changing political and social climate of the times, have transformed the eighteenth century into what is currently one of the most exciting locales of historical enquiry. Thus, the older orthodoxies of industrial transformation through technology have been displaced by a new concentration upon the impact of new proto-industrial organizations of work while recent scholarship

upon eighteenth-century politics has sharply swung away from older assumptions of the politics of federations of English country houses[3] to a much more
sophisticated analysis of popular political engagement and practice. Above all,
many of those historians working in the 1980s upon the eighteenth century
have, like their academic forebears of 200 years ago, rediscovered the role of the
market and its power to modernize and to transform.

This rediscovery of the market can be seen in the work of, among others,
Anderson and Latham whose *The Market in History*[4] emphasized both the
ubiquity and the continuity of the concept of the market as agency and the
market as ideological impetus over a very long time period. Confidence in the
powers of the market may equally be detected in the work of the 'Cambridge
School' historians such as Hont and Ignatieff. Their painstaking search for the
sources of modern political economy emphasizes and amplifies Smith's
argument that the market mechanism provided the best means of reconciling an
unequal distribution of wealth and property with an adequate provision for the
labouring poor.[5] The motif of the market may also be seen to run strongly in the
revisionist work of McKendrick and others on the role of consumers in the
eighteenth century and on the importance of consumption through the market
in the formation of both manufacture and distribution.[6]

Even social historians of the riotous crowd have been influenced by the
explanatory status of the market. Thus Williams argued that the actions of food
rioters were informed by 'the imperatives of the market economy' and that these
rioters were in no way hostile to the market system since they 'were, and had
long been, members of the same marketing system'.[7] We may also note that
Bohstedt, whose early work emphasized the 'community politics' of the food
rioters of Devon, has in his more recent writing emphasized that the riotous
crowd did not endorse a value system which was hostile to the free market
principle. Indeed, he claims that food rioters, in common with all, 'voted for its
promise with their feet',[8] while Root, in his comparative study of markets in

---

3 The phrase comes from J. Habbakuk, 'England' in A. Goodwin (ed.), *The European Nobility in the
   Eighteenth Century* (London, Black, 1953), p. 1.

4 B. L. Anderson and A. J. H. Latham (eds), *The Market in History* (London, Croom Helm, 1984).

5 I. Hont and M. Ignatieff, 'Needs and justice in *The Wealth of Nations*: an introductory essay' in Hont
   and Ignatieff (eds), *Wealth and Virtue: The Shaping of Political Economy in the Scottish Enlightenment*
   (Cambridge, Cambridge University Press, 1983).

6 See, for example, N. McKendrick, J. Brewer and J. H. Plumb, *The Birth of a Consumer Society: The
   Commercialization of Eighteenth-Century England* (London, Europa, 1982) and J. Brewer and R. Porter
   (eds), *Consumption and the World of Goods* (London, Routledge, 1993). This is a fast-expanding field
   of enquiry.

7 D. E. Williams, 'Morals, markets and the English crowd in 1766', *Past and Present*, No. 104, August
   1984, pp. 70, 73.

8 J. Bohstedt, 'The moral economy and the discipline of historical context', *Journal of Social History*,
   Winter 1992, p. 268.

France and England, asserts (though without any evidence from England) that the moral economy served only 'narrow regional and occupational groups at the expense of general welfare'.[9]

Two of the most emphatic advocates of the role of the market, however, are Macfarlane and Kerridge. Macfarlane has little time for views, such as those of Polyani, that, before the eighteenth century, market institutions remained embedded inside society and culture and that it was only with the industrial age that the picture of man as 'homo economicus' was naturalized and turned into the master principle which drove society.[10] Macfarlane confidently asserts: ' "Homo economicus" and the market society had been present in England for centuries before Smith wrote'.[11] Kerridge is prepared to go further in asserting the all-beneficial role of the market. Premising his case upon the view that 'Freedom of property is essential to markets. All property whatsoever is lawfully acquired and protected', itself a highly contentious concept, he asserts:

> Freedom of property once assured, the extent to which markets will develop depends on the innate abilities of their participants and above all on the industry, ingenuity, inventiveness, intelligence and enterprise of the gifted few. At the same time, however, 'the market possesses a wisdom that does not exist, even remotely, in any discrete individual'.[12]

Here we see the Market as modern magic, a *deus ex machina* providing a means to overcome even the deficiencies of the cleverest human agents and assuring economic and social progress.

Before we succumb to this welter of ideological praise for the Market, however, we need to draw breath and enquire whether the reaction to a caricatured Marxist model hostile to the development of market economy has swept us too far. For, as this book will indicate, this capture of the historiography of the eighteenth century for the forces of market change has, to a very large degree, lost sight of the fact that that century was still very much at the intersection of the old and the new, at the junction between patterns of trading relationships and controls which dated back into the early modern period and the new vibrant nineteenth-century economy of the 'Workshop of the World'. The 'long eighteenth century' was not only a period of transformation. It was also a time of tension and stress. This can be seen in industrial relations as new patterns of work, some technologically driven but many more driven by adaptation to new work methods and orders, were slowly evolved and

9 H. L. Root, *The Fountain of Privilege* (Berkeley, University of California Press, 1994), p. 85.

10 K. Polyani, *The Great Transformation* (Boston, Beacon Press, 1957).

11 A. Macfarlane, *The Origins of English Individualism* (Oxford, Blackwell, 1979), p. 199.

12 E. Kerridge, 'Early modern English markets' in B. L. Anderson and A. J. Latham (eds), *The Market in History* (London, Croom Helm, 1984). The quotation cited by Kerridge comes from L. E. Read, 'The miracle of the market' in *Champions of Freedom* (Hillsdale, 1974).

imposed in the context of increasing living costs.[13] It can be seen too in the tensions to be discerned behind the powerful process of agrarian transformation which historians wrap up in the term 'enclosure'.[14] But we may see these tensions most clearly in the food markets, the key location of economic and social exchange for the majority of the population. Tension occasioned by 'the rise of a national market' in grain, by increasing prices of foodstuffs, by increasing fluctuations in supply and availability, fuelled popular unrest to the extent that perhaps as many as two in three of all riots in that most disorderly of centuries were occasioned by food.[15] As this volume will show, change in market provisioning and market practices was a much-contested arena of conflict between the older models of regulation and control and new forces of market freedom and autonomy.

The essays in this volume all in some way deal with the marketing and the provision of foodstuffs, the staple of any market system, and how they changed in the eighteenth century. In particular, all the essays reflect the tensions occasioned by threats to the cultural norms and values which surrounded commodity exchange and availability. Approaching this issue in different manners and forms, they all nevertheless focus upon the question regarding what we may learn from popular protests against market changes to help us understand the development of social, economic and political relations in the long eighteenth century.

THE MARKET ITSELF

Considering the great emphasis placed upon the market by recent historical scholarship, we still know remarkably little about the development of markets in the eighteenth century or about the basic practices of market exchange. Certainly, the eighteenth century witnessed changes in the market place: shops advanced where petty markets retreated and old local regulatory mechanisms clearly came under growing pressure. But the pace of transformation was very varied and its consequences by no means widely understood.

This is true especially when assessing the speed and impact of market integration, for, while assumptions about transformation abound in the literature, the so-called 'rise of a national market' remains somewhat opaque. Thus, while most historians would conclude that a national market followed the

---

13 See J. Rule, *The Vital Century: England's Developing Economy 1714–1815* (London, Longman, 1992) for a recent overview of the economic history of the period. See also L. D. Schwarz, 'The standard of living in the long run; London, 1700–1860', *Economic History Review*, Vol. XXXIII, 1980, which indicates the importance of rising living costs in the latter half of the eighteenth century.

14 J. M. Neeson, *Commoners: Common Rights, Enclosure and Social Change in England, 1700–1820* (Cambridge, Cambridge University Press, 1993), is the most recent and best discussion of the social conflicts around, and impact of, enclosure.

15 G. Rude, *The Crowd in History* (New York, Wiley, 1964), p. 36.

development of a revolution in transport, of coastal and river navigation and, above all, through the turnpiking of inadequate roads, we have only limited knowledge about the impact of these developments upon local markets or upon local perceptions and cultures. Indeed, such issues are rarely touched on by many economic and agrarian historians for they see nothing problematic with market widening. Thus Chartres views the erosion of a public marketing system as inexorable. This was, he believes, the necessary condition for the increased efficiency of the home market which preceded and laid the basis for the Industrial Revolution of the late eighteenth century.[16] Markets and market culture are taken as given. Perren, in his comprehensive account of changes in the structure of food marketing in England and Wales in the eighteenth century, likewise identifies improvements in transport as a key factor leading to the rise of a national market.[17] However, the speed and impact of these changes on the infrastructure of marketing, nationally and regionally, remain open to debate. Furthermore, in much of the literature about market widening, there is little recognition that markets were embedded in wider societal and cultural structures. Changes in marketing practices threatened these social structures.

We should beware of assuming that the 'benefits' of a national market were widely welcomed or clearly and emphatically demonstrated. Here we may usefully note Dr Johnson's perceptive criticisms of the turnpike movement. While Johnson's concern that prices would increase once localities were all connected into a national network of roads is well known, he also foresaw that other wider social and economic changes would flow from this. Localities outside the national price-setting market were, he believed, also outside a national culture that approved and supported the values of a market-oriented society and men who chose to opt out of that society could do so by moving there. Once the turnpike opened up a district to market forces, that option was no longer open. All would be caught up in the treadmill of capitalist innovation. 'Now all refuges were destroyed for elegant or genteel poverty and even had no longer a hope to support them in their struggle through life.' Importantly, Johnson feared that this national market was hostile to older established concepts of community and of family household. 'The roads moreover caused disunion of families by furnishing a market to each man's abilities, and destroying the dependence of one man on another.'[18] The turnpike, Johnson

---

16 J. A. Chartres, 'The marketing of agricultural produce' in J. Thirsk (ed.), *Agricultural History of England and Wales, Vol 5, 1640–1750* (Cambridge, Cambridge University Press, 1985).

17 R. Perren, 'Markets and marketing' in G. E. Mingay (ed.), *Agrarian History of England and Wales, Vol. 6, 1750–1850* (Cambridge, Cambridge University Press, 1989). He also identifies farmers acting as marketing agents, changes in markets and fairs, regional price variations and 'efficient' markets as causative factors.

18 Quoted in J. Latimer, *The Annals of Bristol in the Eighteenth Century* (Bristol, William George, 1893), pp. 275–76.

recognized, brought with it the commoditization of labour. It imperilled the very basis of the existing social and economic order. The 'market widening' achieved by turnpikes was by no means uncontested. As Chapter 3 demonstrates, the issue of turnpikes excited popular opposition in the West of England. This opposition came not only from the lower orders but also from many farmers and petty capitalists and lasted for much longer than might be expected had transport improvements been so obvious a benefit to local society. Protests over turnpikes in Scotland and Wales continued until well into the nineteenth century. The transformative effects of turnpikes on the local market and their symbolic importance as agencies of change should not be underestimated.

The rise of a national market raises questions about the role of the local market. As forums for local exchange increasingly became links in a national chain, their functions also changed and relationships within the market changed with them. This was not missed by contemporaries. Johnson was not alone in distinguishing between those for whom the market was a source of profit and those for whom it was merely a tool of exchange. In the campaign of opposition to the Cider Tax in 1763, Dowdeswell wrote to Hardwicke emphasizing the differences between the cider dealer and the individual household producer with his portion of orchard. The former traded by choice. 'He makes it his option and he makes a profit out of it.' The latter 'takes not up his business by choice. He was trained to from childhood, and is accustomed to nothing else'.[19] Dowdeswell clearly did not see the little cider maker as a marketing agent in Perren's terminology nor as being motivated by profit in a way that was true of the trader.

The transformation of the petty commodity producer into the capitalist tenant farmer may well mark out one of the most important changes of the long eighteenth century. Certainly, that century witnessed a remarkable development of regional agricultural specialism with farmers increasingly becoming drawn into an enlarging market economy.[20] That transformation was assisted by taxation, including turnpike tolls which were certainly classified by their opponents as a form of taxation. Such additional burdens made the margin of subsistence narrower and drew the householder deeper into a monetary exchange network which, by making householders release some of their assets, undermined their ability to sustain household reproduction. A report in *Felix Farley's Bristol Journal*, written during the Cider Tax campaign, captured the double-edged nature of such taxation when it referred to the tax as making 'an Exciseman as Overseer in his family'.[21] The use of the word 'overseer' was significant, intimating not only the influence of taxation as a controller of

---

19 See below, Chapter 4, p. 74.
20 For a useful summary of these changes, see Rule, *Vital Century*, pp. 51–54.
21 *Felix Farley's Bristol Journal*, 2 April 1763.

household decisions but also the threat of impoverishment and dependence upon the parish should the family fail to sustain itself in the new market culture. Growing dependence upon the market may well have been the experience of many, but this did not necessarily reflect improvement. Eden in 1797 contrasted the independent self-sufficiency of the northern labourers with the growing dependence of the southern labourers on the market, not only for their staple foods such as baked bread and manufactured beer but also for clothing and 'luxuries'. Significantly, he thought that the northern labourer fared better.[22] This should alert us to the question of the social as well as of the economic effects of market expansion and commoditization. There is no doubt that the market for 'luxuries' was growing throughout the eighteenth century, a fact much lamented by some traditionalists, Eden included. Many of these were 'groceries'—sugar, tea, tobacco—from the expanding commerce of Empire or consumables connected to them such as crockery. Historians of the 'consumer revolution' have, however, concentrated their attentions on the middling sort. Little research has been carried out as yet into changing plebeian patterns of consumption. Indeed, Medick points out that much research carried out by modern scholars does not yet match the degree of penetration achieved by eighteenth-century observers.[23] The boundary line between the consuming classes and the poor may have been set rather higher than some of the more optimistic accounts of market penetration might presume.[24]

While the speed and impact of the rise of a national market remains only partly understood, very little historical attention has been paid to the actual units of transaction utilized within that supposedly burgeoning national market. Yet here, particularly in measures of grain, we find astonishing heterogeneity in the early eighteenth century. Historians of the market, in so far as they have noticed this, have tended to assume that these older measures must have disappeared with the rise of a national market and that, with the increasing mobility of corn, a standardization on the prescribed Winchester model must have been inevitable since transaction costs would otherwise have been high.[25] Even Hoppit, in a careful and comprehensive examination of the eighteenth-century governmental attempts to achieve standardization, is forced to resort to the imperative, convinced that 'knowledge' would have displaced local and, by

---

22 Sir F. M. Eden, *The State of the Poor* (London, 1797), p. 555.
23 H. Medick, 'Plebeian culture in the transition to capitalism' in R. Samuel and G. Stedman Jones (eds), *Culture, Ideology and Politics* (London, Routledge and Kegan Paul, 1982).
24 See, for example, Lorna Weatherill, 'Consumer behaviour, the ownership of goods and early industrialization' in *ESRC Working Group on Proto-industrial Communities*, Warwick, University of Warwick, 1985, pp. 161–65.
25 See, for example, Perren, 'Markets and marketing', which sees the standardization of weights and measures as an inevitable consequence of the growth of large urban markets and modern marketing methods.

assumption, regressive, measures with those of Winchester.[26] As the study of the persistence of customary measures in the West of England in Chapter 2 makes clear, however, such assumptions are not necessarily sustained by the evidence. Indeed, in that region at least, the survival of customary measures was remarkable. Such persistence there cannot be dismissed as indicative of the 'backwardness' of the West of England in coming within a 'national market'. The counties of Gloucestershire and Wiltshire, far from being remote, were in fact pivotal in the supply of grains to the Bristol, London and international markets throughout the century and growing ever more significant. Yet here the corn trade continued and grew, unhampered by the very standardization of measures deemed so necessary to the development of a national market. The evidence for Oxfordshire likewise indicates the persistence of old customary measures into the nineteenth century.[27] Until similar studies are conducted upon other regions, we can only reserve judgement on what this means for the picture of an increasingly homogenized national market. The evidence of the West, however, indicates that caution is necessary before historians fix the 'modernization' of the national grain market too early in the modern age.

Advocates of the free market in the later eighteenth century were concerned to argue that the removal of regulation would ensure regularity of supply and could not play into the hands of speculators and monopolists. Popular opinion was by no means assured and the ancient distrust of the middleman continued to inform crowd and paternalist thinking alike. How far these fears were based on reality continues to be debated. Thus, in an early response to Edward Thompson's paper on the 'Moral economy of the English crowd',[28] Coats emphasized the Smithian line that markets were self-clearing and that the scope for manipulation would have been very limited.[29] Clearly, in the growing national market, the role of dealers and factors grew ever-more important. Buying and selling, both extant commodities or 'futures', were, then as now, areas in which large capitals were involved and large fortunes could be made or lost. Yet little research has been conducted into the ways in which such men operated in the eighteenth century.[30] One of the many revealing insights into the Irish food market in Roger Wells' Chapter 8 is the evidence he has

---

26 J. Hoppit, 'Reforming Britain's weights and measures, 1660–1824' in *English Historical Review*, Vol. 426, 1993.

27 W. Thwaites, 'The Marketing of Agricultural Produce in Eighteenth Century Oxford' (unpublished PhD thesis, University of Birmingham, 1980), p. 192.

28 E. P. Thompson, 'The moral economy of the English crowd in the eighteenth century' in *Past and Present*, No. 50, 1971.

29 A. W. Coats, 'Contrary moralities: plebs, paternalists and political economists' in *Past and Present*, No. 54, 1975, pp. 130–33. Thompson responded to this in E. P. Thompson, *Customs in Common* (London, Merlin, 1991), pp. 268–69.

30 R. B. Westerfield, *Middlemen in English Business, 1660–1760* (New Haven, Yale University Press, 1915), remains one of the few books on the subject. R. A. E. Wells, *Wretched Faces: Famine in Wartime*

unearthed of the operations of the prominent Dublin corn merchanting firm of Jebbs in conditions of scarcity and of dearth. Wells shows how dealers, in anticipation of being able to cash in on higher prices, were prepared to utilize their capital to withhold stocks from market or even to purchase at high prices grains coming on to the market in order to secure higher prices for their own later shipments, the very forestalling complained of by both crowd and 'paternalists'. Likewise, Thwaites' work shows that the crowd's belief that large magazines of grain remained hidden during times of scarcity, magazines of which their rulers were ignorant and which an idealized Smithian theory of the market would presume were accessible for sale, was indeed based on real knowledge.[31] The reality of scarcity, then as in the modern world, was that those with knowledge of the market and the economic power to hold the consumer to ransom had few qualms about so doing. It was the actions of the crowd which provided the only real check to such market manipulation.

While Parliament may be portrayed as leading the way towards a free market with the repeal of the old statutes concerning forestalling and regrating in 1772, central government also acted in ways which distorted the market in grain.[32] Thus, the failure of government in 1766 to lift the export bounty on grain at a time when many across the country were aware that stocks were low and the current harvest likely to be a disaster proved catastrophic and hastened the manipulations of both factors and farmers alike. The pull of a growing continental food crisis was compounded by the positive incentive to dealers to reverse the normal flows of corn from the grain-producing regions to the industrial and urban districts and send it towards the ports. The result was a series of extensive disorders.[33] The concerns of the government to protect English grain supplies in 1800 produced stresses in the provisioning of Ireland where Cornwallis feared a 'war of bounties between the two kingdoms'. Emphatic assertions of the importance of free markets did not, as Wells shows, impede more covert market manipulation.[34]

The role of government in the development of the food market remains under-researched. Likewise, the evolution of opinion in the eighteenth century concerning the role of the state in economic matters, especially the age-old question of balancing good returns for farmers and landlords with the maintenance of an adequate provision for the poor, has been much neglected. This problem was the subject of a complex debate which occupied a large place

---

England, 1793–1803 (Gloucester, Alan Sutton, 1988), is the only modern investigation of this important issue.

31 See Chapter 7.

32 See, for example, the discussion in Wells, *Wretched Faces*, Ch. 11.

33 W. J. Shelton, *English Hunger and Industrial Disorders: A Study of Social Conflict during the First Decade of George III's Reign* (London, Macmillan, 1973), Ch. 1.

34 See Chapter 8.

in the expanding print media of the developing 'public sphere': books, pamphlets, newspapers and journals. While the ideas of free markets were growing in importance from the mid-eighteenth century onwards, there remained a very extensive body of opinion which continued to emphasize the importance of regulation and moral economic values in the food market.[35]

We also lack much in the way of modern detailed studies of the basic practices of exchange in eighteenth-century markets. Certainly, old local regulatory mechanisms were being gradually eroded across the country. But here again we should resist being too easily swept up in a model of modernity. Local market practice in many major markets in the early eighteenth century was carefully regulated and controlled by the local civic authorities. The continuation of control over the market by local authorities remained a fundamental feature of market practice into the nineteenth century in many places, the rise of a national market notwithstanding. In this respect, the study of Oxford and its markets by Wendy Thwaites in Chapter 7 should be noted as a caution to those who blithely assume that the rise of a national market must inevitably set the terms of trade for the local market. The extraordinary persistence of carefully-regulated marketing practices there owed everything to enlightened self-interest on the part of the town's elite and to their concerns to maintain steady supplies and domestic tranquillity. This was done in direct and conscious opposition to governmental pressure and 'market imperatives'. The Oxford authorities had no intention of finding their town the focus of disturbance simply to facilitate flows of foodstuffs to the metropolitan or the Birmingham markets.

Oxford, with its strong University presence, may well not have been a typical eighteenth-century market. But the Oxford emphasis upon regulation and control was shared by many other towns and cities in eighteenth-century Britain. Even those cities most committed to free markets in the eighteenth century were not prepared to push ideology before public order. This can be seen in Steve Poole's study of Bristol, the second city of the country and a major port, in Chapter 5. Here a clear, early and reiterated civic assertion of the importance of political economy proved no brake upon the development of a sophisticated and carefully managed attempt to influence and ameliorate the food markets by civic intervention. The serious disturbances of 1753 provided an eloquent example of the consequences of allowing markets forces to dictate events. It was a warning which subsequent civic authorities did not intend to ignore. Their intervention in the international market to secure food supplies for a large populace was an option open only to a rich trading city, but their continuous, forceful and contested manipulation of the assize of bread to keep

---

35 This is an area currently being researched by Richard Sheldon at the University of Birmingham for his thesis, 'The Politics of Bread in Eighteenth-Century Britain'.

bread cheap is clear evidence that even those most concerned to maintain free trade did not shrink from market intervention to safeguard social welfare and social and political order.

It is clear, therefore, that while the role of the local market was changing during the eighteenth century, the pace of change was by no means rapid everywhere. Moreover, this change was by no means uncontested. What were the values which informed these contests?

MARKET CULTURE[36]

The eighteenth-century market was not merely a location for economic transaction between buyer and seller, still less merely an abstract agency. The market and the market place also formed a concrete physical location and the centre for community interchange, not only economic but also social and political. The market was the principal focus of community identity. It was a place where relationships were made and developed, where news and gossip were exchanged, where values, attitudes and opinions were disseminated, acquired or debated. Much more than the church or the public house, locations with relatively small and self-contained audiences, the market was the one place where all classes would meet, where all groups in a highly socially stratified society could mingle cheek by jowl. Here was the lifeblood of community. In that community, the values and the culture of the market of the majority remained, in the eighteenth century, in many respects firmly fixed in the regulatory economy of the past. What were the values espoused by those whose lives revolved around the market?

The plebeian culture of the market placed high importance both upon honesty and upon generosity. Those who dealt in illegal measures or who adulterated food could expect little sympathy from the crowd. Thus, when the crowd which had fixed the price of wheat and butter in the Salisbury market in 1766 marched out to the 'town mill' at Fisherton and found not only grain and flour but also large quantities of 'ground chalk, lime and horse beans', it set to and pulled down the bolting mill. It was a response followed by crowds throughout the county. Food rioters were also ill-disposed to those who sought to trick them. In Gloucestershire the same year, a touring mob visited a Mrs Dormer, near Cheltenham, in its search for hidden food reserves. Claiming to have neither cheese nor flour on the premises, she agreed to allow two delegates

---

36 Reddy uses the concept of 'market culture' in his study of market relations in the nineteenth-century French textile industry labour market. 'The advantage of the word *culture* is that it at least raises the possibility of a disjuncture between perception and reality and forces us to interpret rather than blindly accept language used to describe or restructure social life.' The concept is of equal utility in studying eighteenth-century food markets since, as we shall see, the values, rhetoric and reality of the market were all undergoing changes which did not necessarily accord with each other. W. R. Reddy, *The Rise of Market Culture* (Cambridge, Cambridge University Press, 1984), p. 1.

into her house to look. These she greeted with wine and 'entertained long enough for them to have searched'. Unfortunately for her and for the delegates, the rest discovered that they had been tricked, returning to find over 50 hundredweight of cheese and a large quantity of wheat. The cheese was distributed free to the poor as punishment, though the wheat was sold out at 4s.6d. a bushel.[37]

In the market place, the crowd expected its measures heaped, not narrowly levelled, and public execration might befall anyone who displayed the sort of meanness shown by a market woman in Wellington who in 1812 adjusted the weight of a pound of potatoes exactly by biting off part of the final potato to achieve an exact balance. Such was the anger of the purchasers that they hired the crier to broadcast what she had done.[38] The varying treatment accorded to farmers and dealers in times of riot, some being treated with respect, others having their goods destroyed or taken without compensation, may well have reflected local memory and knowledge of earlier examples of generous or parsimonious treatment of the customers.

Honesty was also expected of the consumer. The case of Ruth Pierce offers striking evidence of this. Pierce, a widow from Potterne, joined with three other women in Devizes market in January 1753 to buy a sack of wheat from a farmer, Nathaniel Alexander, for the sum of 17s.

> When the Farmer summ'd up the Dividends it wanted Three pence of the price agreed for which by evidence it appeared to be Ruth Pierce's right to pay. She the said Ruth was accused with it she declared she had paid it and called upon the Almighty for Wittness and wished she might drop down Dead that Minute if she had not paid it the Raish Wish was repeated a second Time and immediately From the VISITATION of the GREAT and ALMIGHTY GOD was struck Dead upon the Same.

A wooden board detailing this event was immediately erected at the Market Cross for all to read. When in 1814 a new stone Market Cross was erected, the story was again engraved upon it, 'to transmit to future times the record of an awful event' and 'as a salutary warning against the danger of impiously invoking Divine vengeance . . . to conceal the devices of falsehood and fraud'.[39]

The distrust of middlemen, so striking an attitude since the middle ages and perhaps before, remained deep-seated within market culture. They were immediate suspects whenever prices rose unaccountably. Word of mouth

---

37 A. J. Randall, 'Labour and the Industrial Revolution in the West of England Woollen Industry' (unpublished PhD thesis, University of Birmingham, 1979), pp. 134–35, 160.

38 See below, p. 41.

39 An account appears in *Wiltshire Archaeological and Natural History Magazine*, Vol. 12, 1870, pp. 256–57. The 'lesson' of Ruth Pierce continues to reach a modern audience. Adrian Randall remembers having the story read to him from the Market Cross by his own mother in the 1950s with the appropriate warnings 'not to tell lies'.

undoubtedly conveyed most news but the printed medium also was often used. Thus, in 1765, the *Bath Chronicle* reported: 'We are informed that papers tending to inflame the minds of the people against corn jobbers have been stuck up in most of the market towns in this neighbourhood.'[40] Some commentators lamented this public hostility towards the factors and dealers. It was foolish to blame the badgers for the shortages, argued John Pitt, Lord Hardwicke's land steward, in 1766:

> in fact they are the friends on many occasions of the poor for though they prevent any commodities from becoming a drug, yet they never suffer it to get over dear and by that very certainty of a market they occasion, wet up the industry of the farmer.

This was not a sentiment which attracted much sympathy from consumers at any stage in the eighteenth century. Certainly, in 1766 'it was not the most politic of political economy'.[41] The food rioters in 1766, in 1795 and in 1800– 01 all exhibited a common animosity towards the middlemen and dealers who were deemed to be manipulating the market. Wiltshire food rioters in 1766 were reported to be 'burning and pulling down the mills of those whom they know to be concerned in sending meal to Bristol for Exportation, a term become as shocking as that of a Bounty to starve the poor . . . They touch no mills but such as deal to their oppression.'[42] A Gloucestershire crowd the same month forced its way into the farmhouse of John Collett where it seized over six tons of hoarded cheese.[43]

This popular analysis that the cause of food shortage and high prices could be laid at the door of the dealers was by no means confined to the lower orders. The middling sort and the gentry likewise all showed their contempt for the factor, the forestaller and the regrater. Thus, as Poole shows for Bristol and Thwaites for Oxford, the press and the authorities were quick to condemn the activities of those who were deemed to have deprived the local market of food supplies or to have artificially inflated prices. This might even be seen to encourage crowd action. Thus Poole notes that in 1795 in the very week when Kingswood colliers were seizing food, the main Bristol paper stated: 'We trust . . . considering the abundance of potatoes that have been grown this year, the public will see that there are no grounds for advancing their price and will accordingly resist any such attempt.'[44] Pitt blamed the clothiers and the press in Gloucestershire for the food riots in 1766:

> the first riots . . . were occasioned by the lower sort of labourers in the clothing trade, who finding work scarce and provisions dear, grumbled until a hint given in the

40 *Bath Chronicle*, 25 March 1765.
41 A. J. Randall, 'The Gloucestershire food riots of 1766', *Midland History*, Vol. X, 1985, p. 88.
42 *Aris's Birmingham Gazette*, 29 September 1766.
43 Randall, 'Gloucestershire food riots', pp. 80, 85.
44 See below, p. 110.

public newspaper was recommended to them by their employers of regulating the markets . . . The badgers and factors were pointed out as the cause, and the mob were hallooed on to them.[45]

The distrust of the dealers and middlemen indicates that the culture of the market remained for the majority of the community a culture of control and regulation. The forms and the theatre of the market remained deeply embedded in the cultural infrastructure of the community. We get insights into the mechanisms of the market's regulatory practice only occasionally, and this has led some historians to assume that such examples of regulation as come to light were anachronistic revivals to fend off crowd hostility. Yet, the ways in which the various forms of regulation were carefully enacted in times of scarcity and popular protest should alert us to their symbolic importance as totems of a deep-rooted normality. Thus in 1766, John Pitt, land steward to Lord Hardwicke, complained to his employer:

> resolutions were agreed to at all the meetings that all buyings and sellings of provisions but in open market were illegal . . . you could not buy an egg or a pound of butter but at the tingling of a bell and on a particular spot.[46]

Such practices may well have lapsed in some places prior to the riots, but the folk memory and the expectation of regulatory action made such devices an immediate necessity if social order was to be maintained. Clearly they held significant resonances for the consumer, both real and ritualistic. The alacrity with which the authorities reinstated and reinforced the old ways everywhere whenever protest threatened underscores that these were the forms and practices which the community as a whole believed were the only legitimate ways of operating. Likewise, the pronounced belief in justice, whether in the 'just price' or in the popular punishment of 'offenders', even to the extent of symbolically destroying food at times when it was scarce, evidences this deep-rooted community determination to uphold a popular market culture in marked contrast to the free market culture of the Classical Economists.

While we have only fragmentary evidence of the opening and closing of pitching markets by the ringing of a bell other than in times of crisis,[47] the continued enforcement of the assize of bread, what Clapham perceptively dubbed 'a kind of economic common law',[48] demonstrates the importance attached by all involved to this most public example of control. The chapters in

---

45 British Library, Hardwicke Mss., Pitt to Hardwicke, 21, 20, December 1766.
46 British Library, Hardwicke Mss., Pitt to Hardwicke, 21 December 1766.
47 See, for example, *Bath Journal*, 3 November 1755. It is worth noting that sales in the Yorkshire cloth halls were regulated in exactly the same way. See A. J. Randall, *Before the Luddites: Custom, Community and Machinery in the English Woollen Industry, 1776–1809* (Cambridge, Cambridge University Press, 1991), p. 36.
48 Sir J. H. Clapham, *An Economic History of Modern Britain: The Early Railway Age* (Cambridge, Cambridge University Press, 1950), p. 344.

this book clearly evidence the real presence of the assize. There can be no doubt that, had the popular will not demanded such time-consuming activity, local market officials would not have spent so much time or endured so much aggravation for themselves in maintaining it. The authorities well knew the outcry which would befall allowing this arena of scrutiny and control to lapse into desuetude. Where the consequences of a failure to appear to be in command of the marketing process were greatest, as in London with its huge and potentially very dangerous crowd, the assize of bread was maintained well into the nineteenth century.[49]

We would be wrong to assume that the market mechanisms of the eighteenth century were necessarily remote from the consumers, merely a theatre provided by the authorities to maintain orderliness. In Coventry, the freemen were obliged to play an active part in the regular and participative task of monitoring the markets. This involved taking turns to carry out the burdensome and time-consuming tasks of checking weights and measures, including ale measures, monitoring market exchanges, taking samples of 'clean wheat of different prizes' to the mayor to assist him in setting the assize of bread and generally patrolling the markets to preserve good order. The freeman franchise of Coventry was very wide and perhaps as many as one in three of the male members of the city might have been involved at some stage in the maintenance of market control.[50] In such a context, we need not wonder at the popular insistence upon the open and regulated paternalist model of marketing throughout the eighteenth century.

Likewise, it is clear that the paternalist model of marketing was not merely something which the gentry rolled out in response to or in anticipation of crowd disturbance. The adherence of many gentlemen in the West of England to the customary market measures in the face of considerable pressure to conform to the Winchester standard is well attested in Chapter 2 and reflected not only a powerful parochialism but also a deep-seated mistrust of the ambitions of the large dealers and middlemen. Here we may note the actions of the magistracy in Tewkesbury in 1769. Faced with the order from the Quarter Sessions that they enforce the Winchester bushel, and recognizing that the populace shared their distrust of the motives of the dealers and large farmers who were calling so vociferously for adherence to the statutory measure, the magistrates demanded that all farmers bringing their grain to the market would honour the pledge made at the earlier Sessions that, not only would the farmers sell only by the

---

49 J. Stevenson, 'The "moral economy" of the English crowd: myth and reality' in A. Fletcher and J. Stevenson (eds), *Order and Disorder in Early Modern England* (Cambridge, Cambridge University Press, 1985), p. 230.

50 We are grateful to Jill Shepherd for this information from her research at the University of Birmingham for a thesis on 'Controlling the City: politics and administration in Coventry, 1760–1784'.

Winchester bushel, but that they would lower their prices to those current at the Bear Key market in London. Unsurprisingly, no farmers came to market to pitch their grain on these terms. Thus could the justices do what they were bid by the Sessions while ensuring that customary measures continued to be used.[51] Here we see the plain evidence of that powerful parochialism which repudiated the centralizing forces of county and country in the name of popular community accountability. This sense of hostility towards those who were acting within the law but against customary perceptions of community culture can be seen in the hostility displayed towards the two informers who threatened to bring actions against those selling by the customary measures in Gloucester in 1810.[52] A parallel situation faced those who sought in 1753–56 to enforce the new and hated Cider Tax.[53] There was little support for law which was deemed oppressive or which threatened customary practice.

POPULAR PROTEST

The guarantors of market culture were, for the most part, the crowd. It was the crowd which most actively resisted changes in marketing practice, the crowd which ensured that those who sought to break old market customs and culture encountered real and effective intimidation or retribution. Some historians have argued that food riots *per se* were too infrequent and scattered across the country to have achieved much impact.[54] Such arguments ignore the fact that 'riots' are both notoriously difficult to count[55] and that a fully-blown market riot might not be necessary to secure the crowd's aim. Smaller market fracas or peaceable demonstrations could well alert the authorities to the need to intervene, to regulate or to punish those who were transgressing established market rules and culture. Moreover, the impact of an assertive crowd went far beyond a single event, both temporally and geographically. Even if it remained 'quiet', the potential power of the crowd could not be discounted. The threat to public order, to the commercial life of the town or city and to the 'face' and standing of the local ruling elite in the eyes of the Lord Lieutenant and Westminster posed by the potential of mass action, meant that account had to be taken of popular attitudes. In large trading ports such as Bristol and London, the authorities had to be careful to be seen to be supportive of the market culture of the crowd.

We owe a good part of our understanding of the actions and context of food

51 *Bath Chronicle*, 26 January 1769.
52 See below, p. 34.
53 See below, Chapter 4.
54 See, for example, Williams, 'Morals, markets', pp. 69–70. Cf. A. Charlesworth and A. J. Randall, 'Comment: morals, markets and the English crowd in 1766' in *Past and Present*, No. 114, 1987, pp. 200–13.
55 See, for example, R. Wells, 'Counting riots in eighteenth-century England', *Bulletin of the Society for the Study of Labour History*, Vol. XXXVII, 1978, pp. 68–72.

riots to Edward Thompson. In his seminal paper, 'The moral economy of the English crowd in the eighteenth century', Thompson sought to rescue the study of eighteenth-century food riots from 'crass economic reductionism'. Such riots, Thompson believed, were 'a highly complex form of direct popular action, disciplined and with clear objectives' which 'were informed by the belief that they [the crowd] were defending traditional rights or customs' which, taken together, 'can be said to constitute the moral economy of the poor'. To Thompson, this moral economy was not a static, tradition-bound entity. It was a selective reconstruction of paternalist legislation which became more, rather than less, sophisticated in the eighteenth century.[56]

The concept of the moral economy and the cultural approach to the study of riot has led to ongoing debate and discussion among historians. Was the moral economy a holistic notion, a value system hostile to a free-market model, widely shared across classes and across the country as Thompson implies, or were consumers in fact fully fledged and willing participants in a modernizing market economy, as Williams asserts and Bohstedt implies?[57] Was the moral economy of the crowd not a value system at all but rather merely a tactical device utilized by the crowd only in certain circumstances and settings, a case argued in their differing ways by both Bohstedt and Stevenson?[58] Were food riots after all little more than rebellions of the belly?

There is not the space here to venture deeply into the historiographical debate on the moral economy, but the material in this book and in related publications can certainly provide us with some pointers as to the broad questions of the actions and motivations of those involved in protests against market changes.

One thing which comes over strongly in all the chapters in this volume is the community character of protest. The rioting and the demonstrating crowd was keen to involve as many as possible in the process of reasserting common 'rights' and customary practice. Dallaway noted of the Gloucestershire food riots in 1766: 'The rioters come into our workshops and force all the men willing or unwilling to join them.'[59] The crowd at Oxford likewise swept up supporters for its actions.[60] Kingswood colliers, a notoriously united riot force, were reported to be touring Wiltshire in 1753 following their violent defeat by the Bristol tradesmen in order to gather more recruits for a return.[61] As Wells

56 Thompson, 'Moral economy'. See also his later thoughts upon the issue in *Customs in Common*, Ch. 5.
57 Williams, 'Morals, markets', p. 70; Bohstedt, 'Moral economy and the discipline of historical context', p. 268.
58 J. Bohstedt, *Riots and Community Politics in England and Wales, 1790–1810* (Harvard, Yale University Press, 1983), Ch. 9; J. Stevenson, 'The "moral economy" of the English crowd'.
59 Public Record Office, P.C. 1/8/41, Dallaway to Conway, 20 September 1766.
60 See below, p. 147.
61 See below, p. 98.

shows in his 'rescue' of Irish food riots, food rioters there sometimes were part of wider community movements with wider community agendas. Thus, in Munster the injunctions of Captain Slasher covered not only the forced sale of foodstuffs and their price level but also what might be fed to pigs and cattle and even the usage of land. Such was the scale of the 'threat' to the free marketing of produce that the government equated it with the dangers of militant nationalism, warning that 'any person presuming to stop provisions of any kind, or fixing prices, on being apprehended, would be punished as principally furthering the Rebellion' and dealt with under martial law.[62]

The military, brought in to restore or uphold social order, were also not infrequently the initiators of price fixing. They experienced the same problems of food supply and cost as the ordinary consumer. Thus in Bristol in 1795, the East Devon Militia were accused of complicity in the serious riots against butchers and fishmongers of that year,[63] while the soldiers in Ireland in 1800 were such frequent transgressors of the free movement of food that Cornwallis was forced to issue a circular warning of the direst consequences should such actions persist.[64]

The objects of the crowd's wrath were not chosen at random. Wendy Thwaites notes that 'the extreme orderliness of the [Oxford] price-fixing of 1766 suggests restraint, care, complex motivation, that is the desire to punish appropriately as well as to obtain cheaper food'.[65] The frequency with which the crowd paid for its supplies, at the 'just price' or not, indicates that the food rioters were not taking advantage of the overturn of the forces of order to make off with goods for free. There was often 'No plundering'.[66] Further, the destruction of foodstuffs, at times when supplies were frequently extremely short, likewise indicates that punishment of offenders against the market culture of the crowd was as much their purpose as their own provisioning. Targets were selected not only according to their current behaviour but also on account of their previous actions. Thus William Money, whose house was destroyed by the Norwich crowd in 1766 and who was a target of vexatious prosecution the following year, had previously threatened customary rights. 'Did not the Old rogue Whip the Gleaners off his Lands?', an angry rioter retorted to a passer-by.[67] Riots provided the opportunity to avenge 'injustices' over a wider time frame.

---

62 See below, pp. 184–85.
63 See below, p. 106.
64 See below, pp. 186.
65 See below, p. 147.
66 For an example of the orderliness of even a very large crowd (over 1,000 according to one estimate), see the account of the crowd which marched from Stroudwater to Cirencester market in 1766 in Charlesworth and Randall, 'Comment: morals, markets and the crowd', p. 210.
67 See below, p. 123.

The composition of the riotous crowd reflected the social and economic make-up of the community. Thus weavers, textile workers and miners figure frequently in the accounts of and among those taken up for food disturbances. However, the protests against the new turnpikes around Bristol reveal that a wider cross-section of society might be involved in actions against threats which impinged upon wider interests. Thus farmers, small traders and colliers joined in the Jack-a-Lent protests in 1749.[68] Furthermore, the protests against the imposition of the Cider Tax in 1763 drew upon a very wide cross-section of popular opinion since the threat posed was seen to cover so wide a social stratum.[69]

The varying character and scale of protests, depending upon the issue and the events concerned, should alert us to the fact that a 'tradition' of protest need not be dependent upon full-scale food riots. Compartmentalizing protests might be neater for the historian but the community experience of protest embraced and included a variety of actions and forms. Market protests stretching from a minor mêlée around the market women's baskets to a wide-ranging quartering of the country in search of hidden granaries coexisted in the community memory alongside industrial protests and disorders, conflicts over the collection of fuel from the local woodland or over gleaning and disputes over rights to the commons. In these and in other ways, a repertoire of protest forms was developed. In this way, as Charlesworth and Randall have argued, 'the defence of particular customs became experiences that justified and reinforced belief in the moral economy and gave the crowd further resolve to go on to the streets to assert other customary rights when occasion arises, thereby further enriching the tradition'.[70]

Most of the historical writing concerning both food riots and the moral economy centres around the lower orders, the middling ranks, where they appear, doing so either as apologists for the free market, supporters of 'order' or as the active destroyers of the customary economy of the poor. Yet, as Simon Renton shows in his study of Norwich in Chapter 6, we would do well to interrogate such a view. The evidence from that city in 1766 shows that, while the middling sort were not prepared to take an active part in market disturbances, they might endorse the crowd's actions in a clear and meaningful way. Moreover, utilizing the real powers they might exercise within the corporation, they were also prepared to express their hostility towards those at whom the crowd's ire had been channelled. The middling sort of Norwich, the artisans and urban tradespeople, proved themselves supporters of a moral

68 See below, pp. 51–52.
69 See below, pp. 76–78.
70 Charlesworth and Randall, 'Comment: morals, markets and the crowd', p. 208.

economic stance not only for their own material self-interest but also from the weight of the political culture of Norwich.

The privileged insight into the workings of the power relations within that city accorded by the remarkable survival of the presentment jury records raises the question as to how far the attitudes of the Norwich middling sort may be considered typical. Yet, even in Bristol, a city with a very different economic trajectory and with a long-asserted faith in free market capitalism, Poole has discovered some very interesting evidence of organized boycotts of foodstuffs and of dealers by the middling sort in Bristol in the 1790s. He notes that, while the respectable citizens might not approve of the riotous form of much popular protest, 'boycotting, like rioting, exploited collective strength to impose a "just" price over the rights of individual retailers'.[71] Renton is prepared to go further: 'A deep commitment to a world view structured by a discourse of rights and entitlements, in which communities had obligations to protect their weaker and poorer members from the ill-effects of both natural and man-made disasters, was required to make them behave in this way'.[72]

Further careful research is needed on the middle-class role in times of market disorder before we can ascertain whether the moral economy of the crowd did indeed have a wider social audience than even Thompson suggested. The evidence from two such different cities certainly suggests that it may well have. While the middling sort might share the moral economic values of the crowd, they frequently possessed the opportunity to exercise some choice, the power of money to buy alternative commodities or the resources to have stored food in other forms. Renton and Poole likewise direct us to look again at the role of the press as moulders of opinion, teetering at times on the edge of endorsing protest against forestallers and yet recognizing the need to maintain order. Indeed, this is the stance which characterized that of the gentry and urban magistracy. This brings us back to the other pole of Thompson's 'field of force', the local authorities.

Just as there was a 'theatre of riot', so too was there a theatre of response from the landed authorities. Riots or the threat of riot were often met with a response which was overtly placatory. In 1766 the government itself may be seen in this role with its proclamation against forestalling and regrating, a proclamation which lent weight to the popular belief that the scarcity was artificial. John Pitt noted sarcastically that while the scarcity was real, 'this necessity was laid to the factors having drained the country. Associations to prosecute were set on foot.'[73] Such associations, and those to organize subscriptions to obtain magazines of wheat to feed the poor, were standard responses. Landlords

---

71 See below, p. 111.
72 See below, p. 134.
73 British Library, Hardwicke Mss., Pitt to Hardwicke, 21 December 1766.

published public notices to tenants warning them not to job in corn or cattle. Yet how far were these actions only tokens? One disgruntled anonymous author from Gloucestershire noted sourly:

> on the first assembly of the Mobb the worthy gentlemen met and declared in public they would use some means to oblige the farmers to reduce the high price of grain and we find all is dropt and nothing done for our extreem necessity.[74]

Yet, as the evidence for Bristol makes clear, civic action or the actions of local gentry in the rural areas could make a positive contribution towards securing supplies of cheaper food and in restraining the dealers. In truth, the local landlords were playing an ambiguous role. As legatees of a paternalist philosophy, they felt obligated to uphold the customary model of social and economic relations. Yet as progressive landlords they were responsible for the enclosures and for the turnpikes which helped create and necessitated the rise of the wider system of marketing which was at the same time undermining the very paternal and regulatory fabric. It is little wonder that their actions were often seen by the food-rioting crowd as confusing.

For some other forms of public disturbance, apparent support from the landed ranks was more obvious. The general distrust of turnpikes meant that even when the cases concerning the Bristol turnpike rioters were heard in Salisbury, the jury would not convict. Punishment was meted out to selected rioters. But the lack of 'vigour' in prosecution demanded by some indicates an ambivalence at best on the part of the local regional authorities.[75]

One aspect of popular protest against market change which also deserves more careful scrutiny is the role of symbolism. Recent work on the popular politics of eighteenth-century England by historians such as Brewer and O'Gorman has emphasized the importance of symbolic devices as a means of rallying support and affirming senses of identity.[76] Thus at elections a rich panoply of symbolism was utilized to convey messages to the widest possible audience. Celebrations of victories or other occasions were marked with bonfires, firework displays and feasts while opposition to enemies or the public execration of those blamed for national disgrace such as the unfortunate Admiral Byng might be marked by effigy burning. This theatre of the streets was a highly effective means of reinforcing political messages to a largely sub-literate populace. The displays of largesse and licence likewise emphasized the paternal care and indulgence of the rich for the poor.

Symbolism, however, was not the sole preserve of the powerful. As the essays

---

74 Randall, 'Gloucestershire food riots', p. 88.
75 See below, pp. 53, 62.
76 J. Brewer, *Party, Ideology and Popular Politics at the Accession of George III* (Cambridge, Cambridge University Press, 1976); F. O'Gorman, 'Campaign rituals and ceremonies: the social meaning of elections in England, 1780–1860', *Past and Present*, No. 135, 1992.

in this book show, the crowd too utilized a symbolism and counter-theatre of its own, often to significant effect. The sound of the cow's horn and the 'flags' made from the bolting cloths seized from mills where the crowd found the means to adulterate flour formed part of a ritual display which food rioters across the country demonstrated. The large crowd, some thousand strong, which left Stroudwater for the march upon the main corn market of Cirencester in 1766 utilized these features but also had its own drums and, apparently, its own music. The Jack-a-Lent marchers in Somerset in 1749 displayed elaborate symbolism: two chiefs on horseback, one with his face blackened, the other carrying a silk handkerchief on a pole as a standard; three drummers and a hunting horn; marchers bearing rusty swords, broad axes and other weapons; and all with emblems in their hats carrying the initials JL. The mixture of carnivalesque and rank intimidation of those who were trying to establish the turnpikes was a potent mixture.[77] Here we see in a most knowing way a counter-theatre of licence that matched the theatre of order and domination of the patricians.

We can see the working of such symbolism most clearly in the response to the Cider Tax of 1763 in the West of England examined in Chapter 4, for here the symbolic trappings of the elite were appropriated by the crowd in an unusual manner. The Cider Tax generated enormous resentment in the West since it was seen by a wide cross-section of the community as a clear and deliberate act of oppression by an unpopular government. The celebrations of the Peace in 1763 turned into major demonstrations against the tax and the administration. Interestingly, there is no evidence of these demonstrations being planned or coordinated 'from above'. They were well received by the press and by those landlords in the West, by far the majority, who shared the popular anger against the measure. However, while the crowd were accorded licence to burn effigies of Bute and to enact their own theatre of protest, it is noticeable that more efforts were made to rein in such demonstrations when respectable opinion began to be directed towards a Parliamentary campaign. The landed classes needed to let those in Westminster know the anger of the crowd in the region. But they did not want to lose face by appearing unable to manage the crowd.[78]

Such popular responses to threats of change and transformation provide us not only with valuable insights into the class relations of eighteenth-century Britain. They also reflect some interesting patterns concerning the symbols of an emerging national political culture.

---

77 See below, Chapter 3.
78 See below, Chapter 4.

CONCLUSION

What may we conclude from the foregoing *tour d'horizon?*

The eighteenth-century market was an evolving and developing entity, subject to and the author of a variety of economic and social changes. Study of the role of the market in the eighteenth century raises a variety of conceptual and methodological issues and gives rise to considerable debate because, as Thompson noted, 'the "market" turns out to be a junction-point between social, economic and intellectual histories, and a sensitive metaphor for many kinds of exchange'.[79] This volume approaches the market from the social and cultural direction and it does not claim that this approach is the only or the most 'valid' one. Our collective concern is to examine the market as a focus for changing social, economic and political relationships.

These examinations strongly suggest that we should resist the notion that the process of modernizing change in the market in the eighteenth century was an uneventful or an uncontested picture of adaptation. Rich and poor alike in the eighteenth century were the inheritors of social and economic attitudes which stretched far into the past and which had become deeply embedded into popular culture. Those who wished to bring about change did not by any means find the process an easy one. The confident modernism of the Enlightenment found its advocates. But they also found many more opponents, who, if their numbers were diminished by the turn of the century, had little liking for the free market and unfettered capitalist world order they foresaw. That even the mercantile elite in Bristol, much given to pontificating about the importance of free trade, should have preserved the moral economic principles of the older world speaks volumes. Forces for change were undoubtedly growing increasingly powerful by 1800, though their triumph was secured rather more by the political circumstances of the propertied's fears of social revolution than by the perceived defeat of older value systems. But the forces of continuity were likewise powerful. The tensions which this titanic clash generated within the social order are only slowly being uncovered.

79 E. P. Thompson, *Customs in Common*, p. 259.

Chapter 2

POPULAR PROTEST AND THE PERSISTENCE OF CUSTOMARY CORN MEASURES: RESISTANCE TO THE WINCHESTER BUSHEL IN THE ENGLISH WEST

RICHARD SHELDON, ADRIAN RANDALL, ANDREW CHARLESWORTH AND DAVID WALSH

Pre-nineteenth-century British systems of weights and measures are notoriously complicated and difficult for the modern observer to understand. As is well known, a profusion of apparently quaint and archaic weights and measures were to be found in use in the market place and farmyard into the eighteenth century and beyond. Thus, there were windles, rods, ells, elns, lagens, firkins, kilderkins, tuns, terses, pottles, poles and perch. One could have a bolt of oziers, a curnock of barley, a firlot of beer, a hobbit of wheat or a poke of wool. This abundance of frequently unrelated measures continues to bequeath problems to the modern historian from the pioneer quantifiers in economic history to the present-day cliometricians.[1] They create major difficulties of comparability which hinder our understanding of prices and quantities. They raise questions as to how transactions were managed in the market place. Further, their survival contrasts strongly with the notion that during the eighteenth century there was a clear and sustained development of a national market in commodities, particularly in grain. Hence, much of the recent writing on the issue places emphasis upon the success of the campaign to standardize weights and measures which came increasingly to fruition at the end of the eighteenth and early nineteenth centuries.[2] In these accounts, metrological reformers, informed by the 'quantifying spirit' of the Enlightenment (an impetus to quantify, measure, categorize and order the earth and its products),

---

1 See, for example, J. E. Thorold Rogers, *History of Agriculture and Prices in England*, 7 vols (Oxford, Clarendon Press, 1866–1902), and William H. Beveridge, 'A statistical crime of the seventeenth century', *Journal of Economic and Business History*, Vol. 1, 1928–29.
2 The best guide to British evidence is R. E. Zupko, *A Dictionary of English Weights and Measures* (Madison and London, University of Wisconsin Press, 1968). See also G. Harrison, 'Agricultural weights and measures' in Joan Thirsk (ed.), *The Agrarian History of England and Wales, Vol. 5, II, Agrarian Change* (Cambridge, Cambridge University Press, 1985) Appendix I.

are portrayed as part and parcel of a process of modernization, driven on the one hand by the force of developing commerce and on the other by the enlightened gentlemen who ran the country. It was, it is suggested, a campaign which gradually but firmly triumphed over a narrow and uninformed localism. Thus Hoppit notes in his detailed and careful account of the reformers that 'One would also expect that, as networks of trade spread, *ignorance* would gradually lessen' (our italics).[3]

However, the setting of weights and measures is not a purely scientific and technical problem pursued by disinterested philosophers and scientists: it is also an exercise of power and one that might threaten to affect materially the fragile margins of the budgets of the poor. Its history is one that is also 'replete with injustice and dramatic struggles'.[4] Thus Linebaugh has demonstrated how the redefinition of the measures used for commodities, especially tobacco, in the maritime trading centres of the Atlantic economy also meant a drive towards the abolition of customary perquisites for labourers, consequently becoming an arena for some skirmishes in the class struggle. While the rational-calculating 'reformers' came to the field armed with new techniques of accounting and novel notions of economy and efficiency, the labouring poor were buttressed with a customary consciousness and practice that opposed excessive zeal in calculation and quantification. As Linebaugh writes:

> For most people, notions of metrology were determined by the practices of the 'moral economy', whose theory owed much to those Mosaic limitations upon commodity production found in the biblical commands against unequal weights, against taking more than can be used, and against reaping a field too cleanly.[5]

The purpose of this chapter is not, then, to describe the progress of 'reform', nor to engage with the technical problems of translating archaic measures that bedevil the historians of prices, nor yet with the specialized discipline of historical metrology.[6] It is rather to examine the sources and values of the stubborn resistance to the implementation of the Winchester bushel in the eighteenth century with particular reference to the West of England as a case

---

3 J. Hoppit, 'Reforming Britain's weights and measures, 1660–1824', *English Historical Review*, No. 426, 1993, p. 92. Though not primarily concerned with English evidence, see also T. Frangsmyr, J. Heilbron and R. E. Rider, *The Quantifying Spirit in the Eighteenth Century* (Berkeley and Los Angeles, University of California Press, 1990). S. Schaffer, 'A social history of plausibility: country, city and calculation in Augustan Britain' in Simon Wilson (ed.), *Rethinking Social History* (Manchester, Manchester University Press, 1993) is also relevant and highly suggestive, though not dealing directly with metrology.

4 W. Kula, *Measures and Men* (Princeton, Princeton University Press, 1986), p. 3. This source is the most important work on the social significance of weights and measures.

5 P. Linebaugh, *The London Hanged* (Harmondsworth, Penguin, 1993), p. 162.

6 On this, see Zupko, *A Dictionary* and R. D. Connor, *The Weights and Measures of England* (London, HMSO, 1987).

study in what might be termed 'the anti-quantifying spirit'. In doing so, we are mindful of Marc Bloch's contention—cited by and extensively illustrated by Kula—that 'The persistence of measures is closely bound up with the questions of communal memory'.[7] A marked feature of many different forms of 'pre-industrial' societies is that they display a marked animosity towards those who exert excessive zeal in weighing, measuring and counting. Bad luck can come from measuring the harvest.[8] And in England, at least as late as 1697, the idea that weights and measures were born of diabolic interference, the invention of Cain, could still be seriously discussed in polite and literate circles.[9]

We must also remember that the market place, as a site for economic and extra-economic activities, occupied a crucial role in the plebeian consciousness. The market place was not merely a centre of economic exchange. It was also a theatre and one of its regular performances was the public regulation of commercial transactions: the assize of bread, the testing of weights and measures by the clerk of the market, and the public burning of those measures found to be deficient. A key prop was the corn bushel itself. Medieval historians are familiar with the notion of the corn measure being a centre-piece of community life. Even in the later eighteenth century when the practice of sale by bushel was on the retreat, in many markets it still possessed a potent symbolism. Thus, in 1796 Lord Romney proved his 'benevolent intentions' by reviving the custom of sale by bushel in Maidstone market. The corn was drawn into the market with staged ceremony: 'the first parcel was drawn by a good old-fashioned team of English oxen, truly emblematic of the days of yore, and highly gratifying to the inhabitants of that town'. No person was allowed to purchase more than a single bushel, enough to feed him- or herself and family but no more.[10] Notions of the 'just measure' linked closely with the moral economy of the crowd. In the early summer of 1753, a year which saw regionalized food protests in areas where grain supplies had been run down by export, the crowd rose in Taunton, 'women as well as men to the number of about four or five hundred'. Their first complaint was 'on account of milk being sold by a small measure'. The obnoxious pails were destroyed and the crowd then moved on from the town to settle scores with local millers.[11]

7 Cited in Kula, *Measures and Men*, p. 111.
8 Thus Kula cites, in a passage that richly illustrates the anti-quantifying mentality, the views of peasants from the Vladimir *gubernya* in the mid-nineteenth century: 'What the Lord has provided, even without counting, will find its way into our barns; it is not for us to assess the verdicts of providence. There is no way in which you can summon God to a court of law. He who calculates the yield of the harvest from our fields, sins. We gain nothing by counting.' *Measures and Men*, p. 13.
9 See, for example, N. Drake, *A Sermon Against False Weights and Measures* (London, 1697). See also Kula, *Measures and Men*, p. 3. Drake contended, however, that the author of weights and measures was more probably Tubal Cain, son of Lamech rather than Adam as the old legend had it.
10 *Gentleman's Magazine*, November 1796, p. 960.
11 British Library, Add. Mss. 32, 731, ff. 214–16, Poulett to Newcastle, 11 July 1753.

It is, we would argue, important to recognize and to seek to understand the sources of such resistance to standard measures in their regional and local context. This is worthwhile not only for the insights it provides into the attitudes of all involved towards market practices in themselves. Such a study of the persistence of sturdy localism also raises questions about the very character of the developing eighteenth-century economy and whether we can speak of the triumph of a national market in grain by this date. Indeed, Harrison points to the continuing diversity in weights and measures as a sharp reminder of the extent to which, by 1750, 'England and Wales could [still] be described as a chain of local and regional markets at this date than as one emerging national market'.[12]

I

The Winchester standards had a long history. Indeed, they may, ironically, have been in use for a longer period than many of the customary measures. Capital of the Anglo-Saxons, Winchester's great fair occupied a prominent role in the early nation's economic life and hence its standards emerged as a model for England. Thus Edgar the Peaceable ordered in the late tenth century that 'the measure of Winchester should be the standard of the realm'.[13] The Winchester bushel, the major measure of capacity, was defined physically by a large metal container which held eight gallons of grain. Nonetheless, it is clear that, despite many concerted attempts to impose this measure between 1603 and 1824, progress was slow and crab-like. 'Decades, even centuries, were necessary to bring about reform, and then all too often the results were impaired by ineptly conceived and poorly worded legislation, defects of various magnitudes in the standards, and inexperience, excessive competition, and corruption among those chosen to enforce the reforms.' The greatest difficulties encountered by the reformers concerned the abolition of local variations.[14] An ever-present obstacle to change was a dogged resistance by the lower orders of town and country against any innovation that threatened to replace local customary standards. Thus, in 1620 a West Country correspondent wrote of the hostile reception accorded to a Royal Proclamation in favour of Winchester measures: 'I cannot persuade the corne seller to make his price according to the abatement of the measure. Beside I understand that the clerk of the markett in the Countie of Devon hathe bene so rudelye dealt with there as of late as his lyfe hathe bene hassarded twice by the Countrye people'.[15]

In 1670 legislation was passed which codified and reasserted the several

---

12 Harrison, 'Agricultural weights and measures', p. 815.
13 R. E. Zupko, *British Weights and Measures* (Madison, University of Wisconsin Press, 1977), p. 11.
14 Zupko, *British Weights*, pp. 94, 95.
15 State Papers Domestic, James I, 24 June 1620, cited in Beveridge, 'A statistical crime'.

existing relevant statutes pertaining to the sale of corn and salt. The Winchester bushel was defined more precisely and prescribed as the sole legal standard. A brass exchequer bushel was sent to all the corporate towns, cities and boroughs with instructions for it to be chained in position in the public market. Fines were laid out (40s.) for any persons selling by measures not agreeable to the Winchester bushel. In addition to this, a penalty was stipulated (£5) to which the 'mayor or any other head officer' would fall liable if he did not enforce compliance to the law in this matter.[16]

II

While it appears that the Winchester bushel was widely used in the South East of England throughout the eighteenth century, it is clear that it enjoyed no such popularity in the West of England counties of Gloucestershire, Somerset and Wiltshire. Thus attempts were made by the Gloucestershire Quarter Sessions to enforce compliance with the legislation of 1670 in 1709, 1767 and 1769, but their efforts came to little.[17] Well into the nineteenth century, it is clear that 'customary' measures still held sway, if declining sway, in that county and even the principal corn factors continued to conduct their business in the old measures. As late as 1810, a particularly well-briefed pair of informers were found to have on them a target list of major corn dealers who still dealt in customary measures. These dealers included three each from Gloucester, Tewkesbury and Wilton, near Ross, two from Hereford and 'several' from Worcester, Shrewsbury and Banbury.[18] The situation in the neighbouring counties of Wiltshire and Somerset was the same. In this respect, the West of England counties replicated the experience of Oxford where, according to Wendy Thwaites, the Winchester bushel was not widely used until after 1813.[19]

We must emphasize that none of these West of England counties were in any respect 'remote'. Indeed, all were major centres of grain production and crucial to the supply of grain to the capital throughout the eighteenth century. Warminster and Devizes in Wiltshire were notable corn markets of national significance. Cirencester and, to a lesser degree, Gloucester and Tetbury fulfilled the same role in Gloucestershire. Nor was local demand insignificant. Bristol, the second city of the land, drew many of its supplies from its hinterland counties, as Steve Poole shows in Chapter 5. Additionally, the Gloucestershire and Wiltshire producers had to supply their own large and growing industrial populations of textile workers and miners. Thus, a major region in the

16 Car. II, cap. VIII. See also, Car. II, Cap. XII (2).
17 See the draft petition drawn up by Gloucester Justices in 1709. Gloucestershire County Record Office, D214/b10/4.
18 *Gloucester Journal*, 3 September 1810.
19 W. Thwaites, 'The Marketing of Agricultural Produce in Eighteenth Century Oxfordshire' (unpublished PhD thesis, University of Birmingham, 1980), p. 192.

developing national market in grain appears to have resolutely stood out against standardization.

While the eight-gallon Winchester bushel was widely ignored (though it was said that Taunton was using the Winchester bushel in 1772[20]), the measures customarily used in most of the markets of the West of England varied considerably. Ascertaining what measures were used where is by no means simple since evidence is both fragmentary and frequently contradictory. Around mid-century, the usual measure was nine gallons to the bushel, as recorded at Tewkesbury in 1769.[21] But in 1810 evidence referred to the 'customary' 9.5-gallon bushel[22] and in 1766 the Earl of Chatham was reported to have ordered wheat on his farms to be sold out at 7s. per bushel or 4s.6d. per Winchester bushel,[23] indicating that the local bushel there may have been some 12.5 gallons. We should note that the West of England was not alone in this heterogeneity. As late as the 1790s, the author of the Board of Agriculture's report on Staffordshire could point to wide variations in standards within the county:

> the custom of Wolverhampton market is eighteen ounces to the pound of butter, one hundred and twenty pounds to the hundred of cheese, nine gallons and a half to the bushel of barley, oats, beans, and pease, and seventy-two pounds to the bushel of wheat, while that of other markets in the county varies, some being more and some less.

Interestingly, the same author added, 'much complaint has been made about a regulation of weights and measures, and obliging every person to sell by the statute or standard weight or measure; but I can't think it a matter of much importance'.[24]

III

From our twentieth-century perspective and in the context of attempts to create a single market across Europe, this all appears extremely confusing. However, we must avoid projecting twentieth-century modes of business rationality back into the eighteenth. The changing significance of the notion of price is illuminating. Our conception of the price as a variable factor based upon a fixed quantity of a commodity and a fluctuating sum is a relatively recent one. For centuries the equation was seen in a different light: a fixed amount of money was exchanged for a variable quantity of goods, as, for example, with the 'penny loaf', the size of which was regulated by local officials as in the old assize of

20 *Bath Journal*, 22 June 1772.
21 *Bath Chronicle*, 26 December 1769.
22 *Gloucester Journal*, 3 September 1810.
23 *Bath Journal*, 22 September 1766.
24 Cited in J. Donaldson, *Modern Agriculture; or, The Present State of Husbandry in Great Britain* (Edinburgh, 1795), Vol. 4, p. 108.

bread. This is precisely one of the ways in which the old Thomistic notion of the 'just price' was able to retain its significance over the centuries, despite the constant ebb and flow of changing prices in subsistence foodstuffs. Rather, we must ask ourselves how the market appeared to the contemporary actors and how they managed, successfully, to conduct transactions when measures varied so widely?

We might suppose that the foremost group demanding the unequivocal establishment of the Winchester bushel would be the principal corn dealers. Customary local measures would create no difficulties for local deals in local markets. The seller and buyer would be used to them and would fix their prices accordingly. But the large-scale London dealers and middlemen who dealt at the region's main markets clearly needed to deal in measures which were known to them. Economic historians have rarely enquired how dealers coped with local variants. The answer is that they used their own ready-reckoners, such as, for example, John Hewitt's *The Corn Dealer's Assistant* (London, 1736), to convert local measures to Winchester measures, much as the traveller and trader today convert goods from one currency into another, to ascertain their costs and profit margins.[25] No doubt there were certain transaction costs in such a system and, as today, there were those who wished for a 'common currency' to facilitate exchange. But it is striking that, as far as the evidence allows us to judge, the large dealers were *not* the ones at a regional level pressing publicly for strict imposition of the Winchester norm, though it is of course possible that they did so privately. Certainly, had their trade been harmed as much as the advocates of strict observance of the 1670 statute claimed, one would have expected rather more fuss from them over a much longer time frame.

Dealers might indeed see advantages in a multiplicity of measures since it provided them with the opportunity to enhance margins within transactions. Kula notes that in the early modern economies of Europe it was possible for traders to profit, not only in spite of, but precisely because of variations in the capacity, weight and usage of standards. Thus, a dealer might buy grain in a heaped measure and sell it in a struck (levelled) measure, his profit lying in the 'top'.[26] Dealers clearly were a powerful force in the market place, the more so when, on occasions, they formed 'rings' or combinations to manipulate market prices. Thus, a witness from Surrey informed a Parliamentary committee in 1734 that:

> The mealmen have combined together under a penalty, to buy no more corn pitched in the market, and that all corn should for the future be bought by samples. And thereby the mealmen, not being contented to take the market bushel, fix the price of

25 See also R. Harvey, *The Farmer's and Corn-Buyer's Assistant* (Norwich, 1764), and, for the nineteenth century, The *Agriculturalist's Calculator*, n.d., n.p.
26 Kula, *Measures and Men*, pp. 102–03 and *passim*.

corn on the farmers and the measure too; for they oblige the farmers to sell them so much corn for a bushel as weighs seventy-two pounds, which generally increases their measure to five bushels the sack, whereas formerly a sack held only four bushels; and they resell it again to the poor at fifty-six pounds only the bushel.[27]

If the main market traders of the region were not apparently disadvantaged by the persistence of non-standard measures, we may well ask who was instrumental in bringing pressure to conform and with what motive?

Support in the West of England for the standardization of measures to the Winchester bushel came from the larger farmers and landholders. This in turn often reflected the increasing influence of small cliques of farmers and dealers who were deliberately making more marginal the role of small traders, especially women, in the market place.[28] Additionally, pressure could come from those with the task of setting the assize of bread who frequently complained that the task was made nearly impossible by the multiplicity of measures.[29]

An elite cadre of the farmers and dealers of Gloucestershire seems to have been vigorously active in the promotion of the Winchester bushel very early. At the county Quarter Sessions in 1711, a petition of the High Sheriff, Justices of the Peace, Grand Jury, other freeholders and farmers of the county petitioned the House of Commons for action against 'the great and unlawful measures' by which corn was sold in the region. This was despite their 'utmost endeavours to have the laws put in execution for regulating the measures' and their attempts to prosecute offenders 'by indictments and informations'. They complained that all this had been to no effect since 'the bakers, maltsters, and other corn buyers utterly refuse to buy any corn by the lawful Winchester measure'.[30] Those present might have been surprised to learn that so dogged was local attachment to the customary bushels that their descendants in office would pass a resolution in similar terms more than a century later.[31]

IV

The non-observance of the Winchester bushel was clearly a source of irritation to some. But the efforts of the bench in the West of England to enforce the

---

27 Cited by E. Lipson, *The Economic History of England* (London, A. & C. Black, 1931), Vol. II, p. 422. For a vivid depiction of the asymmetrical exchange process between buyer and seller in such a situation, see B. Harriss, 'Merchants and markets of grain in South Asia' in T. Shanin (ed.), *Peasants and Peasant Societies* (Harmondsworth, Penguin, 1988).

28 See, for example, W. Thwaites, 'Women in the market place: Oxfordshire c.1690–1800' in *Midland History*, Vol. IX, 1984, p. 34. Cf. the surprise elicited by the appearance of Bathsheba in the corn market in Thomas Hardy's *Far from the Madding Crowd*.

29 See, for example, *Observations and Examples to Assist Magistrates in Setting the Assize of Bread* (London, 1759).

30 *Journal of the House of Commons*, Vol. XVI, 1711, p. 624.

31 *Bristol Gazette*, 15 October 1812.

Winchester bushel were at best intermittent and rarely powerfully sustained. Thus, in 1709 the Gloucestershire Easter Quarter Sessions ordered every constable in the county to ensure that the 1670 law was upheld. Yet in September we find the 'justices, gentlemen, freeholders and farmers of Gloucestershire and Worcestershire who live near to and have recourse for the selling of our corn to the markets of the city of Gloucester and the borough of Tewkesbury' petitioning the crown and complaining that, the Sessions' order notwithstanding, the old measures continued in use due to pressure from the bakers and collusion by the mayor and bailiffs. The complaint, however, did not apparently elicit any action. While the Sessions might make the order, they were clearly not inclined to enforce it. An attempt in 1732 seems also to have suffered a similar fate.[32]

The next sign of a concerted effort to break the persistence of customary measures came in the wake of the food riots that swept through many localities of provincial England in 1766. In June 1767, a subscription fund was established by the promoters of the Winchester bushel to bring prosecutions against any bakers or corn-jobbers who engaged in transactions by old measures.[33] The Sheriff and the Grand Jury were pleased to take up the proposal emanating from some of the 'principal landholders' that the Winchester measure should be made standard. Moreover, they declared that 'it shall not want their utmost Attention for its Establishment'.[34] The measure was to be strictly enforceable from June 1767, at which time the *Gloucester Journal* noted that, while local custom had long resisted standardization, the magistrates were now determined to secure its universal application.[35] The fact that two years later in 1769 the Sessions went through the same performance is ample testament to their failure.[36] In fact, this seems to have been the last such public determination on the part of the Gloucestershire bench in the eighteenth century. When the authorities in Worcestershire announced their determination to enforce the Winchester bushel in 1793,[37] it attracted no reciprocal action from the Gloucestershire bench and even in 1812, when pressure for enforcement increased across the region, the Gloucestershire authorities held their hand. In 1792 Wiltshire farmers held meetings at Devizes, Warminster and Salisbury and announced that they had formed a subscription to prosecute anyone 'who shall in future buy or sell corn in those markets by any other measure than the Winchester bushel'.[38] There is little evidence that this public

32 *Gloucester Journal*, 16 May 1732.
33 *Gloucester Journal*, 22 June 1767.
34 *Felix Farley's Bristol Journal*, 4 April 1767.
35 *Gloucester Journal*, 8 June 1767.
36 *Bath Journal*, 23 January 1769.
37 *Gloucester Journal*, 30 September 1793.
38 *Gloucester Journal*, 6 August 1792.

determination secured any real support from the bench or that the association was successful in eradicating customary measures.

Some might regard the failure to enforce the Winchester measure as evidence of the weakness of the magistracy. The persistence of the non-standard bushels, however, is evidence of the triumph of localism and local economic self-interest and indicative of the pragmatism of the justices. Since trade continued apparently unharmed and indeed grew steadily, the premium upon enforcement of a standard measure was much reduced. Moreover, assaults upon customary measures might well antagonize the crowd to little real advantage.

This can be seen in the actions of the justices at Tewkesbury in 1769 when faced with demands that they enforce the Winchester measure. Recognizing that the populace were not alone in their distrust of the motives of the dealers and large landowners who called so vociferously for adherence to the law, the magistrates played a very shrewd game. They called upon all farmers in the district to honour the pledge they had made at the earlier Sessions that not only would they sell solely by the Winchester bushel but that they would lower their prices to those current at the Bear Key market in London. No farmers came to market to pitch their grain on these terms. Thus the justices were able to point to their efforts to uphold the letter of the law, observing the wish of the Sessions, and at the same time call the farmers' bluff. Thereafter, the Winchester bushel seems to have been quietly forgotten about once more.[39]

How did the local authorities square the circle of upholding the law and at the same time avoiding confrontation? An account published in the *Gloucester Journal* in 1732 gives us an insight into the ways in which the statute law was by-passed. After the arrival of the brass exchequer bushel in the city of Gloucester, a jury met annually to regulate the other measures. The jury came up with an expediency which, it believed, accommodated its practice with both statute law and customary expectations. This is how it proceeded: the official Winchester bushel was first packed tight and shaken with corn so that as much as possible was squeezed into it. These contents were then poured very gently, so as to achieve a lesser density but greater volume of corn, into a customary bushel of about nine gallons, thereby legitimating the local measure which they continued to uphold.[40] This act of 'customization' adds another facet to the problem of customary measures and their reform: the elasticity of their usage.

The reluctance of some members of the gentry to impose the Winchester bushel in some cases indicated a deep-seated paternalism and distrust of middlemen, the traditional bogeymen of the food market. Thus Henry Hunt, the radical son of a Wiltshire gentleman, recalled: 'My father's bushel

39 *Bath Chronicle*, 26 January 1769.
40 *Gloucester Journal*, 16 May 1732.

contained full ten gallons, and when the little bushel was established, four of our bushels made exactly five of the Winchester measure'. So great was the aversion of Hunt senior and junior to the Winchester bushel that, even following a strict enforcement of the standard, or so Henry junior claimed in his *Memoirs*, they continued to fill their sacks of grain with five bushels of corn into a sack 'so that they were always of the same size and weight as they were before the measure was altered'.[41]

As their actions during times of food riot showed, the gentry frequently mixed paternalist pronouncements with pragmatic action to placate the crowd. During shortages it was not at all unusual for the largest landowners to make public declarations of orders to farm stewards or tenants to sell corn at a price set below the inflated market rate, thereby reinforcing their reputation as friends of the poor.[42] Such orders often specified the use of 'old measure', doubly reinforcing the message. Occasionally at such times, local authorities likewise threw their weight behind traditional marketing practices and customary bushels. Thus, in May 1757 it was reported:

> a meeting of the justices and other gentlemen of the county of Somerset, was held at Bruton, in order to settle the price of corn; when the farmers had notice, that they must bring their corn to market, and sell the best wheat for 10s a bushel old measure; and that the poor must be served before the miller or the baker.[43]

It cannot be doubted that such actions served to underline the sense of moral legitimacy associated with customary measures in the same way as the pronouncements of such men condemning the actions of forestallers and regraters reinforced popular belief in the moral economy of the crowd.

V

The justices were right to fear the wrath which attempts to undermine customary measures might excite. It is clear that opposition to the reformers was widespread in the West of England. Opposition to the Winchester bushel came from many who bought in the market, not merely the petty consumer but also from the large ones. Bakers were blamed by the petitioners in 1709 for the failure to secure enforcement of the Winchester bushel: 'the bakers . . . combine together not to buy any of the Winchester measures'.[44] Two years later, a petition from the High Sheriff, justices and Grand Jury complained that 'the bakers, maltsters and other corn buyers utterly refuse to buy any corn by the

---

41 H. Hunt, *Memoirs of Henry Hunt Esq.* (London, 1820), Vol. I, pp. 237–38.
42 See E. P. Thompson, *Customs in Common* (London, Merlin, 1991), p. 300, and for some examples, Ian Gilmour, *Riot Risings and Revolution* (London, Hutchison, 1992), p. 235.
43 *Gloucester Journal*, 24 May 1757.
44 Gloucester County Record Office, D214 B10/4.

lawful Winchester measure'.[45] At Tetbury 'eminent farmers' tried and failed to introduce the Winchester measure, blaming this failure upon the millers who apparently refused to purchase at the new measure in 1767.[46] Certainly the millers and the maltsters could and did exercise considerable influence in the market by virtue of their purchasing power. When combined, they could prove a formidable force. Thus, in 1757 a combination of maltsters forced prices down in Warminster market and, according to one report, was seeking to extend its influence further afield.[47] And, in 1800, the *Bath Journal* contained a report complaining that millers were successfully controlling prices at country markets.[48]

Opposition also came from the crowd. Popular hostility to change can be seen clearly in Gloucester in 1767/8. As noted above, in April the Grand Jury supported a request from leading landholders and announced its determination to implement the 1670 law as from June. However, it is clear that, announcements notwithstanding, there remained considerable resistance to change. Support from the *Gloucester Journal* and a new association of gentlemen and farmers to prosecute those who failed to sell at the decreed measure was forthcoming, but popular hostility is shown by an advertisement placed in the *Journal* in July:

> Whereas a number of public spirited and generous farmers have lately entered into a confederacy for the good of the poor, to bring less measure to Gloucester than is sold in any part of England, likewise to enhance the price of it, according to the old measure, 1s per bushel.

The author went on to propose an alternative market for all farmers 'not tinctured with the leaven of unrighteousness, to meet at Upton on Severn with such lawful measures as sold by all honest men', and signed off under the name 'Pro Bono Publico', with the classic lines of 'moral economy' scripture as his coda: 'He that witholdeth the corn the people shall curse him, but blessing shall fall on the head of him that selleth it (Prov XI, 26)'.[49] Clearly there remained the deep suspicion that dealers and farmers hoped to be able to reap easy profits by buying at the old and selling at the new, smaller, measure.

The same strength of feeling could also be expressed by means of subtle and oblique commentary in the columns of newspapers. Consider the following example:

> A demure old farmer was observing at Gloucester, that he was afraid that bakers and meal-men never read their Bible; but as they always read the newspapers, he desired

45 *Journal of the House of Commons*, Vol. XVI, p. 624.
46 *Felix Farley's Bristol Journal*, 16 July 1767.
47 *Bath Journal*, 10 January 1757.
48 *Bath Journal*, 10 March 1800.
49 *Gloucester Journal*, 6 July 1767.

that they might be given the following texts of scripture:- 'Just Balances, Just Weights, a Just Epah, and a Just Hin shall ye have' Levt. XIX, 36. 'Diverse weights and diverse measures, both of them are alike abomination to the Lord.' Prov. XX, 10.[50]

While some used the press to lambast the supporters of the Winchester bushel, the crowd sometimes took direct action, its deep-rooted suspicion of change erupting in demonstrations or even riots. We may get a flavour of such responses from this account from Tetbury, addressed to the editor of the *Gloucester Journal* in April 1768 (a time of considerable social and political upheaval), when feelings against the Winchester bushel, still running high, were expressed in a surprising but unmistakable display of symbolism and civic 'rough music'.

> Wednesday last, an old venerable bushel containing nine gallons and a half adorned with trophies, was ordered into our market with drums and trumpet, bells and bonfire; and then conducted to the parish church, amidst the acclamation of all orders and degrees of men, regular and secular, and there suspended, to the great terror and amazement of the farmers on the top of our lofty steeple.[51]

The warning to those who sought to meddle with the customary measure could not have been clearer. There is no evidence that the authorities made any attempt to disperse the meeting or to remove the 'venerable bushel'. Again, in December of the same year, the crowd publicly burned Winchester bushels ('little bushels') in the market place of Tewkesbury ('the noblest bonfire that ever was seen in this borough') following accusations directed at the maltsters and bakers 'That they bought by the large measure and sold by the small one'.[52] This action—the public destruction of false weights—emulated the regular legal practice carried out by the clerk of the market or other civic officials for dealing with illegal measures.

In 1795, a year of high prices, scarcity and food rioting, some of the big local farmers were singled out for abuse and ill-treatment by a food rioting crowd at Salisbury. They 'were hustled and insulted; some of the sacks of corn were also cut by the rioters, and the corn let about the market place'. One man in particular, William Dyke of Sycencot, 'one of the largest farmers in the West of England', received the brunt of the popular ire. His coach was attacked and damaged, its windows broken by flying brick bats. By such means, Dyke was prevented from pitching his wares in the market in subsequent weeks. According to Hunt, Dyke had been singled out as a target:

> on account of his being the ring-leader in what the poor called a conspiracy to lessen the size of the bushel and, at the same time, to keep up the price of corn . . . [Dyke]

50 *Bristol Journal*, 28 March 1767.
51 *Gloucester Journal*, 25 April 1768.
52 *Bath Journal*, 19, 26 December 1768.

had been very instrumental in causing the *little bushel*, of the Winchester measure, of eight gallons, to be introduced generally in the county of Wilts, instead of the old bushel, which contained nine gallons, and in some instances ten gallons.[53]

The poor would not countenance paying more for less. There is an unmistakable resonance between the poor's hatred of the 'little' or 'small' corn measure and the elementary rules of economic conduct contained in the Old Testament: 'Thou shalt not have in thy bag divers weights, a great and a small . . . For all that do such things, and all that do unrighteously, are an abomination unto the Lord thy God.'[54]

Such open acts of hostility to the Winchester bushel and its supporters persisted into the nineteenth century. In 1810, a professional informer, a London attorney, travelling with an accomplice, aroused the anger of the crowd in Gloucester. The informer's aim was to persuade farmers to sell him grain by customary measures, whereupon he could turn the hapless vendor over to the courts who, in compliance with the statute, were obliged to hand over half of all the grain included in the contract to the informer. Potential gains, especially at a time of exceptionally high prices, were very large. Informers were an unpopular species in any case and, when news spread of the nature of his charge, an unruly crowd gathered outside the court to meet him:

> upon his retiring from the Tholsey, he was followed down Eastgate Street by a number of persons of both sexes, who, as soon as he had reached the suburbs of the city, began to pelt him with mud and dirt of all descriptions, to such a degree, that he was completely covered and disfigured; nor could the efforts of those who attempted to prevent this outrage restrain the violence of the mob.[55]

The new agricultural societies, largely formed in the later 1790s as engines to awaken interest in 'modern' methods of farming and in science generally, sometimes sought to use their influence to support the standard Winchester bushel. Thus in 1812 the North Devon Agricultural Society attempted to promote and enforce use of the Winchester bushel at Bideford market. Reaction was swift. A member of the society received an anonymous threatening letter:

> Winter nights is not past therefore your person shall not go home alive—or if you chance to escape the hand that guides this pen, a lighted match will do equal execution. Your family I know not but the whole shall be inveloped in flames, your carkase if any such should be found will be given to the dogs if it contains any moisture for the animals to devour it.[56]

---

53 Hunt, *Memoirs*, p. 238.
54 Deuteronomy, XXV, 13, 16.
55 *Gloucester Journal*, 30 September 1810.
56 HO 42/121., cited in E. P. Thompson, *The Making of the English Working Class* (Harmondsworth, Penguin, 1968), p. 68.

The antipathy of the crowd towards the attempts to implement the Winchester measure was informed by fear that it would allow a new degree of deception in the market place. In this their view was shared by many of the respectable ranks. Thus, the reporter to the Board of Agriculture for Somerset found that by 1794 the Winchester bushel was 'pretty general'. However, he noted, it was working 'to the *great benefit of the seller*, and the *great loss of the purchaser*' (emphasis in original).

> The calculation in respect to the comparative price between the old and the new measure, was formed on the difference between eight and nine gallons, but this is erroneous; the old measure of the county was not less than nine gallons and a half, and in some instances, ten gallons, so that the buyer gives seven or eight per cent more than he ought to give.[57]

There can be little wonder that, at times when food was dear, the consumer was bitterly opposed to a measure which deprived him or her of a significant part of the household budget.

The crowd also may have drawn, as in its notions of legitimate and illegitimate practices in other aspects of the moral economy, upon its knowledge of the law in its opposition to rationalized weights and measures. The thick and tangled webs of common law and agrarian practice offered potential sources of support. Thus an official guide printed in 1665 laid down the principle of *conuetudo loci est observanda* in defence of localism:

> This is to be observed, that weights and measures differ much as they are used in different countries. And the custom and vulgar opinion and practice of the country therein, except it be very unreasonable, it is to be observed.[58]

Similar support could be found in the 1780 edition of Burn's *The Justice of the Peace and Parish Officer*, which stated that, although local customs which were in contradiction of statute law were to be declared void, an exception could be made in the case of corn measures: 'the custom of the place is to be observed, if it be a custom beyond all memory, and used without any visible interruption'.[59]

VI

The magistrate who addressed the Farringdon meeting in 1812, Thomas Goodlake, claimed that one major benefit of the Winchester bushel would be to facilitate the implementation of the assize of bread. 'He stated the impossibility there was in ascertaining a correct average price where a diversity of measures are used, and consequently, the impracticability of his brother magistrates and

---

57 J. Billingsley, *A General View of the Agriculture in the County of Somerset* (London, 1794), pp. 188–89.
58 W. Sheppard, *Of the Office of the Clerk of the Market, of Weights and Measures, and of the Laws of Provision for Man and Beast, for Bread, Wine, Beer, Meal, &c.* (London, 1665), p. 26.
59 R. Burn, *The Justice of the Peace and Parish Officer* (14th edition, London, 1780), Vol. I, p. 408.

himself fixing an assize of bread.'[60] A writer to the *Gloucester Journal* from Monmouthshire made the same point, complaining that 'we have measures of such various sorts, that the magistrates would be puzzled to fix a standard for the price of a gallon loaf'.[61] How far the lack of a standardized bushel inhibited the working of the assize of bread is difficult to say, but these claims serve to remind us that customary weights and measures had an equally active existence alongside enforced standards within the market. Thus the 'bakers' dozen', a custom still remembered—if seldom observed—in England, would seem to owe its origin to the stipulations of the thirteenth-century assize of bread. Under that assize, fine calculations were made, taking into account the prevailing price of wheat and the baker's standing costs and allowing a fair profit to the baker at the end of the day. A baker who sold light measure of more than two shillings would face 'the judgement of the body' upon the pillory. Given the perpetual problem of predicting the weight of a loaf after baking and the possible variations, the apprehensive bakers erred on the side of caution and delivered 13 loaves for the price of 12, giving themselves the 'safety net' of a leeway of 8.33 per cent.[62] Memories were long in the eighteenth century and, in the heated atmosphere of the year 1766, historical anecdotes were dredged up for public edification. Newspapers carried stories like this one:

> In the 4th year of the reign of King Edward II, a baker, John of Stratford by name, was, for making bread less than the assize, drawn on a hurdle through the streets of London with a fool's hood and loaves of bread about his neck. And why not the same now?[63]

A complicated body of legislation and common law precept surrounded the use and abuse of weights and measures in the market place. Thus Sheppard's *Office of the Clerk* stipulated the duty of the Justices of Assize to 'once a year over-look the weights and measures, and break and burn such as are defective, and punish the offenders'.[64] Throughout the eighteenth century, the justices and the market authorities were assiduous in the maintenance of control over other weights and measures in the market. There is an abundance of evidence which indicates that in many places scrupulous attention was paid to the weights used by dealers, while the assize of bread—whose status is well described by Clapham as 'a kind of economic common law'[65]—was enforced on a regular

60 *Gloucester Journal*, 30 March 1812.
61 *Gloucester Journal*, 16 November 1812.
62 R. D. Connor, *Weights and Measures*, pp. 198–99.
63 *Bath Journal*, 9 September 1766.
64 Sheppard, *Office of the Clerk*, p. 110.
65 J. H. Clapham, *An Economic History of Modern Britain: The Early Railway Age* (Cambridge, Cambridge University Press, 1950), p. 344. On the assize of bread, see S. and B. Webb, 'The assize of bread', *Economic Journal*, Vol. XIV, 1904. An excellent modern study is W. Thwaites, 'The assize of bread in 18th century Oxfordshire', *Oxoniensia*, Vol. LI, 1986. There is no modern study of the office of the

basis in many markets into the nineteenth century. In this we see in practical fashion that the paternal model of the market was very much alive in small ways.

The execution of the duty of magistrates, clerks and juries was often turned into a public performance of an expected role in a theatre of justice. In the City of Bath, a conspicuous spectacle was made of the regular efforts of the officers to root out short weights, especially in times of high prices and acute disturbance. Thus, in March 1753, the Mayor of Bath ordered his officers to tour the market testing the weight of butter. A 'great quantity', including 25 pounds from one woman, was found to be deficient in weight and so was confiscated and distributed to the poor.[66] Such seizures of short weight wares, especially butter, and their distribution among the poor was a regular practice in Bath and in many other towns. In July 1766, 'a strict examination was made into the weights and measures of this city; when many persons were fined. And Thursday, a great number of gardeners' measures were burnt in the market place.'[67] And in 1808 the county magistrates convicted 45 petty dealers of the country villages surrounding Tewkesbury, finding 199 defective weights and balances.[68] Such actions may have been overwhelmingly directed at petty traders rather than against the large dealers, but they created an expectation on the part of the crowd that the authorities would maintain vigilant guard to ensure that the weights and measures of the market place could not be used to defraud the consumer.

While those found guilty of short weight or unjust measure faced retribution both from the justices and from the crowd, popular ire could also descend upon those who were felt to display parsimony in the striking of an exact balance, as demonstrated by the following event reported to have occurred in the market at Wellington (Somerset) in 1812:

> A singular proof of the poverty of spirit which the severity of the times has induced . . . A poor woman having bargained for a pound of potatoes, the female who sold them not being able with perfect accuracy to make up the weight, actually with her teeth, separated a potato in two portions, and thus adjusted the pound with the extremest correctness! The bye-standers, indignant at the pitiful proceedings, raised a subscription among themselves, and paid the crier for reporting the fact about the town.[69]

---

clerk of the market. For an explanation of his function and duties, see Sheppard, *Office of the Clerk of the Market* (London, 1665) and also Connor, *Weights and Measures*, pp. 325–28.

66 *Bath Journal*, 19 March 1753. For similar examples, see A. D. Leadley, 'Some villains of the eighteenth-century market place' in J. Rule (ed.), *Outside the Law: Studies in Crime and Order 1650–1850* (Exeter, Exeter Papers in Economic History no. 15, 1982).

67 *Bath Chronicle*, 10 July 1766.

68 *Gloucester Journal*, 1 February 1808.

69 *Bath Journal*, 27 July 1812.

Popular notions of legitimate and illegitimate market practices had powerful resonances in market behaviour and practices beyond the eighteenth century. An incident that took place in Glastonbury, occasioned by rumours of sharp practice among the town's bakers, can serve to demonstrate the durability of these notions and their continuing association with matters of day-to-day sustenance. In 1867 (a year of high prices marked by the reprise of food-rioting in some West of England locations), the Guy Fawkes' day procession—an occasion often appropriated for symbolic protests concerning local issues—was marked in the following manner:

> Between eight and nine a procession was formed by some hundreds of people . . . and an effigy, about seven feet high (got up in capital form by a local artist, Percival) and illuminated with fireballs, was carried through the town on the shoulders of a dozen men, headed by the brass band, tar barrels, fireworks, &c. The effigy represented injustice partly blinded, holding a scale in the left hand with a loaf of bread in it, short weight, and a sword in the right hand; it was standing on a labourer lying down with a spade by his side, and curled round the waist of the effigy was a serpent. On arriving opposite the baker's a halt was made, and groans of 'short weight' and such like were given.[70]

VII

It is clear that in the years from 1810 onwards, efforts to establish the Winchester bushel began to take a more decisive hold upon the market. The case noted above concerning the unsuccessful attempt to impeach a dealer in 1810 led the *Gloucester Journal* to warn farmers and corn dealers to be on their guard 'as there are comparatively few, we presume, who are even aware of the existence of the penal statute in question'.[71] In March 1812 it was again warning of travelling informants who had recently laid informations against farmers at Farringdon. Public meetings followed, at Farringdon and at Stow in April, 'to consider the propriety of introducing the legal or Winchester measure in place of that now used'.[72] And, in November 1812, the Quarter Sessions yet again resolved to 'enforce the existing laws'.[73] This was followed by a meeting of farmers 'to consider the propriety of introducing the legal or Winchester measure in place of that now used'. An association was formed which pledged to implement the Winchester bushel as sole measure in the county after 14 November 1812.[74] It is clear that, unlike the previous reprise of this tune in 1768, this time the resolutions took more effect. In part, this may have been a

---

70 *Taunton Courier*, 13 November 1867. On the food riots of 1867, see R. D. Storch, 'Popular festivity and consumer protest: food price disturbances in the Southwest and Oxfordshire in 1867', *Albion*, Vol. 14, Winter 1982.

71 *Gloucester Journal*, 3 September 1810.

72 *Gloucester Journal*, 30 March 1812.

73 *Gloucester Journal*, 16 November 1812.

74 *Gloucester Journal*, 13 April 1812.

reflection of the increase in the prosecutions for failing to use the Winchester measure. Much was made of the threats to the capitals of dealers found guilty at the behest of professional informers. Yet this begs the question as to why such informers had not succeeded in cashing in upon this potential gold mine earlier. The petition of 1709 had claimed that farmers were in fear of prosecution, yet there is little evidence to suggest that, odd scares apart, they were in any real sense influenced in their marketing practices for the rest of the century. Certainly, had the informers proved successful, there is little doubt but that dealers would have been much less willing to continue to trade in customary measures. And, since the parish was entitled to secure half of the fine in such cases, some benefits might be assumed to have accrued to the poor. Yet, as we have seen, informers threatening the customary bushel received short shrift from the crowd.

While change certainly began to spread after 1812, the implementation of the Winchester measure remained a protracted one. Thus William Marshall noted in his *Review of the Reports to the Board of Agriculture from the Western Department* (York, 1810) the following passage from Plymley's report on Shropshire:

> An attempt was made by order of sessions some years ago, to introduce an uniformity of weights and measures, and it was accomplished in Bishop's Castle market, by the perseverance and activity of a neighbouring magistrate; but as the same attention was not continued in other markets, the old measures were in time introduced again.[75]

More work needs to be done in other regions of the country before we can with any confidence advance reasons for the belated triumph of the Winchester bushel. We may perhaps point to factors including the political situation in 1812 with grain prices at their peak, well beyond the crisis levels of 1795 or 1800, a national emergency threatened by Luddism, a war with both France and now the USA, and a philosophy of *laissez faire* increasingly dictating government policy. But in truth it is hard to sustain. While a sea change may well have been taking place, the reasons for the apparent collapse of sturdy localism in defence of customary measures are much harder to account for.

VIII

What can we conclude from this examination of the protracted resistance to the implementation of the Winchester bushel in the West of England in the eighteenth century? Does much of the evidence we have surveyed point towards a 'conservative' and backward-looking mentality among labouring consumers and small farmers? Perhaps, to some extent. Malinowski and de la Fuente posed the same question in an ethnographic study of Mexican markets in the 1940s.

---

75 W. Marshall, *A Review of the Reports to the Board of Agriculture from the Western Department* (York, 1810), p. 226.

Their findings and reflections may throw some light on our question. The Mexican government had for some time endeavoured to implement standard metric measures for the commerce of maize. Popular custom, however, resisted, favouring instead the old Spanish 'almud', a wooden measure.

> The poor Indian and peasant prefer the almud, not because they are 'conservative' or 'dislike innovations', but because this measure enters into all their domestic calculations in a manner which has been standardised for centuries, and they are accustomed to calculate with it. Thus they know how many tortillas can be produced from one almud, or how many cups or bowls of atole (maize drink); in short, how many almudes per week their budgets require. Thus, they prefer to buy in terms of this old measure.

Likewise, vendors knew the measure well and preferred to sell by it. Grain was more easily seen in the almud, giving the buyer a greater feeling of security and trust. 'For all these reasons, buyers and sellers are even more opposed to measure their produce in metric measures.'[76]

Given the fact that the Winchester bushel itself had a long pedigree and claim to customary usage, resistance to attempts to establish this measure in place of local customary measures might be better understood, not as blind acts of hostility to the new, but as improvised defensive performances drawn from a repertoire of customary claims based upon a historical memory open to selective recall.[77] Historians need to pay more attention to the artefacts of material culture and to everyday practices, for both of these reflect and embody social relations and expressions of power.

We may, for example, gain some illumination from more recent events. Eighteenth-century Britain is not to be seriously compared with twentieth-century Africa, but consider the following two events. On a Saturday market day in Carmarthen in March 1795, 'a mob' assembled in the market place, marched on the corn market where they 'forcibly carried away the Winchester measure belonging to the corporation, and bore it away in triumph to a neighbouring iron forge, where they burnt it to pieces'. Later, they returned to the market where they 'insisted on being supplied with corn, butter, and other necessaries of life at reduced prices'.[78] As the present chapter was typed in 1994, protestors took to the streets in Brikama, The Gambia, following news of the privatization of the water supply and the introduction of a new price system. The town elders stated that 'sale of water by bucket may god forbid'. 'We had our wells before,

---

76 B. Malinowski and J. de la Fuente, *Malinowski in Mexico. The Economics of a Mexican Market System*, ed. Susan Drucker-Brown (London, Routledge & Kegan Paul, 1982), pp. 176–77.

77 Here, see especially the work of J. C. Scott, in particular his recent overview of strategies of resistance, *Domination and the Arts of Resistance* (New Haven and London, Yale University Press, 1990), which is full of suggestive insights.

78 *Felix Farley's Bristol Journal*, 7 March 1795.

they brought the taps as a sign of progress. Now they want to charge us for each bucket of water.' A crowd of up to 2,000 gathered in the market and marched on the offices of the area council:

> It is reported that the rest of the staff deserted the building before the crowd arrived. Once they arrived, the buckets which were designed to be used for measurement were seized and crushed beyond repair.[79]

Weights and measures are social institutions which can tell us something about the society and economy in which they operate. While analysis of prices, taxes, rents and wages has always formed the most important pillars of the discipline of economic history, the significance of weights and measures, both in themselves (rather than as technical problems for the historian) and as social institutions mediating relations of exchange and exploitation as well as power, has been neglected. We need to extend our knowledge of their roles, not only in the market place but also in the workplace, as in such industries as mining or textiles where again, this time as producers, the labouring crowd were acutely conscious of their real and symbolic importance. The ubiquity of the scales of justice or the notion of the just measure as symbols redolent of justice and fair play in general suggests that this may be a fertile avenue of investigation for scholars of other periods and places. This preliminary study of corn measures reinforces, we would contend, the importance of the study of the interface between customary practice and economic and social change.

---

79 *Daily Observer* (Banjul), 5 April 1994, quotations from *Foroyaa*, 15 April 1994. Thanks to Guy Roberts-Holmes and Pamela Kea for information and references.

Chapter 3

THE JACK-A-LENT RIOTS AND OPPOSITION TO TURNPIKES IN THE BRISTOL REGION IN 1749

ANDREW CHARLESWORTH, RICHARD SHELDON, ADRIAN RANDALL AND DAVID WALSH

I

In 1754, a correspondent to the *Gentleman's Magazine* argued a case for good roads when he wrote, 'Whatever quickens and cheapens the transportation of goods, and makes their migration more easy from place to place, must of course render a state more wealthy.' For the most part the correspondent was referring to good turnpike roads where 'smoothness, spaciousness and the advantage of celerity in passage' achieved these objectives.[1] Popular opposition to turnpikes in certain localities throughout the first half of the eighteenth century suggests that others had a less optimistic view of such highways and the trusts that administered them.

Turnpike trusts were set up by Act of Parliament. Groups of local people (trustees) were thereby granted temporary powers to maintain and upgrade defined stretches of road, the cost of which was borne by charging tolls at gates along the route. As Langford notes, 'By 1770 they covered 15,000 miles of road, administered by more than five hundred separate trusts'.[2] Opposition sprang from the fact that, as Langford and others have pointed out, the tolls charged were 'in the nature of a tax, supplementing one form of highway rate with another', for the trusts operated on roads which 'were usually ancient thoroughfares, previously maintained by statute labour and travelled free by all who used them'.[3] It is important to emphasize that 'before the eighteenth century the highway was not so much an actual body of land reserved and maintained for the convenience of traffic as a "right of passage" for every subject of the Crown over another's land'.[4] The right of passage was a communal property right, intended for the benefit of, and to be exercised by, all

---

1 *Gentleman's Magazine*, August 1754, p. 347.
2 P. Langford, *Public Life and the Propertied Englishman, 1689–1798* (Oxford, Clarendon Press, 1991), p. 163.
3 Langford, p. 164.
4 E. Pawson, *Transport and Economy: The Turnpike Roads of Eighteenth-Century Britain* (London, Academic Press, 1977), p. 64.

people. The trusts sought to realign such property rights and abrogate the right of free passage. What heightened the sense of grievance felt by ordinary people was the fact that tolls had to be charged ahead of the actual improvements. Thus the benefits were future ones. Moreover, the benefits fell unevenly or were perceived to fall unevenly between different communities and different groups within the same community.

The level of opposition, particularly in terms of popular protest, has been the subject of debate between historians and historical geographers in the last twenty years.[5] Historians have been faced with the problem of how to assess the level and extent of that opposition. For many economic historians, as for some historical geographers, the problem is easily negotiated. Count the number of protest events and then map them, count the number of county petitions to turnpike Bills and arrive at an aggregate figure for the eighteenth century, and there are your measures of opposition. It is hard quantifiable evidence, much more reliable, they would argue, than contemporary literary evidence that might suggest at the very least an antipathy among certain classes to the innovation. To those familiar with the historiography of popular opposition to that other ubiquitous innovation of the eighteenth century, enclosure, this is all very familiar. Yet research on that latter topic, particularly by Neeson, suggests that the problem of determining the level of popular opposition and its regional variations is more intractable.[6] However, with persistent interrogation of a variety of sources and by placing opposition, however expressed, in its proper historical context, a much richer and more complex picture emerges.

This study of turnpike protests in the West of England in 1749 seeks to do this. The opposition found there gives us insights not only into the plebeian, rebellious culture of the region but also into the way local and central government viewed the activities of the turnpike trusts in the first half of the eighteenth century.

II

Turnpike disturbances appear to have begun in the Bristol region in 1727 with the passage of two Acts that affected the roads running eastward from Bristol

---

5 D. G. D. Isaac, 'A study of popular disturbances' (unpublished PhD thesis, University of Edinburgh, 1953), chapter 5; Pawson, *Transport and Economy*; W. Albert, 'Popular opposition to turnpike trusts in early eighteenth-century England', *Journal of Transport History*, New Series, Vol. 5, No. 1, 1979, pp.1–17; E. Pawson, 'Debates in transport history: popular opposition to turnpike trusts?', *Journal of Transport History*, 3rd Series, Vol. 5, 1984, pp. 57–65; W. Albert, 'Popular opposition to turnpike trusts and its significance', *Journal of Transport History*, 3rd Series, Vol. 5, 1984, pp. 66–68; M. Freeman, 'Popular attitudes to turnpikes in early-eighteenth-century England', *Journal of Historical Geography*, Vol. 19, No. 1, 1993, pp. 33–47.

6 J. Neeson, *Commoners: Common Right, Enclosure and Social Change in England 1700–1820* (Cambridge, Cambridge University Press, 1993).

through Kingswood Forest.[7] The colliers of the region, in particular those of Kingswood, immediately demonstrated their opposition to the new tolls. Gates were destroyed and the Kingswood colliers marched through the city itself, refused to deliver coal to Bristol and then levied their own tolls on travellers. Gates further afield were then attacked. Disturbances also occurred on roads running north to Gloucester and in the Stroud–Dursley region. In 1728 a new Act of Parliament was passed, increasing the penalty for attacks on turnpikes so that a second offence became liable to transportation for seven years. In 1731, a new Act for turnpiking exempted pack animals carrying coal from payment of tolls, one of the colliers' grievances. With these two new Acts in place, the trustees began to re-erect the gates. Again the colliers, with some 'country people', retaliated on those turnpikes where the exemption of coal traffic did not appear to be applied. Other disturbances broke out in Herefordshire, so in 1732 another Act was passed, this time making first offences liable to transportation for seven years. Gates were re-erected and again attacked, but this time the authorities acted swiftly to re-assert their authority.

If that show of determination worked, it only did so within that particular locality, for, two years later, attacks on turnpikes broke out again in Herefordshire and Gloucestershire. The region affected stretched from Tewkesbury in the north to Stonehouse in the south and westward to Ledbury. One report suggested that gates as far south as Bristol were also attacked. These gates had been in some cases established for over thirteen years. The reaction to this fresh outbreak of disturbances was severe. In 1735, turnpike cutting was made a capital offence. Nevertheless, when the gates of the Ledbury Trust were re-erected later that year, the local people destroyed them. Fearing that local support for the rioters might make conviction through due process difficult, two of the rioters who were captured were tried under the infamous Black Act for being in disguise during the attack. One was hanged, the other was reprieved on turning King's evidence. At Worcester, others were hanged under the 1735 Act. The passing of these draconian sentences may also have been related to the fact that there were renewed disturbances in the Bristol region. These re-occurrences suggest a deliberate challenging of the law on the part of the protesters. Malcolmson notes that there was a popular belief that the Turnpike Acts could not have been sanctioned by the King.[8] In 1736 there was another attack near Ross.

---

7 The following account is taken from R. Malcolmson, ' "A set of ungovernable people": the Kingswood colliers in the eighteenth century' in J. Brewer and J. Styles (eds), *An Ungovernable People* (London, Hutchinson, 1980), pp. 85–127; Albert, 'Popular opposition'; Freeman, 'Popular attitudes'; and Isaac, 'Popular disturbances'.

8 Malcolmson, ' "A set of ungovernable people" ', p. 97.

III

It is against this background that the 1749 disturbances need to be seen. The Bristol Trust trustees petitioned Parliament for a new Act in that year, partly because the previous Acts, which had only been granted for 21 years, were about to expire. The commissioners clearly foresaw trouble and in June and July 1749 they published in the regional press an extract from the 1735 Act which referred to attacks on turnpike gates being a capital offence. The fact that turnpikes had been destroyed at Barnard Castle in that same month may have strengthened their fear that they were not going to achieve their ends without resistance.[9]

The exact date of the first turnpike disturbance in the Bristol region in 1749 is unclear.[10] The levying of tolls began on 19 July. The first clearly documented attack occurred on a turnpike at Bedminster on the south side of Bristol on the night of Monday 24 July. Here 'a great body of the country people of Somerset . . . making prodigious shouts . . . fell to work with hatchets, axes, etc.'[11] The gates and toll house attacked were at the very beginning of the newly-turnpiked Long Ashton Road. The reports of an attack on turnpike property on the Toghill Road on the east side of Bristol the next night suggest that the attack on the Long Ashton gates was not the first in the region. Press reports mentioned that the Toghill Road disturbance on 25 July was the second such occurrence, so another attack must have taken place at that gate some time during the previous week.[12] All other accounts seem to have missed this point and assume that the attacks on the Somerset side of Bristol were the first. That the Toghill Road disturbances were among the first such protests in 1749 underlines the continuity with the previous disturbances in 1727, 1731 and 1732, pointing to the continued disaffection with turnpiking in the communities to the east of Bristol.

At first sight the Kingswood colliers, the main protagonists of the events of 1727 and 1732, do not appear to have been involved at the commencement of the protests in 1749. It was the 'country people on the Gloucestershire side' who were the protesters. But the report in the *Gentleman's Magazine* did note that the second attack on the Toghill Road involved boring holes in the large

---

9 *Bath Journal*, 3 July 1749.

10 The following account of the disturbances draws upon: *Western Flying Post*, 7, 14 and 21 August 1749; *Bath Journal*, 31 July, 7 and 14 August 1749; J. Latimer, *The Annals of Bristol in the Eighteenth Century* (Bristol, William George, 1893), pp. 274–75; *Gentleman's Magazine*, August 1749; and, with reference to the involvement of the Kingswood colliers, Malcolmson, ' "A set of ungovernable people" '.

11 *Western Flying Post*, 7 August 1749.

12 *Western Flying Post*, 7 August 1749. The report notes that the protestors on the night of Tuesday 25 July 'came and destroyed a second time the turnpike gates and turnpike house at Don John's cross on the Toghill Road'.

posts of the toll gates and blowing them up with gun powder, which might suggest a connection with miners.[13] Whatever the exact composition of the crowd at the Toghill gates, some of them came 'naked with only trousers on, some in their shirts' and several, despite the Black Act's death penalty for blacking, appeared with blackened faces.[14] Both gates and turnpike house were destroyed.

After these protests there began a cycle of confrontation between the turnpike commissioners and the protesters, with the former re-erecting gates, rebuilding toll houses and placing guards on their property and the latter either returning to the scene of their first attacks or seeking out new targets. After the first attack on the Long Ashton Road, the commissioners offered a reward of £100 to anyone who would give information about these or future attacks. For those actively involved in the protests, 'his majesty's pardon' would also be granted. The size of the reward is clearly indicative of the commissioners' concern that, from past experience, the resistance to the new turnpikes was going to be determined. The fact that communities to the east of Bristol were again involved could have given them no cause for optimism. No one came forward: the solidarity of the local communities held.

The commissioners took other precautions. The tollkeepers were to be protected by 'some stout men'. On the new Long Ashton Turnpike, the commissioners took it in turns to stand guard at the gates in bodies of about a dozen, 'to give an awe to the people, and oblige them to pay the toll'. This was immediately met by defiance from Somerset farmers attempting to force a passage for their cattle and colts which they were bringing to a fair in Bristol. The commissioners were insulted and one farmer held the butt end of his whip over the head of one of the commissioners. A further fracas broke out as farmers returned from the fair. The gate was untouched, however, owing to the stiff resistance of the commissioners and their assistants. Three protestors were arrested. However, on the next night, 26 July, the 'country people . . . in a prodigious body, with drums beating, and loud shouting, armed with cutting instruments fixed in long staffs', returned to the same gates.[15] Some of the protestors were disguised for the first time as women. This time the gates were destroyed as well as the house which was in the process of being rebuilt after the previous attack two nights before. A gate on the Dundry Road was destroyed for the first time. 'A body of gentlemen . . on horseback', according to the *Gentleman's Magazine*, went into Somerset, took one of the rioters prisoner, 'and brought him pinion'd behind one of their servants'.[16] The city prepared for

---

13 *Gentleman's Magazine*, August 1749, p. 376.
14 *Western Flying Post*, 7 August 1749.
15 *Western Flying Post*, 7 August 1749.
16 *Gentleman's Magazine*, August 1749, p. 376.

further attacks and seamen were enlisted to act as protectors of the turnpike gates. Prisoners had by now been lodged in the prison and there were threats that the country people would come to rescue them.

The following Tuesday at eight in the morning, some three or four hundred people, chiefly farmers and labourers, came from Somerset to the Ashton Road gates. They were so confident that they had given advance warning that they would come in broad daylight. They succeeded in taking down the gate posts, making a bonfire of these together with the broken posts from their previous attacks. The Dundry Road gates were destroyed in similar fashion. At nine o'clock at Bedminster, where two turnpikes met on the very outskirts of the southern part of the city of Bristol, the Somerset people came together, led by 'two chiefs on horseback; one with his face black'd, and the other a young Gentleman Farmer of Nailsey, well known, carried the Standard, being a Silk Handkerchief on a long staff . . ..' The rest, attended by three drummers, were on foot and armed 'with some weapon or others promisciously, as rusty swords, pitchfork, broad axes, guns, pistols, clubs'. On their hats and caps they had the initials JL to signify they were the 'Jack-a-Lents' and all were to be addressed as 'Jack'. Outside the George Inn, they ranged themselves 'by beat of drum, huzzas, and a hunting horn'.[17]

The target of this great procession was Stephen Durbin, the constable who had taken three persons before the justices on a charge of destroying turnpike property. The crowd entered his house, drank freely and then broke all the windows. But this was not felt to be retribution enough so the older of the two 'chiefs' ordered that the house should be completely demolished.

While there had been a predetermined plan to seek a public redress of Stephen Durbin's behaviour, after that had been completed there was uncertainty as to what to do. They had threatened the previous week to take their three comrades out of the prison, but it is clear that no definite plan had been made to carry this out. Emboldened by the lack of resistance to their attack on Durbin's house, however, they marched forward towards the city. At Redcliff Hill, they halted and consulted and decided to return home the way they had come, 'but on a sudden they wheel'd about and the word was given to go forward'. Finding their way to the city barred, they moved around the outskirts to Totterdown and proceeded to level the turnpike gates, houses and sentry boxes there. There they were surprised by a body of men comprising commissioners, constables and seamen. The Riot Act was read, 30 prisoners were taken, 3 of whom received severe cutlass injuries. The crowd let the seamen know what they would do to them if they ever got hold of them. The City of Bristol had been thrown into turmoil by these events: all business was suspended, the fair closed and shops were shut up. It was no wonder then that

17 *Western Flying Post*, 14 August 1749.

the streets were lined to see the prisoners brought to the Council House before being committed to the bridewell.

It was at this point the 'country people' to the east of Bristol went to Kingswood to gain support from the Kingswood colliers. Some degree of coercion was needed apparently, though one newspaper report suggests that the Kingswood miners had to be induced to join the protests by paying them.[18] Whatever finally made them join, they set out to finish 'what the Somerset people left undone'. One account claimed 'almost all the turnpikes, with their houses, round the city, are now laid waste, burnt and entirely demolished'.[19] The miners also demanded the release of all prisoners committed in the disturbances. Yet the Kingswood men were not totally united on the issue of turnpikes and some began to drift away after the first day and returned to their normal work, taking coals into the City of Bristol. They were warned by local gentry of the consequences of their actions if they continued to defy the law. Even so, on Friday 4 August, some hundreds still gathered in large bodies in Kingswood, demanding money from all who passed, saying they could not 'live by the Air'.[20] They also threatened to destroy the turnpike at Stokes Croft that night and to go to Bristol the following Sunday to release the prisoners. The attack at Stokes Croft did take place but they succeeded only in partially destroying the gates. A large body of gentlemen, other citizens, soldiers and seamen had been alerted to the attack and the miners retreated on the arrival of such a large force. On the next day, the soldiers in Bristol were strengthened to six troops of dragoon guards by the arrival of a further two from Gloucester. The commissioners also ordered the turnpike posts and chains to be re-erected nearer to the city 'so that it must be a very bold step for any to presume cutting them down so near the houses'.[21]

Somerset miners were eventually coerced to join the protests against the turnpikes. The Kingswood men had hoped to see them join with them but the 'threatenings' of the Kingswood men took longer than they expected to have an effect. When the Somerset colliers did come across the river into Kingswood, they were angered to find the Kingswood men had already dispersed. The former 'were very near on the point of dispatching one of the Kingswood leaders and pulling his and some other of the principal colliers houses down'.[22] They must, however, have been involved in some of the earlier protests with their fellow county men because that same day they halted the coach of a circuit judge travelling to Bristol and declared: 'Sir, we have cut down the turnpikes'. He replied: 'I am sorry for it; you had better have let them alone'. They then

18 Latimer, *Annals*, p. 275.
19 *Western Flying Post*, 14 August 1749.
20 Malcolmson, ' "A set of ungovernable people" ', p. 110.
21 *Western Flying Post*, 21 August 1749.
22 *Western Flying Post*, 21 August 1749.

demanded money from him but, as Latimer reports, 'his firmness awed the rabble, and he was allowed to proceed' without giving them anything.[23] The Somerset miners later in contrite mood told three JPs who visited them to reproach them for their actions, that they regretted what had happened and vowed vengeance on the Kingswood colliers for involving them in the first place.[24]

Of those arrested in the disturbances, at least five died of smallpox in prison in Bristol while awaiting trial and some others were dangerously ill with the disease.[25] One of those who died was identified as a farmer; he had been already wounded by a cutlass blow. The rest were sent to Taunton and Salisbury for trial. At Taunton nine were sentenced to death, but only two, Thomas Perryman and John Roach, were executed. The seven who were reprieved included John Derrick, who turned King's evidence, and Thomas Cox, one of the leaders of the protests, whom the jury found to be a lunatic. In April 1750, 18 prisoners were taken under strong guard for trial at Salisbury. In the 1735 Act, provision had been made to try offenders in an adjacent county. The authorities were certain that gaining a conviction in the accused's home county would prove more difficult, given the support for turnpike protesters, even at gentry level, in their locality. Isaac Coles was tried first as 'one of the most active among them in cutting down a turnpike on the Whitchurch Road' but, 'even with very full and clear evidence to that effect', the Wiltshire jury acquitted him.[26] A new jury did the same with another leader of the protests, William Denmead. The Crown's case collapsed. Eleven were bound over to answer for other misdemeanours at the next assizes.

The disquiet among the Somerset farmers was to last all through August. There were still threats to destroy gates, though these would be night-time affairs. Moreover, to put pressure on the mercantile class and the authorities in Bristol, a month-long blockade of provisions coming into the city markets was proposed. Not only would this have brought the market trade to a halt in the city, but it could also have caused disorder over food shortages and prices. By the last week of August, threatening letters were being sent to the Mayor of Bristol. One threatened that 'if the turnpikes were not taken down by Wednesday next the city would be set on fire'. Another from 'the same quarter'

---

23 *Western Flying Post*, 21 August 1749; Latimer, *Annals*, p. 275.
24 Malcolmson, ' "A set of ungovernable people" ', p. 109.
25 The account of those arrested and of the trials comes from *Western Flying Post*, 25 September, 2 October and 27 November 1749; *Bath Journal*, 4 and 11 September 1749; *Bristol Weekly Intelligencer*, 23 September, 7 October, 18 November 1749, 31 March 1750, 7 and 17 April 1750; *Gloucester Journal*, 17 and 24 April 1750; Malcolmson, ' "A set of ungovernable people" ', p. 110–13. The *Gloucester Journal*, 24 April 1750, mistakenly referred to the 18 Bristol prisoners as all being coalminers. As Malcolmson shows, it is unlikely any of the arrested were in fact colliers. Malcolmson, ' "A set of ungovernable people" ', p. 113.
26 *Gloucester Journal*, 24 April 1750.

detailed the proposed threat and noted, 'what a sad thing it would be to see that noble fabric the exchange, and other fine edifices of this great city reduced to ashes'.[27]

Peace had also not returned to Kingswood. Whatever had caused the Kingswood colliers to divide over the issue of turnpikes, such divisions closed up when the community came under attack. When a party of armed country bailiffs came in September to arrest one of the leaders of the bands of Kingswood coalminers who had attacked the turnpikes in August, they were beaten back. Patrols of colliers armed with pitchforks and fire-arms were then established in the woods to prevent further such attempts. On one occasion, they came out of Kingswood as far as the outskirts of Bristol on the expectation of meeting a party bent on making arrests and left a calling card by firing some slugs into turnpike lodge.[28] According to Malcolmson, no collier was apprehended during the whole of the disturbances.[29]

IV

What is striking about the turnpike protests of 1749 was the central role of the 'country people' in the disturbances. Turnpike riots, particularly in the Bristol region, had up until that time been the work of the Kingswood colliers. 'Country people' were rarely central figures in collective protests in eighteenth-century England. Riots were usually instigated by 'ungovernable people' like miners, nailers and textile workers, those who lived in communities beyond the ken of resident gentry or clergy. This is not to suggest that small farmers, farm servants and agricultural labourers were subservient and accepting of the status quo. Given the nature of eighteenth-century agrarian society, however, they usually had to use means of expressing their grievances other than direct collective action.[30]

Given their past vigilant opposition to turnpikes, it would have been surprising if the colliers of the region, in particular those of Kingswood, had not taken the opportunity to reassert their opposition to such innovations. Any hopes of the Kingswood miners taking no action in the face of renewed turnpiking were always premature, despite the exemptions on coal carriage conceded to them for certain turnpikes and the convictions obtained against their colleagues in 1734, leading to the transportation of two colliers.[31] The colliers' previous direct and threatened actions had seriously frustrated the

27 *Western Flying Post*, 11 September 1749.
28 *Western Flying Post*, 25 September and 2 October 1749.
29 Malcolmson, ' "A set of ungovernable people" ', p. 113.
30 See A. Charlesworth, *An Atlas of Rural Protest in Britain 1548–1900* (Beckenham, Croom Helm, 1983); J. Bohstedt, *Riots and Community Politics in England and Wales 1790–1810* (Cambridge, Mass., Harvard University Press, 1983).
31 Malcolmson, ' "A set of ungovernable people" ', pp. 98–103.

efforts to construct turnpikes in the Bristol area. The effect of exemptions, the memory of the severe penalties meted out 15 years before and the new draconian law on turnpike cutting was not only to delay the entry of the Kingswood miners into the 1749 dispute but allowed some in the community to think better of taking direct collective action 'and so', as one report said, 'divided from their brethren' after the first attacks by colliers on 2 August.[32] This division within the ranks of the Kingswood colliers also undermined the attempt to coordinate concerted attacks on turnpikes by them and the Somerset coalminers. Even so, the links between the 'country people', the Kingswood colliers and the Somerset coalminers all suggest that we should beware sweeping statements suggesting that labouring communities in the eighteenth century had horizons limited to their locality and hence could not sustain cooperation across communities and occupational groups. The evidence of the 1749 protests points to the fact that we need to contextualize clearly the circumstances surrounding particular communities' and groups' mobilization to collective protest.

One element that did bind communities and groups together was their ability to articulate their protest through a distinctive cultural fund of rituals and symbols. In this sense, the turnpike disturbances of 1749 had a number of features common to all eighteenth-century popular protest. As Thompson has pointed out, organizational frameworks in the eighteenth century were 'bound to expose one to detection and victimisation'.[33] Yet, as Scott explains, 'subordinate groups must find ways of getting their message across'.[34] Protesters were thus thrown back on such cultural resources for collective action. As Pettit and Seal have argued, common to both customs of plebeian culture and collective protest were such features as disguise, processing, levying, the wearing of unusual garb or adornments, noise and/or music and mock violence.[35] Understanding such customs and the way they were incorporated by protestors is important to the historian in that these instances allow the 'hidden transcript of . . . important subordinate groups' to become public where for all practical purposes they are usually irrecoverable.[36]

Disguise in whatever form was intended to allow the person so concealed to lose their individual identity and become a representative of and a voice for the

---

32 *Western Flying Post*, 14 August 1749.
33 E. P. Thompson, 'Patrician society, plebeian culture', *Journal of Social History*, Vol. 7, 1974, p. 401.
34 J. C. Scott, *Domination and the Arts of Resistance: Hidden Transcripts* (New Haven, Yale University Press, 1990), p. 138
35 T. Pettit, ' "Here Comes I, Jack Straw". English folk drama and social revolt', *Folklore*, Vol. 95, 1984, pp. 3–20; G. Seal, 'Traditional agrarian protest in nineteenth-century England and Wales', *Folklore*, Vol. 99, 1988, pp. 146–69. These two articles have informed our discussion of the links between customary rituals, folk drama, disguise and social protest. See also N. Simms, 'Ned Ludd's Mummers Play', *Folklore*, Vol. 89, 1978, pp. 166–78.
36 Scott, *Domination*, p. 138.

community. It also, with the unusual garb and adornment and the noise and music, marked off the ritual and the protest from everyday behaviour. In the case of protest, these features proclaimed to all, participants, onlookers and those being attacked or harangued, the special nature of the event and the importance that should be attached to the crowd's grievance. Often, as with 'rough music', they signified an occasion when the community was setting its own laws and rectifying what it saw as injustice. The blackened faces, the dressing up in women's clothes, the use of silk handkerchiefs for flags, the use of drums and hunting horns, all were deployed in the protests by the 'country people' of Gloucestershire and Somerset in the last week in July. Moreover, ritual elements such as processing, levying and mock violence were used to encourage the participation of others and hence to create solidarity in the community. Processing heightened the sense of occasion and the excitement of the moment, both of which would draw others into the riot. The protestors' march to Durbin's house in Bedminster echoed Lord of Misrule processions, where a company of men waited on 'the Lord', who was accompanied by pipers producing a great noise. Pettit notes that the Kingswood colliers' march on Bristol in 1727 was of a similar type. Moreover, the Lord of Misrule and his retinue imposed exactions on passers-by. During the 1749 protests, money was levied on different occasions, for example, at the attack on Durbin's house and on the highway itself. Where the rioters asked for payment for passage through an area, they were not only indulging in 'the logic of festive topsy-turvydom that the objectionable official tolls are replaced by unofficial ones', they were also closely paralleling the traditions of Hocktide. On those days (Monday and Tuesday after Low Sunday, the Sunday after Easter), 'men and women . . . were traditionally licensed to exact money from members of the opposite sex . . . "The favourite method was to stretch a rope across the road and impose a small toll on passers-by" '.[37]

Customary mock violence can be seen in the threatening tactics used in eighteenth- and early nineteenth-century protests. The threats to gain the participation of the Kingswood and Somerset miners paralleled the verbal threats and manhandling that took place on festive occasions between the main participants, for example mummers, and their audience. By means of such mock violence, members of the latter were cajoled into participating in the performance.

As Seal points out, many of the elements in protest events were contained in mumming. 'The play itself generally [involved] one or more men with blackened faces together with a man dressed as a woman.' The players, with a

---

37 Pettit, ' "Here Comes I" ', p. 14. Other doleing customs are discussed in relation to popular protest by B. Bushaway, *By Rite: Custom, Ceremony and Community in England 1700–1880* (London, Junction Books, 1982), Chapter 5.

crowd of onlookers, perambulated the settlement visiting various houses where contributions were solicited.[38] Such a comparison is apposite for, by drawing on the rituals and symbolism of plebeian culture, the rioters were like a large repertory company enacting a play where all the members of the company knew the basic plot and were able to step into any of the roles. Moreover, the local gentry and the turnpike commissioners were not so divorced from popular culture that they could not understand this counter-theatre.

If we were to view the crowd behaviour in 1749 from a European viewpoint, we would describe many of the elements as carnivalesque.[39] This is most clearly embodied in the incidents surrounding the protest against the constable Durbin. This is not only in respect of the masking and the fact that some of the crowd were armed, but also that the crowd announced its intention that the attack was to take place in 'open day' ahead of time. The event was enacted on 'the main street, before the George Inn, by beat of drum, Huzzas, and a hunting horn, three drums attending them'. There was an 'audience', who were 'very numerous', and a collection was taken at the end of the 'play', the destruction of Durbin's house, which was 'directed' by 'their elder chief'. The crowd 'drank freely'.[40] As Burke has pointed out, 'the excitement of the occasion and the heavy consumption of alcohol meant that inhibitions against expressing hostility to the authorities or private individuals' were at their weakest on such carnivalesque occasions.[41] Moving off from Durbin's house, the crowd cried ' "They were afraid of no man" '. There are two further parallels with carnival in the Durbin incident. First, Durbin, the object of the crowd's attack, was the constable who had tried to prevent the crowd's earlier attacks by arresting some of their number. As Bristol notes, abuse of constables at carnival times was common. Such officials were charged with surveillance of the crowd's licence and hence were a focus of resentment and resistance to such social control.[42]

Second, Durbin's house was destroyed. This again was a symbolic act associated with the topsy-turvy principles that underlay all carnival customs. The act of destruction was often done using tools usually employed for

38 Seal, 'Traditional agrarian', p. 151. Sir Walter Scott made reference to both white-shirts and blackened faces as costume and disguise in his description of old Christmas customs:

Then came the merry masters in

. . .

White shirts supplied the masquerade
And smutted checks the visors made

Quoted in Pettit, ' "Here Comes I" ', p. 15.

39 For the best analysis of carnival, see P. Burke, *Popular Culture in Early Modern Europe* (London, Maurice Temple Smith, 1978), Chapter 7.

40 The account of the Durbin incident is taken from *Western Flying Post*, 14 August 1749.

41 Burke, *Popular Culture*, p. 203.

42 M. D. Bristol, *Carnival and Theatre: Plebeian Culture and the Structure of Authority in Renaissance England* (London, Methuen, 1985), p. 69.

construction. Also, by so destroying the house, the owner of the house, the person of wealth, was forced to use that wealth in the rebuilding and refurnishing of the house and hence sustain the livelihood of the petty producers and craftsmen.[43] This may suggest that in the Somerset crowd there were not only small farmers but the former groups as well. What was clear to the attackers, however, was that Durbin had sided with the turnpike promoters, the wealthy. He must therefore be made to pay for that by recompensing the petty producers. This may also be another factor in explaining why toll houses were destroyed during attacks. Such destruction took time and the longer the crowd stayed at the scene of a protest, the greater chance of their being caught. That risk was taken because the more complete the destruction of the toll houses, the more the turnpike trust would have to expend on rebuilding. Thus, the attackers ensured that even if they lost their battle on the turnpikes, some money flowed from the trust to the local community via local craftsmen and timber suppliers.

There are two other links with the carnivalesque that refer to the form of dress adopted by the protestors. First, in the earlier incident at Bedminster there were 'some naked with only trousers, some in their shirts'. This has, like the cross-dressing incidents seen during the 1749 protests, both role reversal and sexual overtones. A man's trousers or 'breeches' were a symbol of his masculinity and manly virtues. This was underlined by a Somerset JP who, in haranguing the Somerset colliers for their ready acquiescence to join in the turnpike cutting because of threats from their counterparts in Kingswood, advised the former ' "to pull off their Breeches, and give them to their Wives, who perhaps might make a better Use of them!" '.[44] The element of ridicule in the JP's speech also points to the power of such symbolism and the need on the part of the authorities to curb it.

Second, one of the major themes of carnival, as Burke explains, was sex. 'Carne' was not only animal flesh, that is food, but also 'the flesh'.[45] To be naked, to be without trousers, in public, was not only to call into question both gender norms and the normal standards of daily behaviour, but it was also to release the power of the crowd's licence by invoking the carnivalesque rituals of

---

43 Bristol, *Carnival and Theatre*.

44 Quoted in Malcolmson, ' "A set of ungovernable people" ', p. 111. An incident recorded in the *Gloucester Journal*, 26 June 1739, shows the important symbolism of 'breeches' in a literal battle of the sexes:

> Alford Wilts June 19:
>
> Twenty five married women . . . having cut off their hair in order to dispute with their husbands their RIGHT TO THE BREECHES, went on Wednesday last to an ale-house, the place of their rendevous, where the Amazons soon routed them and that so effectually, that but few of the conquered have been since heard of. They made Mrs. T---s, generalissima, in order if the conquered should again rally their forces to be ready to engage in a second battle.

45 Burke, *Popular Culture*, p. 186.

their society. As Scott argues, 'Carnival, in its ritual structure and anonymity, gives a privileged place to normally suppressed speech and aggression . . .'. It was in the crowd's 'interest to exploit this opportune ambiguity to the fullest'.[46]

The most distinctive feature of the protests of 1749 that drew on customary ritual and symbolism, some of which again was carnivalesque, was the practice of the Somerset farmers calling themselves Jack-a-Lents and wearing the 'JLs' in their hats and caps. Though Latimer's nineteenth-century account links all the attacks in July to the Jack-a-Lents, the contemporary reports make it clear that, though disguise was used in the protests before the attack on Durbin's house, this was the only incident in which the Jack-a-Lents made their appearance.[47]

Jonassen calls Jack-a-Lent 'a complex and multifaceted offspring of popular festival culture'.[48] First, it was the puppet used as a target for a children's street game in Lent, a symbolic scapegoat. Second, it was an effigy in festival pageants at the end of Lent; not only was the element of scapegoat present here, but also the Jack-a-Lent procession was meant to convey the Christian sentiment of repentance. Third, as Burke notes, Jack-a-Lent was the English male equivalent of the pallid, thin, female figure of 'Lent' of continental carnivals, the archetypal oppositional of the male gargantuan falstaffian figure of 'Carnival' itself.[49] As Jonassen notes, 'though puny, reviled and battered the Jack-a-Lent nevertheless possessed the satirical power of Carnival to reduce the mighty to a laughing stock and thus perform a function that critiqued and ameliorated the injustices of society'.[50] Jack-a-Lent rhymes in the mid-sixteenth century provided the poor with a mouthpiece to criticize and ridicule the authorities. The Jack-a-Lent became a symbol of satirical protest who spoke what the people thought but could not openly say.

---

46 Scott, *Domination*, pp. 181–82.
47 Latimer, *Annals*, p. 274.
48 F. B. Jonassen, 'The meaning of Falstaff's allusion to the Jack-a-Lent in *The Merry Wives of Windsor*', *Studies in Philology*, Vol. 88, No. 1, 1991, p. 51. The following analysis of Jack-a-Lent draws on Jonassen, 'The meaning . . .', pp. 46–68 and Bristol, *Carnival and Theatre*.
49 Burke, *Popular Culture*, p. 191. There was also a doleing custom in Oxfordshire that occurred in Holy Week where children went around asking for 'presents' to celebrate the end of Lent, which links with Jack-a-Lent. The song the children sang was:

    Herrings, herrings, white and red
    Ten a penny, Lent's dead
    Rise, dame, and give an egg
    Or else a piece of bacon,
    One for Peter, two for Paul,
    There for Jack-a-Lent's all
    Away, Lent, away.

    Quoted in C. Hole, *English Custom and Usage* (London, Batsford, 1944), p. 140.
50 Jonassen, 'The meaning', p. 51.

In processing the Somerset farmers sought to get the turnpike commissioners to repent of their sins: exploitation of the poor and the abandonment of the ancient custom of free passage. In signing their caps and hats 'JL', they collectively became the Jack-a-Lent of rhyme and ballad, openly proclaiming what the people think but do not say about turnpikes. As the report in the *Western Flying Post* had it, 'it was observ'd the term Jack was the signature to all'.[51] Here was the crowd signing themselves with 'the most versatile and familiar name for every nameless hero of plebeian culture', the name of the little person who was able to triumph in situations of impossible odds.[52] Similarly, in identifying themselves with Jack-a-Lent, they saw themselves as puny, reviled and battered but with the ability through such symbols to attack the rich and powerful in society.

The elements of disguise and cross-dressing in the West of England had regional specificity that Howkins and Merricks have missed in their study of such phenomena.[53] In the case of turnpike disturbances in the West of England before 1749, protestors had been reported to have been disguised with blackened faces on two previous occasions, wearing women's clothes on three previous occasions and 'high crown'd hats' on two previous occasions.[54] With the use of disguise and partial and cross-dressing in 1749, this spatial concentration of such symbolic behaviour during turnpike protests is worth reflecting on. In contrast, in Albert's account of the West Yorkshire riots in the 1750s, there is no mention of disguise. Logue notes men in women's clothes on one occasion only for the attacks on toll gates in the Central Lowlands of Scotland at the end of the eighteenth century.[55]

Moreover, cross-dressing was not only used throughout the West of England in the eighteenth century. It had been employed in the Western Rising of the early seventeenth century. These were protests against the disafforestation of the Royal forests. In the Forests of Dean and Braydon, the leaders adopted the name 'Skimmington', a name borrowed from this region's particular variant of 'rough music' in which processions a man in women's clothing represented symbolically the one to whom the community was directing its disapproval. In the case of Braydon, the prefix 'Lady' was added to 'Skimmington' and all three male leaders wore women's clothes. Later, when convicted, they had to stand in the pillory at the Western Assizes so dressed.[56] Underdown notes that the word

---

51 *Western Flying Post*, 14 August 1749.

52 Bristol, *Carnival and Theatre*, p. 205.

53 A. Howkins and L. Merricks, ' "Wee be black as hell": ritual, disguise and rebellion', *Rural History*, Vol. 4, No. 1, 1993, pp. 41–53.

54 Albert, 'Popular opposition'; Malcolmson, ' "A set of ungovernable people" ', p. 95.

55 Albert, 'Popular opposition', p. 10–11; K. J. Logue, *Popular Disturbances in Scotland 1780–1815* (Edinburgh, John Donald, 1979), p. 180.

56 B. Sharp, *In Contempt of All Authority* (Berkeley, University of California Press, 1980), pp. 100–08.

'skimmington' originated in Somerset and North Wiltshire, whence the term spread over much of Southern England.[57] The turnpike disturbances occurred in a society whose cultural fund contained the ritual symbols of disguise, particularly that of dressing up in women's clothes.

V

The Jack-a-Lents, it can be argued, only came to administer retributive justice, their own justice, on a local official who had stood up against the turnpike protestors. This was against a background where some men of standing were tacitly supporting opposition to turnpikes. Latimer wrote of correspondence between the Mayor of Bristol and the government, complaining of the inactivity displayed by the country gentry throughout the disturbances.[58] He also noted what he terms a 'remarkable entry' in an account book four years after the protests. A Mr Gore recorded a payment to a Mr Hardwick 'for cutting down the turnpike £10'.[59] Whether the passage of time allowed Mr Gore to feel that he could so openly declare his attitude to turnpikes and his part in the recent troubles or whether this betokens continued opposition cannot be discerned. It is, however, the clearest sign we have of opposition from other quarters than the protestors themselves. Moreover, the Attorney General requested again that the trial of those accused of turnpike cutting be tried 'in some county adjacent to Somerset, where there may be the most disinterested jury'.[60] As we have seen, the sympathy for the prisoners went beyond their home county. There was also a history of opposition to transport innovations in the Bristol region. There had also been resistance from local interests to the Avon Navigation between Bristol and Bath in the first decades of the eighteenth century.[61]

Certainly there were divisions within the Bristol elite. Although, by the second week of disturbances, the Bristol authorities were acting in tandem with the turnpike commissioners, they were unhappy with the way in which the commissioners had gone about their work. The Mayor of Bristol noted in letters to the Duke of Newcastle the 'haste measures of the acting trustees in carrying the Act for errecting the turnpikes into execution'.[62] The commissioners' offer of both a reward of £100 and a promise of immunity from prosecution for those active in the riots but prepared to give evidence against others was made immediately after the first attacks.[63] The trustees had also published a handbill setting out how the city would be defended against protestors intent on rescuing

57 D. Underdown, *Revel, Riot and Rebellion* (Oxford, Clarendon Press, 1985), p. 102.
58 Latimer, *Annals*, p. 275.
59 Latimer, *Annals*, p. 275.
60 Public Record Office, SP 36/111, Attorney General to Newcastle, September 1749.
61 F. Walker, *The Bristol Region* (London, Nelson, 1972), p. 213.
62 Public Record Office, SP 36/111, Mayor of Bristol to Newcastle, 1 August 1749.
63 Latimer, *Annals*, p. 274.

their fellows in the Newgate prison without any consultation with their city magistrates.[64] The strength of popular opposition and such division among the local elites ensured central government took turnpike disturbances very seriously. At least two royal proclamations, three Special Acts of Parliament and a number of government directed prosecutions were concerned with attacks on turnpikes.[65] The response of the authorities to the 1749 disturbances must be seen in the light of the continuing opposition to turnpikes in the first half of the eighteenth century. John Wesley and other Tories thought that it should be the wealthy who should pay for the new roads, and no doubt they would have had some sympathy with the Herefordshire farm labourer who said that 'he looked upon such gentlemen as were for erecting turnpikes about Ledbury [as] the same as persons that robb'd on the highway'.[66]

First, the protests occurred at a time when, as Langford points out, party strife was still intense, yet a Whig majority held sway in the Commons.[67] As Malcolmson points out, this is not a simple matter that the commissioners were Whig and the magistracy Tory. Local politics were more complex than that. Moreover, as Malcolmson notes, there were substantial risks for any Tory gentlemen who actively supported popular discontent in this period of Jacobitism and opposition to the Hanoverian succession.[68] Yet that context would of itself mean that a Whig government was suspicious of such open and persistent opposition as the popular disturbances against the turnpikes in the West of England. Furthermore, the level of party strife and the partisanship of the times meant that the Whig government could not be completely even handed in its dealings with its own kind in the country. For example, in Bristol in 1749 the turnpike commissioners were mainly Tory. As Malcolmson indicates, their criticism of the inactivity of the predominantly Whig magistrates met with little support from Hardwicke, who was both the Lord Chancellor and High Steward of Bristol. He wrote to Newcastle that, though the party allegiances should not affect the merits of the case, 'I dare say Your Grace will think that a Sett of Magistrates so well affected to this Majesty's Person & Government, who act so worthily in administering the affairs of that great & popular City, & I verily believe intended to do their Duty, on this occasion, deserve all that Regard & Countenance, which Justice & Reason will admit'.[69]

Second, as Lord Chief Justice Hardwicke noted after the second Ledbury riot in 1735:

64 Public Record Office, SP 36/111, Mayor of Bristol to Newcastle, 1 August 1749.
65 Albert, 'Popular opposition', p. 13.
66 I. Gilmore, *Riot, Risings and Revolution* (London, Hutchinson, 1992), p. 92; E. P. Thompson, *Whigs and Hunters* (London, Allen Lane, 1975), pp. 256–57.
67 Langford, *Public Life*, p. 131.
68 Malcolmson, ' "A set of ungovernable people" ', pp. 105–06.
69 Malcolmson, ' "A set of ungovernable people" ', p. 112.

For my own part I have some time look'd upon this sort of rising as one of the worst symptoms in the Kingdom; and have thought it my duty in the few charges I have made to take particular notice of them, and to inculcate into men's minds the dangerous consequences that must follow from suffering people to get the better of the Laws and, as it were, to overrule the Acts of the Legislature.[70]

Turnpiking, like enclosure, needed special legislation before a turnpike trust could be set up. Thus the volume of turnpike and enclosure legislation dominated the English statute book. Yet for the 'suffering people' to get their way and overturn such legislation could be seen as an attack on the whole legislative process, on government itself. That could not be allowed to happen. The Attorney General in 1749 described the protests as an 'open public insult upon government and upon the laws'. He saw them as 'a matter of very great consequence to the peace of that part of the Kingdom and of [a] most dangerous example to that and the rest'.[71]

Third, the issue of 'taxes and public payments' is something that exercised Hardwicke in 1735. In 1727 the Kingswood colliers were purported to have sent a poem to the trustees of the Bristol Trust that called the tolls 'The Hardest Tax in all our Nation'.[72] As Hardwicke wrote, 'It is not unnatural to foresee that if they [the rioters] should prevail in any of these violences, the like opposition may in time be found against other Taxes and public payments . . .'.[73] The Ledbury trustees in 1734 had anticipated Hardwicke's 1736 views and spelled out Whig fears:

that if this Insolent and Rebellious spirit, which puts these Rioters and their Secret arbettors upon such illegal and Outrageous attempts be not speedily surpressed, their Impunity may by degrees lead them on to more flagrant Instances of Rebellion; till theye come at length forcibly to oppose the collecting of any tax or Payment, however, legally raised, for the Service of the Public & Support of the Government . . .

Those 'Secret arbettors' were almost certainly the same county gentlemen about whom Thomas Williams wrote to the Duke of Chandos, the Lord Lieutenant of Herefordshire, claiming that it was they who had encouraged the riots in the mistaken belief 'as not to think it their Interests to have Turnpikes supported'. Hardwicke was obviously relieved when he could write to the Duke of Newcastle in 1735 that he had heard that the 'Country-Gentlemen' of Herefordshire had now set their face against the turnpike rioters. He wrote:

---

70 Cited in Albert, 'Popular opposition', p. 13.
71 Public Record Office, SP 36/111, Attorney General to Newcastle, 15 September 1749.
72 Malcolmson, ' "A set of ungovernable people" ', p. 97.
73 This and the following three quotations are cited in and taken from Albert, 'Popular opposition', pp. 5, 7 and 13.

As this is the first instance in which I have heard that the Country-Gentlemen have opposed themselves against attempts of this nature with spirited vigour, it seems very desirable that they should be strongly supported.

Fourth, as Albert points out, 'the trusts were similar to enclosures in that they involved a fundamental redefinition in the nature of property. The turnpikes were a new type of property and the attacks on them were seen as a threat to the authority of the law by which all property was defended'.[74] Thompson has pointed out that during the eighteenth century, particularly the early part of it, 'property and the privileged status of the propertied were assuming, every year, a greater weight in the scales of justice . . . this elevation of property above all other values was a Whig state of mind'.[75] Indeed, as Thompson notes, if the 'emergency' of the forest disturbances had not precipitated the enactment of the draconian Black Act in 1723, 'it is probable some other "emergency" (turnpike or food riot or highway robbery) would have occasioned it . . . in the same decade'.[76] As it was, at each successive outbreak of turnpike disturbances the legislation concerning such attacks came closer in line with the penalties to be exacted against offenders under the Black Act.

One of the curiosities of the 1749 disturbances is why those arrested were not prosecuted under the Black Act. The Attorney General, writing to the Duke of Newcastle, wanted to make an example of the rioters. This was particularly necessary, given the long history of disorder over the issue of turnpikes in the West of England and in the Bristol region in particular. He wrote that 'Gentlemen of the County immediately concerned want to strike a Terror in the most effectual manner . . .'.[77] By the 'Gentlemen . . . immediately concerned', the Attorney General meant the turnpike commissioners. They had met the week previous to the Attorney General's letter and had agreed to write to the Duke of Newcastle to request a speedy trial.[78] The Black Act was, however, never used despite the protestors blacking up and being disguised. Whether this was due to irregularities in the proceedings concerning the 1749 Act of Parliament for the erection of turnpikes in the Bristol area is not clear. Certainly, as the *Bath Journal* noted in December 1749, those irregularities, unspecified by the *Journal*, prevented those arrested being tried by a Special Commission, as the Attorney General had originally requested.[79] Moreover, central government in the eighteenth century was dependent upon local sources of information before it acted. Interestingly, the Mayor of Bristol, in writing to

74 Albert, 'Popular opposition', p. 13.
75 E. P. Thompson, *Whigs*, p. 197.
76 E. P. Thompson, *Whigs*, p. 197.
77 Public Record Office, SP 36/111, Attorney General to Newcastle, 15 September 1749.
78 *Bath Journal*, 11 September 1749.
79 *Bath Journal*, 18 December 1749.

the Duke of Newcastle of the protests by the 'Somersetshire men', failed to give any reference to blacking, disguise or costume.[80]

VI

By April 1751, a report in the *Bath Journal* argued that views on the turnpike by Somerset people had entirely changed. The population could now see the:

> great good to the county already produced thereby not only in the great amendment of the roads, which enables the inhabitants and others to travel and bring their commodities to market with greater ease and safety than formerly; but also the farmers and labouring people find great advantages from the considerable sums of money daily laid out thereon, in hawking and labour, all of which they are at present so convinced.[81]

However, given the long history of opposition to turnpikes in the region, the author of the report cautiously tempered such an optimistic evaluation with the news that the expansion of the turnpike network in the Bristol region was still not as extensive as originally envisaged in the 1749 Act. The reason for this was that the revenue and the money to be borrowed on that revenue alone had not been sufficient to capitalize such a project. The latter would only be achieved by voluntary contributions from parishes through which the roads would pass. That is, some element of the local population would have to acquiesce in the project before turnpiking would be recommenced. Popular opinion was still a factor in whether roads were turnpiked or not.

The protests against turnpikes in the West of England had become so well known that a poem published in the *Gentleman's Magazine* at the beginning of 1753 was written in the form of a petition against turnpikes by 'Dick, the Western Farmer'. It surely is no coincidence that a farmer was chosen as the petitioner, given that the prominence of the 'country people' of Somerset and Gloucestershire in the disturbances of 1749 had added to their notoriety arising from their part in earlier protests in the West. The petition was, however, sarcastic in its tone when dealing with the complaints of such people:

> And pray can you make me a handsomer show
> Than a farmer be-lov'd with rich earth, like a bean?
> Where's the pleasure to dream on an uniform plain?
> And what is so cool, as a road full of rain?[82]

Turnpike commissioners could also be ridiculed. In the 1754 pamphlet by Ignoramus, *The World Turned Upside Down*, a turnpike commissioner was one of the targets. Significantly, the author was made to retract publicly the 'scanda-

---

80 Public Record Office, SP 36/111, Mayor of Bristol to Newcastle, 1 August 1749.
81 *Bath Journal*, 29 April 1751.
82 *Gentleman's Magazine*, January 1753, p. 44.

lous reflections'.[83] This again suggests the continuing divisions within the Bristol view of events.

Popular opposition was certainly still present. In the same year as the latter pamphlet, part of a bridge on the Bath–Bradford-upon-Avon turnpike was pulled down.[84] On a Friday night in October the following year, a turnpike keeper at Lechlade in North Gloucestershire, William Collett, was murdered at his toll gate at St John's Bridge.[85] The attacks on and at a bridge are significant in that toll gates in open country could be and were bypassed. A bridge crossing with toll gate was ideal for preventing such toll avoidance, but in so doing focused people's resentment on that one visible sign of the innovation.[86]

In 1758, in printing an address by a Mr Poulett, the *Bath Journal* again sought to convince its readers that the 'common people of this country [who] have a very commendable jealousy of all innovations' had 'become sensible of' the benefits of turnpikes, even those 'who were at first so violently' set against them. This assessment of opposition to turnpikes has to be put in the context of the new Militia Act which was leading to disturbances throughout England. For the address was directed at those in Somerset and Gloucestershire, who would be most affected by the Act – small farmers. This was the group that had been at the centre of disturbances in other areas because the Act deprived the petty producer of essential family labour by taking away younger male members of the household for militia service for long periods of time. Poulett argued that the 'common people' were suspicious of innovations, as they had been over turnpikes, and if not persuaded otherwise would violently protest. In the case of the Militia Act, he sought to persuade them that the militia scheme was not innovatory but 'the ancient method of defence in this country . . .', so protest was unnecessary. Moreover, he argued that the violent opposition to turnpikes had been because the real benefits of the innovation had not been explained to the farmers. As they now understood those benefits, opposition to turnpikes had disappeared.[87]

Albert noted that by 1766, the crowd's opprobrium had been turned on other innovative aspects of the deepening market economy.[88] One of the large perambulating crowds of 'regulators', those seeking out corn and doling out retribution on dealers and millers thought to be holding back supplies, was met

---

83 *Bath Journal*, 26 June 1754.
84 *Bath Journal*, 12 August 1754.
85 *Bath Journal*, 27 October 1755.
86 Similarly, the vehemence of the attack on the Bristol Bridge toll gates in 1793 might be seen as the continuity of ill feeling towards taxing the free movement of goods and people. P. D. Jones, 'The Bristol Bridge riot and its antecedents: eighteenth-century perceptions of the crowd', *Journal of British Studies*, Vol. 19, 1980, pp. 74–92. Cf. M. Harrison, ' "To raise and dare resentment": the Bristol Bridge riot of 1793 re-examined', *Historical Journal*, Vol. 26, 1983, pp. 557–85.
87 *Bath Journal*, 16 October 1758.
88 Albert, 'Popular opposition', p. 11.

by Thomas Prowse, MP for Somerset, and several other gentlemen 'at the Turnpike'. Prowse remonstrated with them and said if they would disperse, he would use 'his best endeavours for their relief . . .'. They continued on their way, clear in their purpose, ignoring both Prowse and the turnpike.[89] The turnpike certainly became a familiar landmark integrated into the customary practices of the Bristol freemen. In 1794, all apprentices and freemen of the city were requested to meet on the turnpike by the Town Commons and thence 'to perambulate the boundaries of their estate . . . and to receive each a pint of ale and a cake'.[90]

Yet, even as late as 1834 there was more than an echo of resentment against turnpikes in the West of England. William Bick, a Gloucester carpenter, was charged with 'unlawfully and maliciously throwing down, levelling and destroying' a turnpike gate.[91] In Britain itself, the issue of turnpikes had not disappeared. Five years on from the charging of Bick, in the South West of Wales, the most notorious and sustained campaign against turnpike tolls was to erupt with the Rebecca Riots.

VII

The 1749 disturbances were a turning point in terms of open opposition to turnpikes in the West of England. The solidarity of the Kingswood miners, the main protestors against turnpikes in the Bristol region, had been brought into question for the first time and their failure to join with their fellow miners in Somerset undermined opportunities for continued opposition to turnpikes. Yet in 1749 we can see for the first time the 'country people' protesting in great numbers against the abrogation of their customary right of free passage. Their protests had been both mobilized through and structured around customary rituals and symbols which reveal both the richness of plebeian culture and the ability of the common people to draw upon such customs to create a counter-theatre of opposition. Many of those symbols and rituals can be seen as carnivalesque. Burke has stated that carnival had its own particular geography, being weakest in Britain and Scandinavia. He did note, however, that local variants 'performed its functions and shared its characteristics'.[92] The evidence of 1749, especially the Jack-a-Lents, suggests that these British variants had more in common with the continental carnival than Burke suspected. It certainly reveals a vibrant plebeian culture. The persistency of turnpike opposition in the West of England, with the continued use of disguise and cross-dressing by the protestors, in the face of increasingly draconian measures

89 *Felix Farley's Bristol Journal*, 27 September 1766.
90 *Bath Journal*, 26 May 1714.
91 Public Record Office, Assi/6, ff. 716, 1 August 1834.
92 Burke, *Popular Culture*, pp. 190–91.

taken by the central authorities in particular, underlines this point. As Thompson argued, such legislation and the way it was applied were part of the Whigs' 'own kind of Terror', used to buttress their hegemony and create a politically stable state. If, as McLynn contends, turnpikes were 'the one real outward sign of social changes in [that] "Augustan" period', then the Jack-a-Lents were the face of a rebellious, plebeian culture resisting such patrician-inspired innovations.[93] In the second half of the eighteenth century, such resistance itself became part and parcel of popular culture, providing a tradition of protest that would be drawn upon by the labouring classes against an ever increasing stream of innovations that sought to erode the basis of customary practice.

---

93 F. McLynn, *Crime and Punishment in Eighteenth-Century England* (Oxford, Oxford University Press, 1991), p. 221.

Chapter 4

THE CIDER TAX, POPULAR SYMBOLISM AND OPPOSITION IN MID-HANOVERIAN ENGLAND

DAVID WALSH, ADRIAN RANDALL, RICHARD SHELDON AND ANDREW CHARLESWORTH

> The peace is good—who dare dispute the fact?
> See the fruits thereof—the Cyder Tax.[1]

On 10 February 1763, Britain signed the Peace of Paris which successfully concluded the Seven Years War. Victory, however, proved costly. The war raised the National Debt to an unprecedented £146 million, of which only £137 million was funded. The result was that the Treasury faced annual debt interest payments of £4.7m. The embattled Prime Minister, the Earl of Bute, his low standing in national esteem slightly raised by the ending of the war, and his Chancellor of the Exchequer, Sir Francis Dashwood, faced a daunting fiscal challenge. Their solution was to impose an Act to raise the excise duty payable on cider and perry.

The decision to raise much-needed revenue by a tax upon one specific commodity of consumption focused the burden squarely upon the 'cider counties' of Cornwall, Devon, Gloucestershire, Herefordshire, Monmouthshire, Somerset and Worcestershire. This was not accidental since it was calculated that these counties paid the least in a compounding of the Land and Malt Tax.[2] The sense that one region was being singled out to fund the debt incurred by the war aroused considerable and immediate anger there.

It was not, however, simply the fact that cider and perry were the government's chosen targets for raising revenue which provoked protest. A tax had been levied on cider since 1643 and had subsequently been amended on three occasions. In 1660 the duty was increased from 1s.3d. to 2s.6d. per hogshead, but the tax fell only on the retailer, not the maker, in order to 'free

---

1 'On the Peace', Anon, published in *Felix Farley's Bristol Journal*, 9 April 1763.
2 Bodleian Library, Oxford, Dashwood Papers, undated memoranda, bundle BL/3/5, 1763. See also *The Parliamentary History of England from the Earliest Period to the Year 1803* (London, John Wright, 1803), Vol. XV, pp. 1308–09.

Gentleman owners of orchards from the visitations of the Excisemen'.[3] In 1697 the tax was increased to 4s. per hogshead, to be paid by the first buyer, in particular the larger dealer, or retailer (re-seller). Finally, in 1743 an Order was issued to the effect that cider made for private use was not liable to any duty.[4] The 1763 Act significantly changed the established policy, shifting the onus of payment from the retailer and dealer on to the maker. As William Dowdeswell, MP for Worcestershire, observed:

> By the manner of laying it on the maker, the old distinction between the public and the private house . . . was entirely laid aside. All cider and perry . . . became chargeable with the duty of 4s per hogshead and private houses became subject to the laws of excise.[5]

The Act gave sweeping powers to the collectors of the excise. By far the most detested of these was the right to search any property suspected of brewing or hoarding cider. To those in the West of England, the new Act therefore not only threatened a commodity specific to the region's consumption and economy but also singled out the region for exceptional treatment by the Excise. This was regarded as a gross invasion of privacy and a manifest erosion of traditional English liberty. The effect of this measure was to generate, in what was in most other respects an economically and socially variegated region, a remarkable community of interest and a concerted and powerful opposition which touched all classes and severely threatened the stability of Bute's government.

I

The first decade after the accession of George III was one strewn with political crises which are well known: the conflict over General Warrants; the ongoing agitation surrounding John Wilkes; the issue of the Stamp Act; and growing disenchantment as to the nature of political representation. The agitation over the cider excise is less well recorded. Although the campaign was regionally specific, it was nevertheless of considerable significance. It was the first of the movements of external opposition which beset the government, and the furore which attended the imposition of the tax in the cider counties reveals valuable insights into the nature of eighteenth-century political culture at various levels. Opponents of the tax forged a series of both formal and informal alliances which ran from the very highest levels of political opinion to the lowest, cutting across

---

3 Cited in P. T. M. Woodland, 'The Cider Excise, 1763–1766' (unpublished DPhil thesis, University of Oxford, 1982), p. 17.
4 C. D. Chandaman, *The English Public Revenue 1660–1688* (Oxford, Oxford University Press, 1975), pp. 41–46. See also J. Owens, *A History of the Excise* (Linlithgow, 1879).
5 British Library, Hardwicke Papers, Add. Mss 35879, ff. 347–54, Dowdeswell to Hardwicke, 6 March 1766.

boundaries of political faction and social status. Further, the coherent nature of the tactics employed by them reveals a degree of articulation and concerted pressure (which were to be successful in a remarkably short period of time) which pre-dated the more historically famous episodes of oppositional mobilizations such as the Association Movement, the Anti-Slavery Campaign or the myriad of particularized pressure groups formed in the first half of the nineteenth century. Additionally, the agitation served to reinforce already powerful sentiments of popular patriotism, of community identity and, importantly, of hostility towards any perceived emanation of centralized arbitrary power. Many of the above features have been examined in a series of well-documented publications by Patrick Woodland, but his emphasis remains focused upon the political elites and their relationships to Westminster.[6] This paper concentrates upon the more popular demonstrations and opposition aroused by the Cider Tax in the West of England and, in particular, on the issue of the use of popular symbolism and its role in developing, sustaining and controlling that popular discontent.

II

Cider played an important role in the economy and society of the West of England. Cheaper than ale, it was widely drunk in the region. Cider had been made for immediate consumption by farmers and labourers from the earliest times, but by the seventeenth century there is evidence of production for local and even wider markets. Worcestershire and Gloucestershire were, according to a Shrewsbury chronicler in 1601, 'refreshed with great store of cider and perry',[7] while in the 1630s it was reported that the coastal areas of south-east Cornwall were being planted with orchards for the Plymouth cider market,[8] Thomas Westcote noting that cider was 'a drink both pleasant and healthy, much desired by seaman for long southern voyages'.[9]

It was not, however, until the Restoration, with the growing interest in all sorts of horticulture and arboriculture, that orchard acreage grew and cider became more widely available and of a better and more consistent quality.[10]

---

6 See Woodland, 'Extra-Parliamentary political organization in the making: Benjamin Heath and the opposition to the 1763 Cider Excise', *Parliamentary History*, Vol. 4, 1985, pp. 115–36; 'Political atomization and regional interests in the 1761 Parliament: the impact of the cider debates, 1763–1766', *Parliamentary History*, Vol. 8, 1989, pp. 63–89; and 'The House of Lords, the City of London and political controversy in the mid-1760s: the opposition to the cider tax further considered', *Parliamentary History*, Vol. 11, 1992, pp. 57–87. There is only a brief outline, in his thesis, of popular displays of opposition to the excise. Woodland, 'The Cider Excise', pp. 259–63, 286–88.

7 P. Clark, *The English Alehouse: A Social History, 1200–1830* (London, Longman, 1983), p. 95.

8 *Cambridge Agrarian History of England and Wales, Vol. 5: 1500–1640*, ed. J. Thirsk (Cambridge, Cambridge University Press, 1967), p. 75.

9 Clark, *The English Alehouse*, p. 95.

10 *Cambridge Agrarian History, Vol. 5*, p. 196; Clark, *The English Alehouse*, p. 95.

Cider production for wider consumption became principally focused on the 'cider counties' of Herefordshire, Worcestershire, Gloucestershire and Devon, though both Somerset and Wiltshire had producers making cider for their local markets as did eastern counties such as Norfolk. Production was not simply for the immediate local or regional market, Davenant noting in the 1680s that Lechlade in Gloucestershire, situated on the newly navigable Thames, was 'the place from which all cider is sent by water to London'.[11] By the mid-eighteenth century, these counties, with the exception of most of Devon where the local market was large, were sending their cider production to towns and cities across the country, the largest markets being London and Bristol, and also to the West and East Indies.[12]

Cider formed an important element in the labourer's diet and domestic economy in the West. Marshall saw the wide consumption of the beverage as having significant social consequences: 'the drunkenness, dissoluteness of manners, and the dishonesty of the lower class might well be referred, in whole or in great part, to the baleful effects of cider; which workmen of every description make a merit of stealing'.[13] The apple crop, and the price of cider, was notoriously liable to fluctuation. When the crop was a bumper, employers complained that it made labourers idle and saucy. When crops were poor, the labourers complained of the impact upon their cost of living. Thus, in 1764, a year after the excise on cider was imposed, it was reported from the cloth-making districts of Gloucestershire and Wiltshire:

> that the woollen manufactory in those counties is greatly decayed, owing chiefly to the Cyder Tax, as the spinners and others employed in that branch are not able to maintain themselves by reason of the excessive high prices of provisions, and that Cyder is now almost as dear as beer.[14]

Not all the poor had to obtain their supplies from the farmer or publican. Some possessed a few trees and brewed their own. The new excise imperilled this. One of the 'greatest grievances' contained in the Cider Act, according to the *Worcester Journal*, was the clause that:

> no one shall lend out his vessels etc for making cyder, the poorer sort of people in the country, who commonly have few apples, but no vessels will be deprived of the only means that providence has sent them, of furnishing themselves with a little of that wholesome liquor.[15]

11 Clark, *The English Alehouse*, p. 211.
12 *Cambridge Agrarian History of England, Vol. 6: 1750–1850*, ed. G. E. Mingay (Cambridge, Cambridge University Press, 1989), p. 270.
13 W. Marshall, *The Rural Economy of the West of England including Devonshire and parts of Somersetshire, Dorset and Cornwall* (London, 1796; repr. New York, Augustus Kelly, 1970), p. 234.
14 *Bath Journal*, 29 October 1764.
15 *Berrow's Worcester Journal*, 24 April 1763.

Cider was not, however, merely another product from the farm. It was also an item which helped to define both social and economic intercourse within the rural and industrial communities within the region. In rural districts, cider formed an important part of the harvest relationship between harvesters and farmer. Like beer elsewhere, cider formed part of the harvesters' perquisites. Low wages in the West were supplemented by an allowance of cider. Thus in South Hams in Devon, it was reported: 'Wages are one shilling a day, and a quart of cider. In harvest, much the same, with as much cider as they chose to drink.'[16] Labourers thus saw the cider harvest as very important to their real and cultural well-being, a view not always shared by the farmers. 'You waste one half of your time making cider', bemoaned an angry Herefordshire farmer in 1794, 'and the other half drinking it. I wish that there was not one apple in the county. You all think of cider, no matter what comes of plough.'[17]

While the product of the tree played an important economic and social role, the tree itself featured in popular culture. Apple tree wassailing was a well-established custom in West Country villages. On Twelfth Night, groups of labourers would tour the orchards of the farmers, sprinkling trees with cider to ensure a good harvest the following autumn. They would then repair to the farmer's house where they expected to be treated with largesse. As Bushaway notes, 'Apple tree wassailing emphasised the bonds of rural society and stressed commensality on the part of the farmers. Food and plentiful supplies of cider were used to strengthen these bonds.'[18] Cider was believed to have curative powers, protecting against rheumatism, gout, gravel and stones.[19] Marshall disagreed strongly but, while he might bemoan the consequences of cider drinking, he recognized that the bonds between the common people of the cider counties and the orchard were powerful. 'Notwithstanding . . . the accumulation of evils arising from the production, use and abuse of cider, the men of Devon are more strongly attached to it than even those of Herefordshire. Their Orchards might well be styled their Temples and Apple Trees their Idols of Worship.'[20]

Cider, therefore, was closely integrated within the daily life and the self-perception of the people in the western counties. The decision of Dashwood to solve the government's financial predicament by focusing on this one commodity as a source of revenue challenged not only a regional economy. It challenged a regional culture.

16 W. Marshall, *Review and Abstract of the County Reports to the Board of Agriculture* (York, 1818), Vol. V, p. 554.
17 J. Clark, *A General View of the Agriculture of the County of Herefordshire* (London, 1794), p. 40.
18 R. W. Bushaway, *By Rite: Custom, Ceremony and Community in England, 1700–1880* (London, Junction Books, 1982), pp. 155–57.
19 F. Willcocks, 'Notes on the Devonshire colic and its connection with cider' in *Transactions of the Devonshire Association*, Vol. XVII, 1885, p. 615.
20 W. Marshall, *The Rural Economy of the West of England*, Vol. I, p. 237.

III

The passage of the Cider Tax aroused immediate indignation among all classes in the West of England and in a relatively brief period gave rise to a very highly organized and sophisticated lobbying campaign. The tax engendered anger which was fuelled not merely by self-interested provincialism. The decision to raise the taxation payable upon cider and to levy the tax upon the maker outraged labourers, farmers and gentlemen alike, as did the prospect of having to endure an interventionist Excise. It is worth paying some attention to the initial motivation of the protestors and to the first responses to the detested legislation.

One of the most thoughtful analyses of the response of the landed, both greater and lesser, to the tax in the cider counties comes in a letter from William Dowdeswell to the Earl of Hardwicke in early March 1766, a matter of months before Dowdeswell himself became Chancellor of the Exchequer and repealed the cider excise. Dowdeswell made it plain that the cider excise was regarded by the political elite in the West as grossly unfair and unjust in its application. While Dashwood emphasized the higher taxation of beer and ale, Dowdeswell denied that the comparison was valid. With beer, the law differentiated between the public and the private house and between, on the one hand, good (strong) taxable liquor and, on the other, 'the more ordinary sorts' which 'became the common beverage of the country for the use of the farmer's family, for the labourers and cottagers in his neighbourhood, and for the manufacturers in the adjoining towns'. Dowdeswell believed that the Act was thereby shifting the onus of taxation on to the individual household and particularly on to working people while relaxing the duties payable by middlemen or badgers. There was, he told Hardwicke, an essential difference between the trader and the private maker:

> The one takes up his business with its burthen. He makes it his option and he makes a profit out of it. His education enables him to conform. He can make himself tolerably master of the Laws if he pleases. He at least knows what is required of him . . . The private person especially the farmer, the occupier of land, the cottager, the labourer with the little orchard in which his house stands . . . takes not up his business by choice . . . He has no stock wherewith to set up other business. He is educated for no other. He can neither read nor write . . . he is unable to defend himself against oppression.

This notion of 'oppression' was reiterated later in his paper. The object of those who were protesting about the tax, he wrote, was:

> to protect from Excise the private house, to protect the farmer, cottager and labourer from those penalties which their want of knowledge so often subjects them to, to guard them from the power of oppression, which is equally formidable, tho' less than oppression itself.

Dowdeswell clearly believed that it was the factors and middlemen, who had escaped liability for taxation before, who should be the appropriate focus of Excise attention, not the cider makers:

> By the factor is meant the man who undertakes the business of selling and disposing of other men's cider and perry, taking commission or some other profit from it. A middle man between a maker and a consumer, acting by choice and from his own benefit and therefore as fit an object for Excise as any dealer whatsoever.[21]

Dowdeswell's remarks were a noteworthy analysis on two counts. Not only were they considered judgements of a man regarded as an expert in fiscal policy[22] and subsequently acknowledged as such by his elevation to the office of Chancellor of the Exchequer. They were also a reflection of opinion in the cider region, expressed by a prominent Member of Parliament for one of the affected constituencies. As such, Dowdeswell was both a leader and a conduit of local opinion. His language suggests that his assessment refracted the feelings of injustice and disgust harboured by many of the plebeians in the region.

While Dowdeswell's paper gives us insights into the considered views of the regional political elite once the Act was enforced, we must turn to the press to gauge the first-hand response. That response was immediate, with a barrage of anger and criticism and frequent allusions to English liberties and foreign oppression. At Worcester, *Berrow's Journal* encapsulated the sense of injustice felt in the region at the imposition of an excise upon such a dietary staple as cider when compared with the staple produce of the country's recent enemy:

> Will it be believed in After-Ages that CYDER and PERRY, the produce of our own Country, and which is the common, healthful Drink of many Counties in England, should have a Duty laid upon it superior to what at the same Time is laid upon French Wine?[23]

Felix Farley's Bristol Journal reported the widespread anger in the region—'How does the Land of Apples already begin to mourn!'—and called upon the City of Bristol to emulate the City of London and instruct its Members of Parliament to fight the excise. The paper emphasized the theme of the threat to the civil liberties of the British posed by the imposition of the excise:

> Let the swarthy, lean, haggard Frenchman dress his vines, under the sultry sun, without enjoying liberty or reaping the fruit of his wretched Toil; but, let not Britain's [farmer] plant orchards in vain, or be deprived of the benefits arising from his

---

21 British Library, Hardwicke Papers, Add. Mss. 35879, ff. 347–54, Dowdeswell to Hardwicke, 6 March 1766.

22 Edmund Burke wrote that Dowdeswell was 'a senator for twenty years and a minister for one, a virtuous citizen for the whole of his life and deservedly lauded for his knowledge of his countries finances and Parliamentary procedure'. *Dictionary of National Biography*, Vol. V, pp. 1290–91.

23 *Berrow's Worcester Journal*, 7 April 1763.

industry, or have an Exciseman as Overseer in his family. The extending of the Excise is evidently subversive to Liberty; that on tobacco would affect but few, but on cyder the whole community.[24]

This combination of appeals to patriotism, fears of loss of liberty and a sense of a whole community under attack was echoed across the region.

IV

While the gentry and the press took umbrage, the crowd too stirred. The juxtaposition of the imposition of the tax with the celebrations of the peace provided a fortuitous platform for protest.

Celebrations of great national events took a characteristic form with formal processions, speeches, feasts, bell ringing, bonfires and sometimes fireworks which provided an outlet for displays of popular approval and patriotic feeling. Thus in 1749, celebrations at Bath of the General Thanksgiving to mark the end of the war were begun by a procession of the mayor, aldermen and council from the Guildhall to the abbey for a service, followed by feasts, military display and general illumination. 'During the day, several peals were rung . . . and the night concluded with public Demonstrations of joy', including a protracted firework display.[25] At Worcester, events followed a similar pattern, with 'the ringing of Bells, and Bonfires blazing in several Parts', together with a spectacular firework display.[26] Such events were sponsored by and usually carefully controlled by the urban elite. Indeed, the names of those who subscribed towards the costs were often published, thereby emphasizing their loyalty and public beneficence. At Shrewsbury, the cost of the firework display, on a scale which occasioned 'the great satisfactory Astonishment of all the Spectators' and left one man dead, three severely burned, one minus thumb and finger and the engineer in charge in bed with a 'burning Fever', was 'rais'd by a Rate of 6d. in the pound on the Inhabitants in the several Parishes'.[27]

The celebrations of the peace in 1763 followed this same form across most of the country. In the West of England, however, with feeling running high over the Cider Tax, crowds used the celebrations to demonstrate their disapproval of the new excise. This was a tactic which seems to have been adopted simultaneously across the region without any obvious prompting from above. Certainly, there appears to have been no 'hint' in the press or attempts at coordination among the political elite.[28] One characteristic of these demon-

---

24 *Felix Farley's Bristol Journal*, 2 April 1763.
25 *Bath Journal*, 1 May 1749.
26 *Worcester Journal*, 27 April 1749; *Gentleman's Magazine*, May 1749, pp. 200–01.
27 *Worcester Journal*, 4 May 1749.
28 Careful scrutiny reveals little which might suggest any common origin or transmission of the model. Even government supporters could detect no coordinating agency or scapegoat.

strations was the elaborate use of symbolism. Thus, the *Bath Chronicle* reported that, when the peace was proclaimed at Stroudwater:

> an apple tree, which had been cut down for that purpose, was carried in the procession together with an effigy as large as life, with the letter B inscribed on the back: at the closing of the cavalcade, the effigy was put into the stocks, then hung up by the common hangman, and afterwards burnt to ashes: the same ceremony, we hear, was observed at Dursley, and other parts of the country of Gloucester.[29]

When the peace was proclaimed at Cheltenham, similar symbolic action took place:

> The stage from whence it was proclaimed, was constructed of a few loose boards upon four cyder hogsheads, which were drank empty. The proclamation was read by a youth in mourning, upon which such joyful occasion the band of music struck up, which consisted of sow-gelders horns only, and the populace were regaled with part of a bottle of wine, but it is asserted by others, that the generosity of the officers extended as far as three, it being a fair and market day.[30]

At Worcester, crowds expressed 'only their joy on account of the peace; but also their great sorrow and concern, at the late woeful tax on cyder'.[31]

One of the most detailed accounts of the symbolic aspects of the displays at this time came from Exeter. The demonstration reflected not only political and social disgust with Bute but also included racial and religious imagery as devices which mock the authority of specific groups. For example, the white wands carried in the procession were the standard emblem of purity and parody the black staffs of office used by the Excisemen.

> At a Publick House, a figure was prepared, the lower part of which represented a Jack-Boot, the upper part of it was dress'd in a plaid Bonnet, with a star. This figure was exposed to view the whole day . . . About six o'clock began another procession in the manner following: First, a man riding an Ass, and on his back the inscription *From the Excise and the Devil good Lord deliver us.* A strip of apples, in Mourning, was hung round the Ass's neck, which was supported by thirty or forty men, each having a white Wand, with an Apple at the top of it, also in Mourning. Next came a cart, with a gallows fixed on it, and the plaid figure hanging by the neck. After that came a cyder hogshead, with a Pall over it, carried by six men in black Cloaks: on the Pall was a number of Escutcheons with Inscriptions to the same effect as those above mentioned. The whole was accompanied by some thousands of People hallowing and shouting through the principal Streets of the City, and at night a bonfire was prepared into which they cast the Figure, and burnt it to ashes.[32]

The power of these images was reflected in the popular verses of the time. In a 'Song on the Present Times' which appeared within a matter of days after the

29 *Bath Chronicle*, 28 April 1763.
30 *Bath Chronicle*, 28 April 1763.
31 *Berrow's Worcester Journal*, 12 May 1763.
32 *Bath Chronicle*, 19 May 1763.

announcement of the excise, the theme was once again that the region and the poor were being singled out for the expense of a war in which they had already paid the full price in terms of both physical and material commitment. However, also included within the song is a sense of history in the view that opposition to acts of oppression was something which should engage the assistance of *all* members of society:

> Our strong beer is taxed, we'er taxed on our lights,
> Yet more would they tax of our natural rights.
> But sooner than yield to a tax on our fruit,
> The Trees, tho' in Blossom, shall fall at the root.
> As Britain enjoys the sweet comforts of Peace,
> How strange to tell her Burthens increase.
> But Englishmen born, who with Freedom are blest,
> Will never submit to be basely oppressed.
> May those who persist in enforcing the Deed,
> For ever more dwell on the North-Side of the Tweed.
> And always abridg'd of that delicate Juice,
> Which Worcestershire Pippins are known to produce.
> Our Fathers before us rejected the Bill,
> Their sons are too stubborn to swallow the Pill.
> And nobly endeavour those measures to Shun,
> Which thirty years past was by Walpole begun.[33]

The spontaneity, similarity of the symbolism employed and geographical spread of the popular displays are impressive.[34] But what are we to make of them?

V

Historians have only recently begun to unravel the meanings of the symbolic and ritualistic actions which accompanied many of the displays of crowd behaviour in the early modern period.[35] Clearly, among the barely literate,

---

33 *Felix Farley's Bristol Journal*, 9 April 1763.

34 There are reports from across the region of demonstrations, combining the celebrations of the peace with displays of mourning at the imposition of the cider excise, for example at Exeter, at Stroudwater and many other places in Gloucestershire and across Worcestershire. See *Bath Chronicle*, 28 April 1763; *Felix Farley's Bristol Journal*, 23 April 1763; *Gloucester Journal*, 18 and 25 April 1763; *Berrow's Worcester Journal*, 28 April and 12 May 1763.

35 Notably the work of E. P. Thompson, *Customs in Common* (London, Merlin, 1991); N. Rogers, *Whigs and Cities, Popular Politics in the Age of Walpole and Pitt* (Oxford, Oxford University Press, 1989); R. W. Malcolmson, *Life and Labour in England, 1700–1780* (London, Hutchinson, 1981); J. Brewer, *Party Ideology and Popular Politics at the Accession of George III* (Cambridge, Cambridge University Press, 1976). F. O'Gorman has examined the symbolism and rituals surrounding elections in his 'Campaign rituals and ceremonies: the social meaning of elections in England 1780–1860', *Past and Present*, No. 135, May 1992; while J. Epstein has looked at symbolism refracted through popular radicalism in 'Understanding the cap of liberty: symbolic practice and social conflict in early nineteenth-century England', *Past and Present*, No. 22, February 1989.

symbols acted as a simple means of communication as in the way that shop or tavern signs made recognizable the goods on offer. They also served as beacons around which trade identities could be expressed as, for example, in the way in which the carrying of an effigy of Bishop Blaze in procession symbolized the solidarity of worsted cloth workers. Among these groups, symbols offered an easily recognizable context of meaning across a range of social and historical contiguities. Symbolism was also widely employed by the political elites to rally supporters. Thus O'Gorman writes that election campaigns took the form of a theatrical performance in which many visual devices such as fireworks, bonfires and effigies were regularly employed:

> Participants in an election had access to an entire world of symbolism which can appear strange and impenetrable to the historian. Such symbolism, however, was central to the meaning of elections, because symbols both defined and affirmed political and social loyalties.[36]

The Wilkite movement, for example, which, when it began, coincided with the agitation surrounding the cider excise, was rich in its use of symbolism. This included the wearing of the colour blue to signify loyalty to the cause, particularly relevant when combined with the cap of liberty, and use of the number 45 to highlight the injustice and arbitrary nature of the issuing of General Warrants.[37]

Symbolism, however, was not simply provided *de haute en bas*. The same audience which responded to the symbols of the elite were equally adept in appropriating these same forms and utilizing them to challenge their masters. Thus, Thompson argues that symbolic action was not merely the preserve of the political power relations of the patricians, from which the lower orders were excluded, but frequently signified direct action by the plebeians themselves in which they would satirize, prod or challenge the sensibilities and authority of the governing elites through what he calls the 'counter-theatre' of the streets. If the politics of state, military power or the rule of law possessed ritual and symbolic content, so too did the culture of the plebeians. 'Just as the rulers asserted their hegemony by a studied theatrical style, so the plebs asserted their presence by a theatre of threat and sedition.' The trappings of symbolism were thus the visible manifestations of wide-reaching social norms and power relations which lay at the very root of eighteenth-century social and political relations.

> Of course, every society has its own kind of theatre; much in the contemporary life can be understood only as a contest for symbolic authority. But I am saying more than that the symbolic contests of the eighteenth century were particular to that century

---

36 O'Gorman, 'Campaign rituals and ceremonies', pp. 94–95.
37 For more on this, see Brewer, *Party Ideology and Popular Politics*, Chapter 9. See also G. Rude, *Wilkes and Liberty, A Social Study of 1763 to 1774* (Oxford, Oxford University Press, 1962).

and require more study. I think that symbolism, in that century, had a particular importance, owing to the weakness of other organs of control: the authority of the Church is departing, the authority of the schools and the mass media have not yet arrived.[38]

Brewer likewise emphasizes that popular symbolism and ritual in the eighteenth century are 'precisely the clues that enable us to decode what is happening when protest occurs', and argues that they represent the 'crowd's "belief system" made concrete'.[39]

Symbols and rituals were therefore vital forms of communication. They could be expressions of approval or admonition, often, in the case of the latter, a powerful reminder to the elites of their responsibilities. Symbolic crowd behaviour acted as an important frame of reference which identified, informed, transmitted and reinforced group solidarities.[40]

Looked at from this perspective, the popular demonstrations which occurred in April 1763 fit into a classic form of popular peaceful protest. The symbols and imagery were, as at Exeter, taken from accepted formal and official ceremonies and rituals, turned back against those who were portrayed as the oppressors and contextualized in a form which made clear the sense of betrayal of customary values and expectations. Such actions served as a political focus point for those firmly outside the formal political contract and were widely observed social phenomena in early modern Europe.[41] The actions of the crowd, the antithesis of the common official form, not only provided the functional benefit of holding up those deemed guilty to public ridicule in a peaceful manner, but also, via the symbols and motifs employed, made it easy for spectators to understand the display and to endorse the message. Held in a centre of population, such as a market or county town, upon an important occasion—the proclamation of the peace was just too good an opportunity to miss—these displays of popular theatre drew an audience not only from the immediate locality but also from the surrounding areas who would take the imagery and the message away with them and in turn relate their experience to their family and friends. Thus, what may have appeared an innocuous satirical sideshow involving no more than a few hundred could have been related and re-told to an eventual audience involving thousands, even without the use of the written word.

38 Thompson, *Customs in Common*, pp. 67, 74.
39 Brewer, *Party Ideology and Popular Politics*, p. 182.
40 This is not to suggest that the use of symbolism by the working class diminished with development of a politically aware industrial working class. Symbols were still a rallying point in the first four decades of the nineteenth century, as the use of such devices as the white 'cap of liberty', the Tricolour and Paine's *Rights of Man* demonstrate. See Epstein, 'Understanding the cap of liberty'. The point is that in the *absence* of a coherent class structure and programme of action, symbols performed a function integral to the wider understanding of what the crowd and the demonstration was all about.
41 See P. Burke, *Popular Culture in Early Modern Europe* (London, Maurice Temple Smith, 1978).

VI

Discussion of the use of popular symbolism by protesting crowds raises the question as to how far the impetus may be seen as arising from a popular base or as planted among the groundlings from above. In the case of elections and such like, it is clear that the political elites frequently attempted to mobilize and utilize the crowd for their own purposes. The initial response in the West to the Cider Tax, however, can by no means be clearly so ascribed. What were the means whereby the forms of popular demonstration might be transmitted?

The dissemination of popular symbolism in the eighteenth century was done at the most basic level by the use of the songs and ballads sung in taverns and market places. Little systematic research has yet been conducted on this form of popular eighteenth-century culture, but it is clear that, in some instances at least, the popular song retained the power to concern the authorities. For example, at the height of the displays of popular opposition against the imposition of the cider excise, one ballad in the West of England reminded George III of the fate of Charles I. This information was fed back to the centre of the state at the highest level.[42] Whether or not this was the overt intention of the writers of such ballads we cannot be certain, but the fact that such manifestations of popular opinion—even those advocating such extreme solutions—did filter back to the government leaders is indicative of the significance attached to popular symbolism and opposition. Another means of dissemination was by the distribution of handbills, squibs, cartoons and other popular pamphlets. These were stuck up on walls or doorways, but such material was also just simply placed in some convenient place where it would be read and, hopefully, influence public opinion.[43]

However, by far the most important medium of popular dissemination in the eighteenth century was the growth of the national and regional newspapers. The growth of improved means of communications through the turnpike system and postal service meant that virtually all areas of Britain were covered by newspaper circulation. In this way, news of the Peace of Paris and of the intended imposition of the excise on cider might reach the affected counties within a matter of days of their announcement in London. The press, then, was an important source of information which could be quickly transmitted to a large number of people across a wide geographic area, both by reading the reports or, as was more likely, by the oral communication of the contents of newspapers at local social centres.

---

42 British Library, Hardwicke Papers, Add. Mss. 35352, f. 345, Royston to Hardwicke, 5 May 1763.
43 This was a method frequently used to generate popular anger against jobbers and factors in times of food scarcity. For example, 'We are informed that papers tending to inflame the minds of the people against the corn jobbers have been stuck up in most of the market towns in this neighbourhood'. *Bath Chronicle*, 25 March 1765.

However, the press was, of course, not merely the transmitter of news. It was also the shaper. Its reports could both inform the readership of an event and take a lead in anticipation of effects. The analysis of the tone of the language used in the press, therefore, offers the historian an opportunity to judge not only the friendliness or otherwise of the writers but also their expectations of their intended audience.

While, as has been noted, the regional press was fierce in its condemnation of the passing of the Cider Tax and in its predictions of economic disaster which would follow—for example, the *Gloucester Journal* described the region as being shrouded in 'universal gloom' as a result of excise[44]—the popular demonstrations which occurred around the celebrations of the peace do not, as noted above, appear to have been in any way influenced by 'hints' in the press or by any coordination. However, the tone of the reports which followed these examples of popular theatre indicated a level of sympathy and an endorsement rarely accorded to such displays. Thus, the events at Cheltenham evidenced above were described by the *Bath Chronicle*, a paper generally not well-disposed towards popular demonstration, as 'whimsical'. Indeed, its tone was invariably friendly. Reports of the celebrations of the peace were combined with an open disdain of the new tax:

> In several market towns where the proclamation of the peace was read, several church bells were toll'd, as for a burial, and cyder and perry were given to the populace to prevent the payment of the excise.[45]

Berrow's Worcester Journal openly told its readers how to avoid the excise with its 'hints to cyder-makers'.[46]

The regional press was not usually so indulgent of popular symbolic action or protest. In the case of the disturbances which broke out in 1766 over food, many papers imposed a news blackout in an attempt to defuse the situation, fearing, no doubt correctly, that reports of riots elsewhere might trigger them locally.[47] Drink, a legitimate item of largesse to the anti-Cider Tax demonstrators in 1763, was, in the circumstances of 1766, returned to its more usual role of instigator of anti-social action. Thus, the *Bath Journal* blamed the start of the riots in Gloucestershire upon four 'idle and dissolute fellows' who, 'being assembled together at Pitchcomb Feast, and there getting drunk, were the first

---

44 *Gloucester Journal*, 28 March 1763.
45 *Bath Chronicle*, 28 April 1763.
46 *Berrow's Worcester Journal*, 30 June 1763.
47 Thus, for example, the *Gloucester Journal*, having reported the successful repulsion of the Stroudwater mob at Gloucester market on 12 September in its edition on 15 September, thereafter kept all news of the riots in the county out of the paper until 6 October when it stated that it had been till then 'unwilling to report the conduct in the manufacturing parts', but that it would now be 'a lack of duty not to relate the dismal consequences' of the riots to its readers. By this stage, the riots had been over for at least a week. *Gloucester Journal*, 15 September, 6 October 1766.

who kindled the flame of disturbance'.[48] Editors were careful not to alienate or offend their readers, rarely participants in popular demonstrations, and they had no wish to offend the existing conventions of rank, social status and the prerequisites of established law. Their wholesale approval of the crowd's actions in their reports about these early popular responses to the Cider Tax is notable and reflected the exceptionally wide social band of disapproval which the measure encountered within the cider counties.

VII

Press reports not only fed news of popular demonstrations back to the region. They also reflected local events back towards London. This was, of course, a quite deliberate and intentional process. Just as the demonstrators themselves had as their intended audience the local power elite and press, the press in turn had every reason to convey the seriousness of the situation to Westminster. In this respect, it was highly successful.

From the earliest stage of the agitation, the central authorities became alarmed. In late April, it was reported at Bath that sources in London:

> expected that some disturbances may happen on the commencement of the additional duties on cyder, we hear, but hope it is not true, that three regiments are ordered to march into the cyder counties, to suppress that which probably will happen there.[49]

Bute's government also received a jolt in London itself when navy seamen openly displayed their dissent to the tax: 'This day a body of sailors went up to St James's in order to have their "R"s taken off; it is remarkable, they all had silk favours in their hats, on which were in gold letters, the words Liberty, Property and No Excise'.[50] In early August, the Earl of Hardwicke wrote to the Duke of Newcastle, informing him that the situation in the West Country had scarcely improved and that the effigy of Bute was still hanging at Exeter with no one daring to cut it down.[51] A similar fate befell Bute at Monmouth.[52] Ilminster in Somerset was said to be in a state of 'fury' more intense than the reports indicated, and the *Sherborne Mercury* stated that 'we shall have a state of war if these disturbances continued'.[53]

Concern at the state of feeling in the cider counties was compounded by the

---

48 *Bath Journal*, 27 October 1766. Yet this same newspaper, some months before the riots took place, was itself prepared to encourage the use of the symbolic form as an agency of stigma and redress against bakers who sold underweight bread. *Bath Journal*, 9 June 1766.
49 *Bath Chronicle*, 28 April 1763.
50 *Felix Farley's Bristol Journal*, 16 April 1763.
51 British Library, Newcastle Papers, Add. Mss. 32950, f. 1, Hardwicke to Newcastle, 1 August 1763.
52 Cited in J. Brewer, 'The misfortunes of Lord Bute: a case study in eighteenth-century political argument and public opinion', *Historical Journal*, Vol. XVI, 1973.
53 *Exeter Flying Post*, 16 May 1763; *Sherborne Mercury*, 23 May 1763.

fear that the agitation might become mixed up with the agitation surrounding John Wilkes. Horace Walpole wrote that, discontent in the West being so great, 'if Mr Wilkes will turn patriot hero or patriot incendiary in earnest, and put himself at their head, he may obtain a rope of martyrdom before the summer is over'.[54] That such a conjunction never occurred was primarily because Wilkes already had much to occupy his energies, but also because there is no evidence that the representatives of the dispute in the cider counties ever approached him.[55] They wished above all to agitate within their own districts and bring the unanimity of their regional protest to the attention of the authorities in London with the strictest legality.

VIII

The organization which sprang up in the cider counties to overturn the Cider Tax was a remarkably effective and innovatory one. In a very short period of time, a structure was established based upon a formal organization of freeholders with county subcommittees who in turn reported to large standing committees which were serviced by salaried clerks. They in turn directed attention towards a concerted lobby at Westminster. Woodland suggests that the movement outside Westminster served as a precedent for the more wide-ranging Association Movement of the later 1770s. He states: 'many of its activities, building conservatively upon the precedent of the county meeting, foreshadow those of Wyvill'.[56]

This organization operated on two inter-related levels: in the provincial constituencies, where associations and regular meetings kept the issue alive and supporters of repeal united and informed of the latest developments; and at Westminster. Although the question remained essentially a regional one, the aim was to influence Parliament and, eventually, government to carry through a repeal.[57]

The support of sitting members was crucial and relentless and concerted pressure was applied. Distrust of their commitment periodically surfaced. In

---

54 Walpole to Montagu, 6 April 1763, cited in W. S. Lewis (ed.), *Horace Walpole's Correspondence* (New Haven, Yale University Press, 1937), Vol. X, p. 57.

55 It is significant to note that Wilkes' main propaganda organ, *The North Briton*, was generally hostile to the excise and towards the Cider Tax in particular: 'The county of Devon furnished the navy with double the number of sailors of any five counties in England . . . And what has been her recompense? The subjecting of her entire Landed Interest, of every Rank, Gentleman and Farmer, to the *unconstitutional Tax of an arbitrary Excise and the abusive Dominion of insolent Excisemen!' North Briton*, 9 July 1763, cited in *Berrow's Worcester Journal*, 14 July 1763.

56 Woodland, 'Extra-Parliamentary political organization in the making', p. 130.

57 The author of the plan was Benjamin Heath, town clerk of Exeter. Heath, *Some Hints submitted to the Consideration of the Owners and Occupiers of Lands in the County of Devon, upon the Steps most proper to be taken in order to obtain a Repeal of the Tax upon Cyder* (no date, Carew Papers, Somerset Record Office). See also Woodland, 'The Cider Excise', pp. 269–71.

the City of Gloucester, for example, a dispute arose between the sitting members, Sir William Codrington and Mr Southwell, as to who was the most supportive of repeal. The acrimony became so bitter that Codrington, when approached by the Earl of Hardwicke to represent his political interests in Gloucestershire, was obliged to decline in order to emphasize his commitment to the cause of repeal.[58] Further evidence of the political effects of the excise can be gauged from the following report made during the Gloucestershire election of 1763:

> The truth is, it [the cider excise] has spread a universal face of sorrow over the cider countries, and men who were but a few months ago irreconcilable enemies, are now united in their opposition to an odious and oppressive excise.[59]

Elsewhere, local Members of Parliament were reminded of their responsibilities. In June 1763, dissatisfaction was being expressed at the 'surprising Indolence' of the Somerset MPs.[60] They received some indication of their public esteem when a Bath paper reissued a satire from the excise crisis of 1733:

> Gentlemen, Yours I received, and am very much surprised at your Insolence in troubling me about the Excise. You know what I know very well, that I bought you. I know what perhaps you think I don't know, that you are about selling yourselves to someone else; and I know perhaps what you don't know, that I am about buying another Borough. And now may the curse of G— light upon you all; and may your Houses be as common to excisemen, as your Wives and Daughters were to me, when I stood Candidate for your Corporation.[61]

The lobbying of Westminster was the least successful area of the three-year campaign against the Cider Tax.[62] Even so, it ultimately achieved its objective. Under the Grenville administration, two modifications were adopted in the operation of the excise, but the real change came with the appointment of William Dowdeswell as Chancellor of the Exchequer in July 1765. Eight months later, the excise on cider was repealed.

IX

The shift towards lobbying Westminster changed the dynamics of the provincial situation from protest to pressure. While the campaign remained very much

58 British Library, Hardwicke papers, Add. Mss. 35692, f. 163, Codrington to Hardwicke, 18 October 1763. Hardwicke was opposed to the cider excise. He had been carefully cultivating the Tory clothiers in Gloucestershire since the mid-1750s in the Newcastle interest, particularly through appointments to the bench. He was thus very interested to learn from John Pitt, his agent in Gloucestershire, of their widespread political defection from Bute's administration as a result of the operation of the excise. Pitt to Hardwicke, 8 October 1763, f. 157. See also N. Landau, *The Justices of the Peace, 1679–1760* (Los Angeles, University of California, 1984), pp. 140–43.
59 *Gloucestershire Notes and Queries*, Vol. II (Gloucester, 1884), p. 88.
60 *Sherborne Mercury*, 13 June 1763.
61 *Bath Journal*, 4 April 1763.
62 Woodland, 'Extra-Parliamentary political organisation', pp. 129–30.

an extra-Parliamentary movement, the provincial leaders of the agitation[63] wished above all to place the movement on a solid basis of legitimacy after the initial outburst of popular clamour. This, they believed, was crucial if the issue was to force its arguments on to the legislature and achieve the ultimate objective of a repeal. This explains why, after the introduction of the Excise Act in July 1763, the emphasis of the regional press was focused on the numerous county meetings organized by the gentry and middle classes while demonstrations of popular disapproval were very much played down. Displays did, however, continue, and on the day the Cider Act came into force it was mourned in the following manner at Ledbury:

> A procession was made thro' the principal Parts of this Town by the Servants of the Cyder Merchants, Coopers, Farmers, and some poor Labourers, with Numbers of poor People, in the following Manner, viz. A man with a Drum covered with black Crape, beating the dead March, Drumsticks reverted; two Mutes with Crape Hatbands and black Cloaks; an empty Barrel upon a Bier, carried by six poor Farmers, dressed in Cyder Hair Cloths, with Hair Cloths covering the Barrel, and Gauging stick in the Bung Hole, and the Pall of Hair Cloths, supported by six others in black; two Men, the one on the Right, with an empty Can upon his Head covered with Crape, upon the Top of which was a Branch of an Apple Tree, with Apples thereon, covered also with Crape; the other on the Left in black, the Tools on his Shoulder necessary to be made Use of in felling of Trees; and in the Rear a Number of poor Objects, with Apples in their Bosoms covered with Crape. The Bells were rung muffled all the Day; and every face expressed a sympathetic Sorrow for the impending Ruin that awaits this Country.[64]

By August, the clampdown on popular demonstrations was largely observed as the local elites concentrated on maintaining the utmost respectability and constitutional legitimacy in their campaign for repeal. This was a clear policy decision as this report concerning a proposed meeting of the leaders of the opposition with the High Sheriff of Worcestershire makes clear:

> For 'tis proper that the Ministry should be convinced, that the Repeal of this Law is contended for, not by a Set of *clamorous* People, *out of place*, not by an insignificant Number of Men, but by the largest and most respectable Born in the Kingdom, acting on principles founded in Reason, justified by Experience, and warranted by the Constitution.[65]

However, there were parts of the region where the writ of gentlemanly control was at the best of times frail and where popular sentiments could not

---

63 The major figures were Dowdeswell in Worcestershire/Gloucestershire, Benjamin Heath in Exeter and the South West and Velters Cornewall in Herefordshire.

64 *Berrow's Worcester Journal*, 21 July 1763.

65 *Berrow's Worcester Journal*, 25 August 1763.

easily be constrained. In the Forest of Dean, for example, a notoriously 'independent' district where the free miners were disinclined to worry over social niceties, the colliers seized an exciseman, 'going his rounds to the cider mills', as a hostage shortly after the Act was invoked. The *Bath Journal* reported that he:

> was instantaneously hurried down 2 or 300 feet under ground, where he now takes up his abode. The colliers, it is said, use him very well, and he lives as they do; but they say the day of his Resurrection shall not come to pass till the Cyder-Act is repealed.[66]

A report one month later noted that the unfortunate officer was still being held captive in the 'subterraneous regions', after which nothing was heard of him again.[67]

The organizing elites were at pains to prove that they were in control of the situation in the cider counties. Velters Cornewall, for example, the leader of the campaign in Herefordshire, claimed to have succeeded in quieting 'the peoples minds' there[68] and it does generally appear that most of the populace were satisfied that their leaders were conducting the business as expeditiously as possible. In this, the press again played its part, emphasizing the unanimity of determination to secure repeal of the detested legislation. However, the writ of the elite did not always run so smoothly. In Monmouth, 'a certain Great Commoner', passing through the town and stopping briefly at an inn, was recognized and 'set upon' by an angry crowd who forced him and his wife to escape by a back door. All the traces on his coach were cut and 'the coach was also destroyed'. According to the report, 'it was apprehended that had he not happily made his Escape, he would have been in great Danger of being killed, so greatly are the People enraged against the favourers of the Cyder Act'. The Riot Act was read and order eventually restored.[69] Elsewhere, excisemen attempting to go about their business were assaulted or threatened. At Bristol two excise collectors were asked why they had suddenly resigned their office, 'as no violence had been offered to them? They answered, that they were only spared upon their solemnly promising never to come there again on that errand: as they were men of honour, they determined not to forfeit their word.'[70] From Exeter, a report in July noted that one of the large number of excisemen sent to the county had ears cut off his horse while he himself had been ill treated by the populace. Far from expressing the usual concern, however, the report pondered on whether the excisemen had any right 'to bring their Horse or Horses in upon

66 *Bath Journal*, 25 July 1763.
67 *Bath Journal*, 29 August 1763.
68 Woodland, 'The Cider Excise', p. 264.
69 *Berrow's Worcester Journal*, 9 June 1763; *Gentleman's Magazine*, June 1763, p. 304.
70 *Bath Journal*, 10 October 1763.

any Man's Land . . . where his Duty may call him without being deemed a Trespass', speculating that civil actions might follow.[71]

X

Repeal in 1766 was a signal for renewed popular demonstrations, on this occasion of celebration. The *Bath Chronicle* reported that at Honiton bells were rung and the local MP, Sir George Yonge, had provided 'sheep to be roasted and seven Hogsheads of Cyder to be given to the Populace':

> A fine large ox was led thro' the town, attended by Drums and Fifes, decorated with Garlands of Flowers, Apple Branches with Apples gilt and crowned with Laurals. A label was painted and fixed between his Horns with this Motto: *The Cyder Act repealed, Freedom restored.* A grand green Flag was displayed; the Motto, *Yonge and Liberty, No Cyder Tax.* The Ox was afterwards killed, and with a great quantity of other Beef distributed the next day to the poor House-keepers. The evening was concluded with a Bonfire, Illuminations, and other Indications of Joy, on this glorious and important Event.[72]

Elsewhere, celebrations were combined with other measures that a popular government had provided for a given district. At Yeovil, for example, it was reported:

> on account of the Repeal of the Cyder-Act, and the Prohibition of the Importation of French Gloves, (Gloving being the principal Trade of that Town) the inhabitants have devoted the greatest Part of last Week to Bell ringing and other Diversions; three sheep being roasted whole on the three last Days, and two Vessels of Cyder continuously running at their Market-House.[73]

Similar reports were published covering all the cider counties, testifying to the mutual satisfaction of elites and plebeians in the repeal.

XI

What can we conclude from this examination of the opposition to the 1763 Cider Tax in the West of England? How far can we view the demonstrations and symbolic actions of the crowds and the actions of the middling sorts as indicative of a popular or widely-shared political consciousness? And what do they tell us of the political sub-culture and values of the people?

It is clear that the common people of Hanoverian England possessed a vibrant and easily drawn-upon culture of opposition which was effectively and meaningfully expressed through symbolic display. Inventive and resourceful, they were able to mount tableaux which satirized the displays of their social

---

71 *Berrow's Worcester Journal*, 28 July 1763.
72 *Bath Chronicle*, 24 April 1766.
73 *Bath Chronicle*, 1 May 1766.

betters in ways in which their views were crystal clear to all who saw them or heard of them later.

It is equally clear that, while the 'mob' could be utilized by the political classes for their own ends, the ordinary people were quite capable of their own independent activity. This was well shown by the ways in which, without any prompting from above, the peace celebrations were converted into parodic protests over the Cider Tax. The spontaneity and widespread geography of these demonstrations are indicative of the vibrancy and the common 'language' of symbolic display across the region.

The campaign against the Cider Tax, however, was able to draw upon the widest cross-section of society. Uniquely, the decision to target this one commodity simultaneously struck the rich and poor in the region as transcendently oppressive. The poor clearly felt an economic threat to their living standards not felt by the richest, but the gentleman, the farmer and the labourer all saw the imposition of the excise and the powers accorded to the excisemen to search the Englishman's castle, his home, as arbitrary and smacking of continental despotism. All shared the sense that the region was being singled out for harsh and unfair treatment by an unpopular and unaccountable government. No other issue in the period managed to outrage so socially and geographically widespread an audience.

Once the movement was under way, however, the scope for propertied support for popular action was much diminished. The need to appear both respectable and firmly in control of those forces of popular outrage they claimed to represent meant that the campaigners could no longer tolerate too much popular spontaneity. As with middle-class radicals later in the century and into the next, the crowd, like the hounds, could be hallooed on to Establishment targets but could not be allowed to roam too freely. These problems of sustaining and controlling popular opinion, a task in which Woodland sees the middling sort who organized the Cider Tax campaign as pioneers, were to grow no more easy over time.

The agitation of 1763 may also be seen as a significant moment in the development of a plebeian political consciousness. The successful repeal of the Cider Tax in one respect appeared to reinforce the traditional route to redress, namely highlighting a grievance to the authorities and, with their assistance, witnessing the eventual triumph of justice. However, in economic as well as in political terms, the world of the plebeians was changing rapidly. The wide sense of community engendered across the whole of the region by the Cider Tax marked a notable but short-lived alliance. This was to be clearly indicated when, in September 1766, extensive food riots broke out across the region. It could well be that the crowd in the West of England, fuelled by their 'victory' over the cider excise earlier in the year, believed that their actions would again produce a prompt resolution. However, as we have noted, the symbolism and the values of the 'regulators' did not receive the same indulgent support from the authorities as had the demonstrations against the Cider Tax only three years before. The sheer size of the crowd's response to dearth brought immediate concessions. But within a matter of weeks, the Special Commission had been sent out determined to make an example of the captured rioters. Without the mobilized oppositional assistance of the elites, the lower orders were extremely vulnerable to the severities of the law. Traditional plebeian attitudes and customs were to find themselves increasingly out of favour as the century continued. The use of symbolism as a means of articulating grievances and expounding messages, however, was to continue as an important facet of developing popular political action.

Chapter 5

SCARCITY AND THE CIVIC TRADITION: MARKET MANAGEMENT IN BRISTOL, 1709–1815[1]

STEVE POOLE

Past studies of scarcity in England have focused primarily upon the reactive behaviour of the labouring poor, and specifically the incidence and cultural precepts of riot. While some studies have laboured over the identification of 'perennially' riotous or non-riotous communities, measures taken by urban elites to manage and alleviate scarcity have been largely neglected. One scholar, John Bohstedt, has discussed the non-viability of 'community politics' in the modern 'city of strangers', setting up telling comparisons between the reciprocal paternalism of rural Devon and the nascent class antagonism that underpinned social relations in booming new industrial towns like Manchester. But studies of towns in which conditions permitted the co-existence of modernism and tradition are something of a rarity.[2] Bristol, in common with many English towns and cities, experienced price rioting in lean years, but it cannot simply be described as a riotous, violent or socially alienated community.[3] Indeed, in many

---

1 I should like to thank the British Academy for awarding me the fellowship which made possible the research for this essay.
2 See, for example, E. P. Thompson, *Customs in Common* (London, Merlin, 1991), Chapters 4 and 5 (on the 'moral economy') and John Bohstedt, *Riots and Community Politics in England and Wales, 1790–1810* (Cambridge, Mass., Harvard University Press, 1983), especially Chapter 3. The exceptionally broad scope of Roger Wells, *Wretched Faces: Famine in Wartime England, 1793–1801* (Gloucester, Alan Sutton, 1988) is a notable exception to this 'neglect'. Walter Shelton's *English Hunger and Industrial Disorders: A Study of Social Conflict During the First Decade of George III's Reign* (Toronto, University of Toronto Press, 1973), pp. 95–121, devotes a chapter to 'the role of the authorities' during the riots of 1766, but confines itself to the abdication of the rural gentry and the inadequate policies of central government.
3 Bristol does not measure up to any of Bohstedt's community models. It was neither a 'stable medium sized town' where dominant horizontal relationships invited frequent rioting, nor a 'big industrial city like Manchester or Birmingham' where vertical relationships predominated and riots among alienated strangers were ineffectual. The author summarizes his case in 'The moral economy and the discipline of historical context', *Journal of Social History*, Vol. 26, No. 2, 1992, pp. 174–75. For a useful critique, see Andrew Charlesworth, 'From the moral economy of Devon to the political economy of Manchester, 1790–1812', *Social History*, Vol. 18, No. 2, 1993, pp. 205–17. For the assumption that some towns were 'almost perennially subject to disturbances, whilst others remained almost completely undisturbed', see John Stevenson, 'Food riots in England, 1792–1818' in R. Quinault and J. Stevenson (eds), *Popular Protest and Public Order: Six Studies in British History, 1790–1920* (London, Allen and Unwin, 1974), p. 67. Stevenson takes issue with the followers of E. P. Thompson for

of the most serious periods of scarcity, disorder was averted in the city despite rioting in surrounding districts. This essay examines the development of a 'civic tradition' of market management in Bristol, under which loosely allied corporate, commercial and middling-class interests acted to promote social harmony, preserving the integrity of what Bohstedt would call 'horizontal relationships' by broadening them in the teeth of recession. It was, it is argued, the unprecedented social violence unleashed by food price disturbances in 1753 which prompted recognition of the need for effective management—both of the market itself, by a variety of means, and of the machinery of law enforcement. Thence, through a mixture of pragmatic paternalism and imaginative free trade, Bristol weathered the storms of scarcity in the latter part of the century. The early inception of such 'modern' practices made later modification virtually unnecessary, for the city's markets suffered their last disturbance in 1812.

I

For much of the eighteenth century, Bristol's claim to be the nation's 'second city' was rarely questioned. The pre-eminence of the port and its dependent home industries encouraged the development of an ethos of self-reliance, proudly reflected in civic ritual and ceremony, and made inclusive by a wide freeman-franchise of 5,000.[4] Authority was highly centralized. Judicial and executive functions were vested jointly in a self-electing Corporation of 42, the city's 12 aldermen—one for each ward—acting as justices for the borough. Independent county status further enhanced local self-governance and enabled corporate control over all civil and criminal law through a wide range of courts. A series of local acts obtained during the century upgraded and improved corporate powers and functions. Income, derived from substantial property holdings, lucrative market rents and shipping dues, generated between £14,000 and £18,000 a year by the end of the century, making it one of the wealthiest corporate oligarchies in the country. The Corporation extended its interests still further through membership of nominally independent bodies like the Turnpike Trust, on which the entire Corporation was represented, the Select Vestries and the Society of Merchant Venturers.[5] As a supervisory body for

---

'general explanations' of riots which construct them as 'universal phenomena, which clearly they were not'.

4 Secondary sources are numerous, but see, for example, W. E. Minchinton, 'Bristol—Metropolis of the West in the eighteenth century', *Transactions of the Royal Historical Society*, Vol. 5, No. 4, 1954, pp. 69–89; Jonathan Barry, 'The cultural life of Bristol, 1640–1775' (unpublished DPhil thesis, University of Oxford, 1985), pp. 301–05. Bristol's borough electorate was one of the seven largest in the country.

5 A standard sourcebook for the background to local government in Bristol remains Sidney and Beatrice Webb, *English Local Government from the Revolution to the Municipal Corporations Act: The Manor and the Borough*, Vol. 2, 1908, pp. 443–75; but see also Mark Harrison, *Crowds and History: Mass Phenomena in English Towns, 1790–1835* (Cambridge, Cambridge University Press, 1988), pp. 62–89.

both the quays and the river pilots, and as a medium for business cooperation and joint enterprise, the Society of Merchant Venturers was a powerful economic pressure group enjoying close ties with a number of Parliamentary committees. As we shall see, its working relationship with the Corporation was to become a major factor in the management of provision.

Despite its impersonal size, visitors were so struck by a sense of collective purpose in the place that 'the mind is immediately filled with the idea of the inhabitants being totally occupied in trade and commerce'.[6] Observers were impressed by the city's capacity to temper recession with broad industrial diversity so that, 'in comparison with many of our larger cities and manufacturing districts, [Bristol] is suffering less than almost any other place in the kingdom'.[7] Large-scale and well-funded charitable enterprises like the Colston Society, originally endowed by the successful merchant, Edward Colston, were both a safety net for the poor and a constant reminder for all Bristolians of the benefits bestowed by their mercantile heritage. Yet civic virtue was always susceptible to attack from 'outsiders'. The threat of attacks against shipping by alien incendiaries like John the Painter, who frightened the burgesses 'out of their senses' in 1777, haunted commercial self-confidence for decades.[8] Volatile communities of colliers and weavers beyond the city liberties took the blame for much eighteenth-century urban disorder and petty crime, just as 'crowds' of migrant Irish fleeing scarcity at home would later be blamed for bringing 'the seeds of disease and death' to Bristol.[9]

The idea that all classes in the city shared equally in the success or failure of business and harvest alike was carefully nurtured by the authorities and business elite. Commercial triumph might be celebrated by merchants showering coin on to the people from upstairs windows, but in dearth 'it will not be one portion of the community alone that will suffer. The suffering will be as general as it will be severe'.[10] Language was carefully chosen. In 1812, a draft entreaty of abstinence which began 'The mayor and aldermen feel it their duty to

---

6 The 1801 census recorded 63,645 people in the city, making it the fifth largest English town after London, Liverpool, Manchester and Birmingham. S. W. Poole, 'Popular politics in Bristol, Somerset and Wiltshire, 1791–1805' (unpublished PhD thesis, University of Bristol, 1993), pp. 3–4; P. T. Marcy, *Eighteenth Century Views of Bristol and Bristolians* (Bristol, Bristol Branch of the Historical Association, 1966), pp. 4–6.

7 *Felix Farley's Bristol Journal*, 12 October 1816.

8 Poole, 'Popular politics', pp. 65–66, 71–72.

9 Poole, 'Popular politics', pp. 65–66, 71–72. For the Irish, see *Bristol Mirror*, 15 May 1847 and *Felix Farley's Bristol Journal*, 25 September 1847. The Corporation tried to discredit demands made by a Cornishman for a public inquiry into its responsibility for rioting in 1793 on grounds that he was a 'factious alien', drawing the similarly stigmatized poet Coleridge's retort, 'I glory that I am an alien in your city': A. W., *A Letter to Edward Long Fox, M.D.* (Bristol, 1795); S. T. Coleridge, *An Answer to a Letter to Edward Long Fox* (Bristol, 1795).

10 For showers of money after the successful conclusion of the city's campaign against the 1766 Stamp Tax, see Kenneth Morgan, *Bristol and the Atlantic Trade in the Eighteenth Century* (Cambridge,

recommend to their fellow citizens . . .' was actually printed as '. . . feeling in common with their fellow citizens . . .'. The ammendment was minor, but not unimportant.[11] Soup kitchens had been established in 1800, it was boasted, 'so that it may not be said to the disgrace of this rich and opulent city that any person is perishing therein for want of food'. But urban cultural sophistication had more to offer than soup. Poetic odes to private benevolence pitied Bristol's hungry 'children of sorrow' in 1784, but, in this 'city of charities', what could the wealthy do but 'cheerfully open their store'? Determinedly upbeat local newspapers pressed the case for cohesion and interdependence. 'Let old Bristol stand forth as the first provincial city', went the cry, 'resolved to do what she can in the present crisis of high prices and diminishing labour.' Famine might be 'at the gates of our city, almost at our very doors', but Bristolians were exorted to work together to repel the danger.[12]

Bristol's markets were extensive and varied in the eighteenth century. Corn and flour came by trow to a number of small quayside market houses from the West Country, Evesham, Hereford, Worcester and Monmouth; there was a twice-weekly fish market in Union Street, and separate markets for Welsh produce, hay, livestock, cheese and vegetables. During scarcity, these markets were busy, not only with local and regional consumers, but with wholesale buyers from landlocked towns as far away as Birmingham and even from competing but smaller ports like Bridgwater. In 1800, Bridgwater managed to attract only one consignment of American flour and so, like most towns in Somerset, became reluctantly dependent on merchants from the 'plentiful market' of Bristol.[13] The dependence of surrounding regions only increased the resolve of the local authorities to ensure generous and uninterrupted avenues of supply. Yet supply could be severely disrupted by popular interference with barge traffic in the producing districts. Blockaded waterways in Gloucestershire put Bristol under severe strain in 1709, 1757, 1766, 1795 and 1800.[14] War with France threatened supplies still further, whether through

Cambridge University Press, 1993), p. 23. For the universality of scarcity, see *Felix Farley's Bristol Journal*, 9 August 1828.

11 Bristol Record Office Town Clerk's Letter Box, 1811–12, unnumbered bundle, draft and printed poster dated 2 May 1812.

12 *Felix Farley's Bristol Journal*, 21 February 1784, 18 October 1800, 15 and 22 May 1847.

13 See the critical analysis charting the decline of Bristol's markets and the 'negligence' of the Corporation in *Felix Farley's Bristol Journal*, 25 March 1826, 1 April 1826; for outside buyers, see Public Record Office, Home Office Papers 42/35, Greville to Portland, 19 June 1795, Stamford to Portland, 27 June 1795, Legge to Portland, 30 June 1795. For the dependency of Somerset towns, see questionnaire replies in Home Office Papers 42/54 (ff. 326 et seq.).

14 British Library Add. Mss. 61609, Blenheim Papers, Bristol magistrates to Sunderland, 26 October 1709; information of N. Harrison, 10 October 1709; *Felix Farley's Bristol Journal*, 19 February 1757, 7 May 1757, 8 November 1766, 5 April 1800; Bristol Record Office, Corporation Letter Book, Smith to Portland, 17 October 1795.

lost overseas markets, exportation to feed British troops abroad or the plundering activities of enemy privateers. Bristol merchants suffered heavy losses to French shipping during the dearths of 1740 and 1757.[15] A decline in the city's share of the grain trade at the close of the century brought mixed blessings. The deteriorating state of the docks had contributed to Liverpool's success in attracting more grain cargoes than Bristol in 1800–01. Consistently lower prices in the northern port led to calls for a dock improvement bill and even a suggestion that Bristol merchants should purchase corn at Liverpool and bring it down by canal. But Bristol was not well served by canals. When the Kennet and Avon canal opened fully for business in 1811, one of the first towns to benefit was Bath, where 840 sacks of wheat were landed from Newbury in the first week. It was probably just as well for the viability of domestic supply at Bristol in the early nineteenth century that the decline of the port was synonymous with the growing independence of surrounding markets.[16]

Subsistence crises were not only confined to periods of serious scarcity. In winter months, freezing conditions in the docks meant not only seasonal unemployment for the watermen, but obstruction to landing cargoes and a consequent threat of price rises at a most critical time. Having pawned their clothing, furniture and 'even their working tools' to buy bread in 1768, unemployed dockers were forced to parade the streets for alms.[17] When general unemployment reached 3,000 in the recession of 1816–17, the awful consequences of a fashionable exodus of wealth from the poorer inner parishes to the leafy suburbs became starkly apparent. In St Phillips, complained a vestry committee, there remained 'hardly an opulent resident' to pay for the maintenance of the poor.[18] 'Charity', it was frequently boasted, 'steps in to supply every deficiency', yet, reliant as they inevitably were upon the continuing subscriptions of the better-off, charitable schemes were gravely tested during longer periods of scarcity.[19] Provision committees made the most of their limited funds by offering relief in soup or in bulk-purchased commodities below market prices. Qualification was usually by written recommendation, a rule designed to informally means-test applicants and to exclude the idle. Yet their viability remained precarious in the long crisis of 1766–68, and in 1800 both the city infirmary and the Strangers Friend Society felt squeezed by the competition for subscriptions. The soup kitchen, despite an income of £2,000

15 Morgan, *Bristol and the Atlantic Trade*, pp. 18–19; *Bristol Weekly Intelligencer*, 30 April 1757.
16 *Felix Farley's Bristol Journal*, 7 February 1801, 11 April 1801, 1 December 1810, 2 February 1811.
17 *Felix Farley's Bristol Journal*, 9 and 16 January 1768; Public Record Office 30/8, Chatham Papers, Smith to Pitt, 21 February 1795. Relief targeted specifically at pilots, bargemen and trowmen was distributed by the Venturers in 1789 and 1800: P. McGrath, *The Merchant Venturers of Bristol* (Bristol, Society of Merchant Venturers, 1975), p. 208.
18 *Bristol Mercury*, 9 December 1816; *Felix Farley's Bristol Journal*, 4 January 1817.
19 *Felix Farley's Bristol Journal*, 17 January 1795.

during the first five months of 1801, struggled hard to maintain supply, 'notwithstanding the most rigid economy'.[20]

There are difficulties in assessing the severity of crises like these on the lives of the poor, for evidence of hardship is patchy and often anecdotal. In 1757, a sudden rise in the price of corn from five to nine shillings a bushel forced overseers in one parish to distribute over 12,000lb of cheap bread to 700 families, but no estimates survive for the city as a whole.[21] This is a larger figure than any claimed during the equally serious crisis of 1766–67,[22] but relatively minor when compared with evidence from 1795. In July of that year, corn peaked at 17 shillings a bushel amid claims that 15–18,000 Bristolians (some 3,000 families and perhaps a quarter of the population) were in 'absolute want'. Discrepancies between the number of people receiving relief and those claimed to be in need are frequent, however. Soup charities in 1800 were serving 7,500 people, but the number calculated to be 'in need' by city vestries, over and above those already receiving parish relief, was 9,000. Similarly, a provision committee in St Phillips in 1817 had sufficient funds to relieve 681 people, but warned there were 'many more' in acute distress.[23] It is unclear how many times a single applicant could receive soup in a week. Although between 6,000 and 8,000 queued every day in 1801, benefactors were urged in 1816 to issue soup tickets to any family no more than three times a week, and only after 'strict inquiries into the character' of claimants. Nor is it clear how many were receiving relief from sources other than the Corporation-supported committee. A number of smaller subscription committees were active in 1801.[24] Dietary deficiency invited early mortality. Fever and agues were described as 'almost general' among the poor of St Phillip and Jacob in 1768, while the Kingswood colliers were in a 'wretched state' and their pit horses dying from malnutrition. The wave of fever that swept the city after the near famine of 1800–01 claimed the lives of at least 28 people in one single house alone.[25]

20 *Felix Farley's Bristol Journal*, 1 February 1766, 14 March 1767, 16 January 1768, 18 January 1800, 1 and 8 February 1800, 5 and 26 April 1800, 26 December 1800; *Bonner and Middleton's Bristol Journal*, 5 July 1800, 14 February 1801.

21 *Felix Farley's Bristol Journal*, 5 February 1757, 7 May 1757; *Bristol Weekly Intelligencer*, 30 April 1757.

22 St Phillip and Jacob parishes were relieving between four and five hundred families a week in 1767: *Felix Farley's Bristol Journal*, 28 March 1767.

23 *Bristol Mercury*, 9 December 1816; *Felix Farley's Bristol Journal*, 18 January 1817.

24 *Bristol Mercury*, 13 July 1795 (letter); *Felix Farley's Bristol Journal*, 18 January 1800, 8 February 1800, 24 November 1816, 18 January 1817; *Bonner and Middleton's Bristol Journal*, 24 January 1801, 14 and 28 February 1801.

25 *Felix Farley's Bristol Journal*, 16 January 1768; J. Latimer, *Annals of Bristol in the Nineteenth Century* (Bristol, William George, 1887), p. 8.

II

Bristol was no stranger to market-place disorders in the eighteenth century. More often than not, it was visiting colliers from Kingswood Chase who challenged the civic order.[26] In 1709 they pillaged city granaries but were easily dispersed by a combination of threats, promises and arrests. Further conflict was avoided by magisterial inaction over the 'escape' of detainees from the Council House, the temporary subsidization of cheap grain from the public purse and by lowering the assize of bread.[27] In 1740, miners again parleyed with the mayor over prices but were deterred from forcing reductions by Colonel Blakeney's regiment of foot, who made a public show of loading live ball outside the mayor's house.[28]

By far the most serious disturbances, however, occurred during a short localized dearth in 1753 when colliers forcibly emptied a barge loaded for exportation after customary parleying broke down. Mayor John Clements' resort to stave-wielding constables and arrests did not calm the situation. Fighting in the streets left shattered windows at the Council House, an alderman and the town clerk seriously injured and the colliers' leader, Job Phipps, confined to the bridewell with a broken arm. In the following tense and uncertain three days, gates were locked and guarded, constables enrolled, troops sent for, scouts sent into the countryside and all 'respectable' tradesmen 'directed' to arm in defence of the city. Shops were boarded and trade ground to a virtual standstill. As expected, the colliers returned to liberate Phipps, but, instead of defending the bridewell, the 'very nervous and unavoidably agitated' Clements took his 50 Scots Greys down the Pithay and across the River Frome to St James' Back. From this position, he was unable to obstruct the advance on the bridewell and the soldiers would have been out of sight of the majority in the crowd. He issued no orders to engage the rioters. Instead, he permitted (or was perhaps powerless to prevent) a disorderly rout by hundreds of armed tradesmen. Of the colliers, 4 were killed, 30 captured and the rest put to flight.[29]

26 The standard text on the colliers remains Robert Malcolmson, ' "A set of ungovernable people": the Kingswood colliers in the eighteenth century' in J. Brewer and J. Styles (eds), *An Ungovernable People: The English and their Law in the Seventeenth and Eighteenth Centuries* (London, Hutchinson, 1979), pp. 85–128.

27 British Library Add. Mss. 61608, Blenheim Papers, Magistrates of Bristol to the Earl of Sunderland, 21 and 23 May 1709; Savage to Sunderland, 24 May 1709; Latimer, pp. 78–79.

28 Public Record Office State Papers 36/52 pt. 2, Clutterbuck to Newcastle, 23 September 1740; State Papers 41/12, Leighton to Wade, 24 September 1740; *Gloucester Journal*, 30 September 1740, 7 and 14 October 1740.

29 The preceding narrative is based on contemporary accounts: Public Record Office State Papers 36/122 pt. 1, Clements to Newcastle, 21 and 25 May 1753; Bristol Public Library, Manuscript Diary of William Dyer, 1744–1801; the contemporary press and an early chronicle, G. Pryce, *A Popular History of Bristol* (Bristol, W. Mack, 1861), pp. 438–41.

Clements' nightmare was just beginning. While a large delegation of tradesmen prevailed upon him to secure and punish all those who had escaped, delicate negotiations were under way in Kingswood for the release of a tradesman-hostage, taken as the colliers withdrew. Moreover, instead of appearing cowed and beaten, bands of insurgents were moving into Wiltshire to enlist recruits for a return bout. A baker's shop was razed just outside Lawfords Gate, and in Bristol itself Clements sensed 'a strong inclination . . . among the lower sort of our citizens to join them', making resistance 'too hard a task for our present force'. He abandoned the usual Restoration Day public illuminations for fear of attracting further crowds. If this was not bad enough, tradesmen who had been looking forward to exemplary justice at the assize were suddenly put in fear of it when friends of a dead rioter secured a coroner's verdict of unlawful killing against three tradesmen and against the draper John Brickdale in particular. The verdict was eventually overturned in the Court of Kings Bench, but only after Brickdale hectored the Corporation into taking the matter up with the Attorney General. The arrival of troop reinforcements secured temporary pacification in Kingswood, and in September a Special Commission found two rioters guilty of treason in absentia and gaoled nine others.[30]

III

The extraordinary events of 1753 were nothing if not an object lesson in the vulnerability of civic order during scarcity, the damage inflicted upon social cohesion and commerce by confrontation strikingly evident, and the limitations of *force majeure* as a means of containing discontent exposed. The very fact that the most persistent threat to the city's peace came from communities of outsiders, over whom aldermanic jurisdiction was extremely limited, only emphasized the difficulty. Moreover, as the 1753 riot showed, straightforward bargaining over the assize had failed to address consumer demands for intervention against the injustice of exportation amid deficiencies in the home market. It was in this period of radical corporate and mercantile reappraisal that more positive and paternalistic initiatives for alleviating scarcity first emerged. Put simply, the key to averting disorder was the maintenance of supply. The return of provision shortages in 1757 put to the test a number of interventionist initiatives that would later become commonplace. With domestic supplies in

---

30 *Felix Farley's Bristol Journal,* 9 June 1753; 8 September 1753; *General Evening Post,* 9–12 June 1753; Malcolmson, "A set of ungovernable people", pp. 118–20; British Library Add. Mss. 35413, Coroner's depositions, 12 June 1753. Brickdale was a Bristol turnpike commissioner who had led similar violent forays against the colliers during disturbances four years earlier: British Library Add. Mss. 32719, *Newcastle Papers,* Brickdale to Newcastle, 15 September 1749 and J. Foster to Newcastle, 11 September 1749. A very similar episode involving a coroner and the shooting of workers at Bristol may be traced during a weavers' dispute in 1729: State Papers 36/16, J. Yorke to Newcastle, 20 December 1729.

constant jeopardy from blockades on the Wye and Severn, the Corporation appealed for help to the Merchant Venturers. After vigorously (and success-fully) petitioning Parliament for an end to import duties on foreign corn, bounties with a total value of £200 were offered on any consignments 'sold . . . to the citizens and other inhabitants for their immediate use and consumption'. Considerable sums of money were put aside for poor relief: £200 in January 1757, and a further unspecified subsidy in June. A total of £123 was spent on the exemplary prosecution of blockaders and plunderers in Gloucestershire. Select vestries raised their own relief funds by subscriptions from the wealthy and the college chapter house was requisitioned for the central distribution of cheap rice to the poor. While rioting was reported at Worcester, Tewkesbury, Hereford, Taunton, Devizes, Frome, Castle Cary and in South Wales, Bristol remained calm and, most importantly, the Kingswood colliers were relieved with bread and stayed at home.[31]

Success in 1757 was consolidated in 1766. In January, several months before the situation in the region became critical, the Corporation petitioned Parlia-ment for a complete ban on corn exports. The supportive press emphasized the morality of public over private interests, reminding readers of the 'several thousand sacks of flour ready for exportation in this city', despite looming domestic shortage.[32] In contrast to their aquiescent attitude in 1753, the Corporation now sought an outright ban on exportation. Corn exports in 1753 had been defended on grounds that it was 'designed for the British plan-tations'.[33] Assured nonetheless of a plentiful harvest,[34] it was not until late September, with crop failure a certainty and the surrounding countryside convulsed by rioting, that the Corporation took any positive steps of its own. Unlimited bounties of £20 per 300 quarter load were offered on all incoming shipments retained for local sale. The MP Lord Clare, a close confidant of the Merchant Venturers, offered £8 more the following week, and within days a first consignment had arrived at the port.[35] As an 'artificial' check on prices, magistrates met late in October and agreed to hold down the assize of bread so that it became completely out of line with the cost of corn. Protesting bakers were indulged:

> our magistrates were so generous and careful for the interest of the poor that, sooner than the bread should be made less, agreed with the bakers to satisfy them for the loss they should sustain till next spring.[36]

31 *Bristol Weekly Intelligencer*, 30 April 1757, 14 May 1757; *Felix Farley's Bristol Journal*, 1 and 15 January 1757, 5 and 19 February 1757, 28 May 1757, 4 June 1757.
32 *Felix Farley's Bristol Journal*, 18 January 1766.
33 *Felix Farley's Bristol Journal*, 26 May 1753.
34 Bristol Record Office, Bristol Sessions Papers, 1763–8, C. Welch to Worrall, 27 August 1766.
35 *Felix Farley's Bristol Journal*, 27 September 1766, 2 October 1766.
36 *Felix Farley's Bristol Journal*, 25 October 1766.

Relations between the Corporation and the Company of Bakers were rarely cordial. In setting the assize of bread, magistrates calculated an allowance to the bakers for covering costs and permitting moderate profits, but the Company complained incessantly of its members' poverty and that theirs was the only trade subject to such strictures. The assize forced such losses in 1767, asserted one baker, that 'att this time I can't by my trade alone gert Bread for my children . . . [or] journeyman's wages by baking which is raley a Great hardship'. The Company petitioned the mayor, claiming the assize had 'Greatly Distressed Every person in our trade, many it has intierly Ruined and obliged to leave their famielies in want'.[37] Magistrates, caught between the complaints of the bakers and the pressing hunger of the poor, had little room to manoeuvre and were sensitive to charges of 'supineness and unconcern'. 'They enjoy fulness of bread and therefore care very little about those who have none', declared one man in 1772. 'Or why do they suffer the bakers to be filling their purses at the expense of the poor and needy?' One baker, John Jenkins, responded by unilaterally cutting his bread prices, for he 'would rather lose money than be the cause of oppression to the poor'. Jenkins' ability to sell 7,000 loaves daily as a result did not endear him to the Company, although a delighted newspaper press lauded his 'truly patriotic' moral economy.[38] Magistrates too were well aware that Jenkins' cheap bread sales permitted the poor to buy bread despite the upward trend of assize prices and feigned deafness to Company bakers' pleas for a prosecution. A Company-financed prosecution for irregularities in the labelling of his loaves was overturned as 'malicious', and a second case—for failure to serve an apprenticeship—was lost. Nevertheless, the Company badgered Jenkins with writs and abuse throughout the following year.[39]

In keeping with the practice adopted in 1766, the price of corn was often assized a full shilling per bushel below the official market return in 1795–96 and the price of the quartern loaf held down accordingly. From June 1795 to March 1796, the standard quartern loaf never once rose beyond a shilling and was often slightly less—a factor which provoked the confrontation when an

37 Bristol Record Office, Petty Session Convictions 1728–1795; Town Clerk's Letter Box, 1766, bundle 8, 'A Baker' to Mayor of Bristol, 12 February 1767; Sessions Papers, 1763–8, Petition of five Bristol bakers, n.d. (1766).
38 Meat was pegged in a similar fashion in 1772, when a committee of gentlemen subscribed £2,000 to set up their own slaughter house and successfully undermined butchers' 'combinations' in the market. Bristol Record Office, Town Clerk's Letter Box, 1772, bundle, Edward Day to Mayor of Bristol, 13 January 1773; Bath Chronicle, 20 February 1772, 5 March 1772, 3 February 1773. For Jenkins, see Felix Farley's Bristol Journal, 17 October 1772, Bath Chronicle, 23 July 1772, 4 November 1772.
39 Felix Farley's Bristol Journal, 25 January 1772, 17 October 1772, 28 November 1772, 5 December 1772; Bath Chronicle, 23 July 1772, 20 October 1772, 8 April 1773, 19 August 1773, 4 November 1773. For Francis Adams, see Public Record Office Home Office Papers 42/36, Adams to Portland, 19 October 1795.

uncomprehending crowd at the nearby village of Keynsham surrounded a county magistrate on his return from Bristol market and demanded to know why their own bread was not this cheap. Following the 1796 Act legalizing the sale of still cheaper mixed grain bread, most Bristol bakers followed the mayor's recommendation and offered wheat and barley loaves for sale, despite concern about that 'laxative quality which is prejudicial to hard working people'. Significantly, the only rioting experienced at Bristol in 1795–96 was sparked off by the cost of meat and fish, not bread. Even when wheat and bread prices at Bristol rose wildly later, they remained below those of Bath. This greatly puzzled the Bath magistrates because, after March 1801, the city's assize was fixed solely from the Bristol returns. The Mayor of Bath wrote frequently to his neighbour for an explanation but seemed unwilling to ascribe the discrepancy to any deliberate policy at Bristol of setting the assize weight artificially high. Aggrieved Company bakers at Bristol also disputed assized weights and were in regular conflict with magistrates in 1800–01 for under-weighing their loaves. Bad feeling escalated to a threat of strike action when the mayor stepped up supervisory checks and commenced a spate of fines. When, after an unexpected rise in market prices in May 1801, the mayor 'refused' to raise the price of the quartern loaf beyond 1s.4d., the bakers simply raised it for him, 'giving rise to very undesired reflections on my character' and ultimately forcing him to abandon the assize altogether, thus 'leaving the bakers to themselves'. By and large, the Corporation maintained an unsympathetic attitude to tales of hardship in the baking trade. Some, they pointed out, usually sold their bread below the assize price, yet 'appear to be in as flourishing a state as those who sell at the regulated price'.[40]

After manipulating the assize in 1766 and lobbying central government for a relaxation of the legal restrictions which bound it to market prices, the Corporation once again turned its attention to petitioning against exportation. The town clerk maintained close contact with the city's MPs at Westminster, urging strong representations against the government's intention to renew embargoes on foreign imports in January 1767. Primed by the Merchant Venturers, Clare argued for a free-port extension until September and won a respite until June. The wealthy sugar magnate, Merchant Venturer and

---

40 Bristol Record Office, Assize of Bread Records 1795–96 and 1800–01, Clark to Ludlow, 5 March 1801, Ludlow to Mayor of Bath, 7 March 1801, and entry dated 21 May 1801; Town Clerk's Letter Box, 1801, unnumbered bundle, Attwood to Mayor of Bristol, 14 April 1801; Public Record Office, Privy Council 1/33 A.87, Harvey to Portland, 30 March 1796; Bath Guildhall Record Office, Assize of Bread Records, 23 and 30 May 1801, 6 June 1801. *Bristol Mercury*, 25 January 1796; *Felix Farley's Bristol Journal*, 16 August 1800; *Bonner and Middleton's Bristol Journal*, 21 February 1801. Bristol Record Office, Corporation Letter Book, Mayor of Bristol to Edward Protheroe MP, 14 May 1813. Magistrates abandoned the assize in similar circumstances in 1815: *Felix Farley's Bristol Journal*, 2 and 16 September 1815.

alderman, Abraham Elton—injured by the rioters in 1753—spent much of that autumn in 'essential service to the publick' as an adviser to the Parliamentary Corn Committee's deliberations over the assize. Several merchants and even the Corporation itself made successful bids for corn cargoes in rival ports during November and December. 'The care of the magistrates', concluded the city's grand jury with satisfaction, 'has greatly contributed to the public tranquility.'[41] Apart from framing petitions of their own to Parliament, the Merchant Venturers set up a standing committee to import corn for local consumption in 1767, voting 'all monies necessary' and purchasing 6,000 bushels at Danzig.[42] Yet the great paradox of capitalist enterprise as a solution to scarcity was that its unpredictability continually frustrated the best paternalistic efforts of the Corporation. Despite pointed criticism from the magistracy at a quarter session three years after the riots of 1753, many city mill owners persisted in the profitable conversion from corn-milling to snuff and copper production. By 1766, the decline of public corn-milling in Bristol had left the distressed poor and the bakers dependent upon market-priced flour for bread making. The Corporation invited entrepreneurs to build public mills on its lands under 'terms and conditions' laid down by the city surveyors, but it took a loan of £200 from the Merchant Venturers to persuade one James Walters to take the risk. Despite the Venturers' support for the 'public utility' of the project, Walters was in debt within a year and only spared eviction by a disastrous fire in the building.[43]

Within the limits imposed by free market practice, then, Corporate and elite patronage successfully averted public disorder and famine in Bristol during the 1766–68 crisis and established a pattern for containment in future years. Bounties from the public purse were extended to fish—a commodity blissfully secure from harvest failure and plentiful enough to attract hauls away from such riot-prone ports as Padstow—in 1772–73, 1795–96 and 1800–01. Nearly £3,000 was paid out in bounty money to fishermen in 1800.

The scarcity of 1795–96 came at a critical juncture in the war with revolutionary France. In February 1795, supplies to the port were 'wholly cut off' by a government embargo on coasting vessels, introduced to facilitate naval impressment. Blockades of the Wye and Severn by starving colliers in Gloucestershire compounded the problem until 'we are deprived of having a

41 *Felix Farley's Bristol Journal*, 20 December 1766; Bristol Record Office, Common Council Proceedings 1762–1772, resolutions of 18 October 1766; Session Papers, 1763–8, Elton to Mayor of Bristol, 27 and 29 November 1766.
42 University of Bristol Library (Microfilm) Proceedings of the Society of Merchant Venturers, resolutions of 28 November 1767.
43 *Felix Farley's Bristol Journal*, 29 November 1766; Morgan, p. 178; Bristol Record Office, Proceedings of the Common Council 1762–1772, resolutions passed 18 October 1766; Proceedings of the Society of Merchant Venturers, 9 December 1766.

supply . . . and therefore nearly left to the quantity already in the city'. Mayor Joseph Smith felt besieged and begged the Privy Council, already inundated with similar requests from other towns, to divert shipments from other ports to Bristol. Smith was warned to expect no special treatment, but finally secured a single consignment of grain from Yarmouth after much personable pleading to the Duke of Portland. Having recently endured four days of market rioting over the price of fish and meat, and convinced that the order from Yarmouth would last for three days at the most, he requested further urgent shipments a week later but was turned down, for 'present circumstances render it impossible'.[44] Forced to find solutions of its own, the Corporation despatched two agents to Southampton, along with the merchant and alderman John Noble, to purchase grain with money from the city treasury. In the course of several months, more than £20,000 was spent in this way and the bulk of the grain sold to Bristolians at cost price, to the evident admiration of a visiting gentleman from Monmouth for whom 'too much could not be said in commendation' of the Corporation's 'foresight and good conduct'. Millers from outside the city were prevented from purchasing any of it by order of the mayor, although a surplus was retained for sale at a comfortable profit in neighbouring markets to regain the investment.[45]

These measures ensured supply, but appear to have delayed the formation of a city-wide Provision Committee to assist those for whom even cost-price grain was prohibitively expensive. Bristol was seven months behind Bath in this.[46] The Corporation's £500 profit from its flour sales was given to the Committee in June, but money was not always wisely spent and the control of distribution remained problematic. In September, the Corporation purchased what turned out to be 'a large quantity of stale flour' to sell cheaply to the city's bakers, but neither it nor the Provision Committee seemed able to prevent its being 'sold to the factors and by them mixed with fresh flour, and sold by them to the bakers at £4.10s. a sack and the bakers assized to the first cost which . . . was no more than 54s. a sack'. This injustice was remembered some 30 years later as a pernicious attack on 'the fair tradesman's legitimate profit'. The bakers demanded regular market hours for the sale of freshly landed cargoes so that they might stand a better chance of attending sales and bidding for flour and

44 Public Record Office, Home Office Papers 42/35, Smith to Portland, 8 July 1795, and Minutes of the Privy Council, 8 July 1795; Home Office Papers 43/6, Portland to Smith 7, 11 and 22 July 1795; Public Record Office 30/8, Chatham Papers, Smith to Pitt, 21 February 1795; Bristol Record Office, Corporation Letter Book, Smith to Portland, 10 July 1795.
45 *Felix Farley's Bristol Journal*, 18 February 1826, 4 and 11 March 1826; *Bristol Gazette*, 22 February 1826; Public Record Office, Home Office Papers 42/35, Harvey to Portland, 15 July 1795; Wells, *Wretched Faces*, p. 45.
46 *Bristol Gazette*, 23 July 1795; *Bath Journal*, 12 January 1795. Most parishes followed a lead given by the wealthy inhabitants of St Augustines, who raised £100 in January: *Bristol Mercury*, 12 January 1795. The Corporation gave the Provision Committee £500 on its formation in July; *Bristol Mercury*, 20 June 1795.

grain. Otherwise, 'when there is any goods come to the Back, it cannot be called a market for it is nearly all promised before it comes to those persons who grasp all into their own hands'.[47]

Relief in 1800 was far better organized. A Provision Committee began collecting subscriptions in January, and although the Corporation wrote speculatively to the city's MPs in February urging them to use their influence to secure a grain shipment 'within a month', it did not labour the point as it had done in 1795. Instead, it launched an unprecedentedly ambitious scheme to buy a way out of trouble, a partnership between itself, the Merchant Venturers and city bankers, wealthy enough to make unbeatable bids for cargoes in friendly international ports. It was a major enterprise. With each Bristol banking house investing £1,000 and the Corporation giving £500, this new merchant-led Committee was soon able to announce a preliminary budget of £15,500 and place an immediate order for three cargoes at Hamburg and one at Milford Haven.[48] Shipments of wheat and rice continued to arrive throughout the spring and summer, earning praise for the Committee from the local press, 'for even if the price be high, the having it at any price, compared with the total deprivation of it, should induce our gratitude'. With accumulating profits for investors, the local market thrived as dealers from all over the South West vied for a share. By mid-May, the city's soup kitchen was able to close despite an 'increasing exigency of circumstances' at nearby Bath. When the West Indian fleet returned home 'fully laden' in July, there was 'general joy' in the streets.[49] Bristolians were therefore 'somewhat suspicious' when prices continued to rise. Rumours abounded that 'the late joyful exportation of corn into this port is in a large measure locked up till the price is higher'.[50] Bristol merchants do not appear to have begun selling their foreign grain to the poor at reduced cost until mid-July when, following early expectations of a succesful harvest, regional prices briefly tumbled. To discourage forestalling and to hold these prices steady, the Corporation now let market stalls to local farmers at a greatly reduced rate. Although corn prices did rise again after a month, Bristol alone among south-western market towns successfully avoided any major public

---

47 Bristol Record Office, Corporation Letter Boxes, 1795, unnumbered bundle, Petition of 32 master bakers to the mayor, 28 September 1795; *Felix Farley's Bristol Journal*, 4 March 1826.

48 *Felix Farley's Bristol Journal*, 4 January 1800, 1 March 1800; Bristol Record Office, Corporation Letter Book, Morgan to Portland, 26 February 1800. Bristol may be contrasted with the smaller southern port of Weymouth, whose magistrates were still anxiously appealing to Whitehall for grain cargoes in October; Public Record Office, Home Office Papers 42/52, Mayor of Weymouth to Portland, 28 October 1800.

49 *Felix Farley's Bristol Journal*, 17 May 1800, 11 October 1800. Grain arrivals are reported in *Felix Farley's Bristol Journal*, 21 June 1800, 26 July 1800, 9 August 1800, 6 September 1800. For Bath, see *Bath Journal*, 19 May 1800.

50 J. Ayers (ed.), *Paupers and Pig Killers: The Diary of William Holland, a Somerset Parson, 1799–1818* (Gloucester, Alan Sutton, 1984), p. 41; *Felix Farley's Bristol Journal*, 19 July 1800.

disturbance until April 1801. Even this might have been avoided if the merchants' committee had not ceased trading in October 1800, just as the soup kitchens were re-opening on an expanded plan.[51]

Welcome though the alleviating ministrations of the elite may have been, however, the recipient poor were not uncritical. The infrequency of serious food rioting is certainly striking after the watershed of 1753, but it should not be assumed that the threat had been entirely defused. Nothing is known about the cause of the 'tumults' that attended the first sales of cheap (but uncustomary) rice in 1757, but in 1766 it was hoped the poor would 'soon be tolerably well reconciled' to dietary substitutes as they 'really are more palatable than any one would be inclinable to imagine'.[52] An abundance of privately subsidized foreign corn in the market might have been relatively inexpensive, but it was often complained of for its 'indifferent quality'; consumers were 'dissatisfied with the bread and the importers rendered unpopular'. John Noble, the alderman deputed by the Corporation to assist with its purchase, admitted in 1801 that most of the city's bread had to be made from 'foreign wheats, very little of which is found sweet, and produces an ill-taste in bread in general'.[53] There were complaints about the quality of the Provision Committee's soup in 1801 and 1816. *Felix Farley's* blamed the 'base efforts' of the city ballad singers 'who go about endeavouring to poison the minds of the lower classes by miserable ditties, designed and calculated to render them unthankful and dissatisfied'. The singers' month-long war against the soup kitchen provoked calls for their 'total suppression'.[54]

IV

Effective though these civic actions undoubtedly were, the Corporation remained justifiably sensitive about preventive policing. Troops were frequently retained and paraded at the first sign of scarcity, helping to make serious disorder infrequent after 1753. Direct confrontation between soldiers and miners was minimal, chiefly because the colliers remained in Kingswood. Rumours of their imminent arrival circulated readily enough during the serious dearth of 1766, but troops were 'all under arms expecting the mob' and the threat did not materialize.[55] In 1795–96, the miners again stayed within their parish, but were far from inactive, blockading the river and roads, striking work and withholding coal. Although the strike was broken by the military,

51 *Felix Farley's Bristol Journal*, 26 July 1800, 11 October 1800; *Sherbourne Mercury*, 15 September 1800.
52 *Felix Farley's Bristol Journal*, 22 February 1766.
53 Public Record Office, Home Office Papers 42/54, questionnaire returns from Corton Dinham, Timsbury and Frome, November 1800; *Bonner and Middleton's Bristol Journal*, 3 January 1801.
54 *Bristol Weekly Intelligencer*, 14 May 1757; *Felix Farley's Bristol Journal*, 11 and 18 January 1800, 1 February 1800, 30 November 1816.
55 *Public Advertiser*, 2 October 1766. Shelton is quite wrong in his description of 'particularly serious disorders' at Bristol in 1766: *English Hunger*, p. 37.

magistrates were forced to parley and discuss terms for a 'promise' that blockades would not be resumed.[56]

The presence of soldiers in the city did not prevent serious rioting against butchers and fish-mongers by Bristolians in June 1795, however. There are various possible explanations. The billeted East Devon militia were considerably under-strength through illness and having to undertake policing duties in the surrounding area at the time of the disturbances. Additionally, relations between regular soldiers and the host population had allegedly been on edge for several weeks and there are indications that the militia had proved unreliable during the colliers' strike in May. On the eve of the June disturbances, a magistrate heard a butcher refusing to serve two soldiers, whose 'reply was fierce and menacing, saying they would have meat for the poor and for themselves—at a fair price!' Although the local press made no mention of it, two anti-ministerial dailies insisted that rioting had been led by men from East Devon. The troop was certainly re-posted immediately afterwards, and it was the Northamptonshire militia who turned out to quell a mutiny of new recruits at Pill docks in July. Finally, the coincidence of the 1795–96 scarcity with the emergence of a radical underground reform movement invites speculation that Bristol's military force had become susceptible to political subversion as well as plain hunger. For example, city radicals were accused of pressing handbills 'of the most treasonable kind' upon the Hampshire Fencibles when they arrived to subdue renewed outbreaks among the colliers in October. The people were arming, declared an anonymous letter-writer, 'a body of colliers is already prepared and we have also three regiments of soldiers on our side'.[57]

Disorder in 1800 was limited to a fairly minor incident over prices and quality at a warehouse 'cheap' flour sale in September. District military commander, Lt James Rooke, dealt with the crowd entirely on his own initiative and, presumably, without waiting for the Riot Act to be read. Having experienced the consequences of magisterial dithering in 1795, Rooke may have felt justified in taking matters into his own hands. His report to Portland, anxious to allay 'false reports' of the action, explained:

> that having previous notice of [the crowd's] intention, the Troops were in readiness to receive them and without waiting for the presence of a Magistrate, the Constables

56 *Felix Farley's Bristol Journal*, 14 November 1795; *Bristol Gazette*, 14 May 1795; Public Record Office, Home Office Papers 42/34, Rooke to Portland, 10 May 1795; Bristol Record Office, Corporation Letter Book, Smith to Duke of York, 5 May 1795.

57 Public Record Office, War Office 1/1083, Walker and Haynes to Yonge, 8 May 1795; 1/1092, Rooke to Wyndham, 23 March 1795; Walker and Rooke to Lewis, 11 June 1795; Public Record Office 30/8, Chatham Papers, Grenville to Pitt, 31 May 1795; Treasury Solicitors 11/944, papers for prosecution of John Vint for a libel; Bristol Record Office, Town Clerk's Letter Box, 1795, bundle 42, anon to Mayor of Bristol, 31 October 1795; *Bristol Mercury*, 8 and 15 June 1795; *Evening Chronicle and Gazette*, 9 June 1795; *Courier*, 11 June 1795; *Bath Journal* 20 July 1795 (The Northamptonshire refused to open fire and it was left to regular dragoons to quell the mutiny).

being obliged to retire, I gave orders for the Cavalry to Charge, which dispersed them, and all remains perfectly quiet . . .[58]

Radicals had tried to rouse support by leaving bloody loaves and anonymous notes around the city in February and by sending an anonymous letter to the mayor, demanding 'are the labourous people to be starved this winter?'. Ignoring the writer's assertion that it was 'better to stand like men than starve in the land of plenty', the mayor was confident that the magistrates were 'exerting themselves in any way that could be devised to moderate the price of corn'.[59] Serious disturbances did not arise in the market until the spring of 1801, when military discipline was once again in question. Lt Rooke received a note purporting to be from his own men expressing a determination 'not to see our Families and the People at large Starve in a Plentiful country . . . Let the mob Do as they please, we will not interfere.' He considered it a forgery, but four militiamen were among those arrested during the April price-fixing riots shortly afterwards.[60] The 'inflammatory bills' fly-posted immediately prior to this disturbance may have been related to the declaration which colliers had been forcing farmers to sign, beginning: 'This is to certifie that provisions is fallen at Taunton', and calling for parity. The colliers' hope that such agreements might override free-market price determination represented a direct challenge to established practice at Bristol and was unequivocally rejected by the magistrates. In the clearest possible language, the Bristol bench distanced itself from developments in Somerset, promising to increase relief payments but to protect *laissez faire* at all costs. By continuing importation, 'the present high price will be considerably reduced; this reduction however cannot be effected by *any interference* of the magistrates'. Price-fixing by crowds, confirmed the recorder when he opened the assize, was unquestionably theft, and 'all persons who stood by and abetted' would be treated as accomplices.[61]

The 1795 and 1801 riots demonstrate the degree to which stability at Bristol remained reliant on effective support from the military, but public animosity to them made the authorities ambivalent and indecisive about their use. Worries

---

58 *Felix Farley's Bristol Journal*, 20 September 1800; Public Record Office, Home Office Papers 42/51, Rooke to Portland, 19 September 1800. Rooke's unadmonished use of troops without recourse to a magistrate predates by more than six months a controversial ruling by the Somerset County bench that independent military intervention against food rioters was admissable 'in cases of great necessity'. For details of the ruling, see *Bonner and Middleton's Bristol Journal*, 11 April 1801.

59 Bristol Record Office, Corporation Letter Book, Morgan to Portland (with enclosures), 26 February 1800; Town Clerk's Letter Box, 1801, bundle 35, anon to Mayor of Bristol, 6 December 1800; A. Braine, *A History of Kingswood Forest* (Bristol, Kingsmead, 1891), p. 180.

60 Public Record Office, Home Office Papers 42/61, Cowell to Portland (with enclosure), 17 March 1801.

61 Bristol Public Library, Dyer Diary, Public Record Office, Home Office Papers 42/61, Cowell to Portland, 20 March 1801; Small to Portland, 14 April 1801; *Courier*, 11 April 1801; *Bonner and Middleton's Bristol Journal*, 11 April 1801.

over the consequences of introducing a military dimension into local conflicts, feelingly expressed in 1791 as rioting 'produced in consequence of the attention of the multitude being excited by the means taken to prevent it', would not go away. In 1792, the mayor requested the military's presence during a disruptive strike-wave, but was still afraid it would cause 'confusion',[62] a reticence that was almost prophetic in the light of events on Bristol Bridge a year later. The introduction of troops to disperse a crowd, protesting against tolls on the bridge in September 1793, left more than ten dead, raised public hostility against military interference and heightened popular prejudice against the civil power for sanctioning the slaughter.[63] Thus, in 1795, fishmongers suffered sporadic violence for two days and one butcher had his house pulled down and all his meat stolen before troops were ordered in. William Gage and two others were subsequently arrested and committed to the assize as examples, but this too was badly managed. Since the only 'independent' witness against Gage was another butcher, his solicitor did not call a number of witnesses who had signed affidavits claiming the accused had been working during the riot. Yet, Gage was convicted of theft and sentenced to death. The popular outcry which greeted this decision threatened to become a national scandal as the opposition press— particularly Coleridge's *Watchman*—elevated Gage to martyrdom. Evidently afraid of reprisals, the magistrates hurriedly granted a reprieve, only to be confronted with noisy demonstrations outside the prosecutor's house as celebratory songs and papers were hawked about by 'ballad singers and other rabble'. With policing and 'other' expenses arising from the riots costing the Corporation at least £500, this exercise in exemplary justice had proved a wholesale disaster.[64] The military were not used against butter rioters in 1811, nor against potato rioters a year later, although the mayor had several regiments of infantry at his disposal. What he wanted, he told the Home Office, was 'a few horse', unobtrusively stationed 'in order that the public may not be unnecessarily alarmed'. Their presence alone, he hoped, 'would very much tend to preserve the peace'.[65]

---

62 Poole, 'Popular politics', p. 64–66.
63 The local impact of the bridge riot is discussed in Philip D. Jones, 'The Bristol bridge riot and its antecedents: eighteenth century perceptions of the crowd', *Journal of British Studies*, Vol. 19, No. 2, 1980, pp. 72–92, and Mark Harrison, *Crowds and History*, pp. 271–88.
64 Bristol Record Office, Session Papers, 1794–7; Corporation Letter Book, Smith to Vicary Gibbs, 17 April 1796; Town Clerk's Letter Box, 1795, bundles 36 & 44, Affidavits 4 April 1796; Gibbs to Mayor of Bristol, 8 April 1796; Lewis to Gibbs, 9 April 1796; Proceedings of the Common Council, 1791–6, entries for June and July 1795; *Bristol Gazette*, 31 March 1796, 17 April 1796; *Watchman*, 6 and 11 April 1796.
65 *Bristol Gazette*, 28 March 1811; *Annual Register*, 1812, p. 55; Bristol Record Office, Corporation Letter Book, Mayor of Bristol to Ryder, 13 April 1812.

V

So far, this essay has considered scarcity as a motivation for action among two broad social groups, those with the capital, authority and influence to manage a crisis, and the labouring poor who experienced dearth at the 'sharp end'. This is not to suggest that Bristol's middling sort were somehow uninvolved in scarcity. The attitudes and activities of this group deserve some explanation, particularly after the riot of 1753. John Brickdale's relegation to the status of fugitive in the aftermath of that incident made the independent arming of the tradesmen's interest an experiment that was unlikely to be repeated. Some organizational responses may be divined from the columns of the city press, for Bristol's large, literate and politically sophisticated freeman electorate ensured a ready market for printed polemics and pamphlet doggerel. By the end of the century, the city could boast five competing weekly local newspapers, all of which took a lively interest in debating issues of local and national importance, invoking consensus through appeals from writers like 'Bristoliensis' or 'Civis'.[66] But newspaper attitudes to riot could be underscored by ambiguity: popular disorder and regulation amounted to unacceptable interference with the principle of free trade, yet challenges to the 'extortionate' prices of retailers and middlemen were considered both proper and necessary. 'The case of the poor has become so desperate that it demands some immediate redress', asserted *Felix Farley's* in 1766. When rioting broke out in Devon a week later, the paper thought the crowds 'behave remarkably well, taking only corn and leaving the value of it in money, at a moderate price'. But what may have been excusable in Devon, it argued, was quite unnecessary at Bristol where the poor had 'prudently' awaited the intercession of the elite: 'Far preferable is it thus for the poor to await the proceedings of those who have inclination and power to redress their grievances than rush headlong into riots'. Yet, in the face of the frequently stated opinion that forestallers and other villains were operating with impunity, remarks like 'riots owe their growth and continuance not so much to any real want or defect of the laws as to the puscillanimity of such as those whose Duty it is to put them into execution . . .' effectively shifted the blame from the shoulders of the poor.[67] Moreover, by carrying letters like the one published in 1784 which pressed magistrates to combat speculation by regulating prices, *Felix Farley's* played on popular mythologies of distress in the midst of plenty and public irritation at the inability of market prices to reflect every twist and turn in the weather.[68]

66 For a useful analysis of the impact of the city's press on the life of the city, see Jonathan Barry, 'The press and the politics of culture in Bristol, 1660–1775' in J. Black and J. Gregory (eds), *Culture, Politics and Society in Britain, 1660–1800* (Manchester, Manchester University Press, 1991), pp. 49–81.
67 *Felix Farley's Bristol Journal*, 9 and 16 August 1766, 4 October 1766.
68 *Felix Farley's Bristol Journal*, 7 August 1784.

In June 1795, the *Gazette* railed indignantly against the 'exorbitant' price of beef, called for a consumer boycott and demanded the arrest of all hucksters. The market-place meat riots began two days later.[69] In the same year, colliers in Kingswood began seizing provisions bound for Bristol market in the very week that *Felix Farley's* declared:

> We trust . . . considering the abundance of potatoes that have been grown this year, the public will see that there are no just grounds for advancing their price and will accordingly resist any such attempt.[70]

The key word, 'resist', may have been intended to inspire a consumer boycott rather than a riot, but the distinction was far from clear. No paper openly countenanced riot. Indeed, by 1800 *Felix Farley's* had adopted a policy of silence when faced with the reality of disorder in Bristol. The nearest it came to acknowledging a flour riot in September was when it announced that it had hitherto:

> scrupulously avoided entering into the particulars of riots in other places for fear it might rather spread the evil than allay the ferment, and we shall continue to persevere in the same line of conduct.

This may have been so, although a week earlier the paper had not shied from printing a letter boldly predicting that unless something was done to reduce prices in this 'alarming present period . . . heaven knows what may be the consequence'. The disturbance was also ignored by *Felix Farley*'s rivals, but revealed nonetheless in an insertion placed by the magistrates appealing for calm.[71] The *Gazette* would not have reported an 1811 disturbance at all, 'thinking the sooner it was forgotten the better', but for the necessity of refuting the *Courier*'s version of events.[72]

For all its fierce hostility to 'popular commotion', some correlation may be divined between press scapegoating of hoarders and hucksters, denials of genuine scarcity and the incidence of crowd activity. Rumour and innuendo were relentlessly paraded as scandalous fact. *Felix Farley's* blamed corn dealers and distilleries for the shortage of 1757 and avaricious retailers in 1784. Greedy grain-exporting merchants were singled out in 1772 and Bristol's export-conscious cheese factors in 1773. In 1795, the *Mercury* blamed flour shortages on hair-powder makers and illegal wartime trading with the French 'after an uncommon plentiful harvest'. In frequently rejecting the reality of dearth and ascribing inflation to 'alarm alone', newspapers offered a natural platform for public demands for lower prices. Having judged the harvest of 1810 'plentiful',

---

69 *Bristol Gazette*, 14 May 1795, 4 June 1795.
70 *Felix Farley's Bristol Journal*, 7 November 1795.
71 *Felix Farley's Bristol Journal*, 13 and 20 September 1800.
72 *Bristol Gazette*, 28 March 1811.

for example, *Felix Farley's* impatiently compared Birmingham and London's more favourable prices with Bristol's and called for a substantial reduction since 'it cannot be much longer deferred'.[73] The simple rhetoric of the press encouraged public action.

The type of action it preferred and actively endorsed, the consumer boycott, was more likely to be organized by the middling sort than the labouring poor. Boycotts were a 'respectable' and extremely effective form of popular price control. Newspapers played a leading role in suggesting, publicizing and legitimizing butter boycotts in 1796 and 1801. Boycotts may have been respectable but, as the angry stall-holders who assaulted two boycotters in 1772 were to demonstrate, they were not necessarily non-violent. When, as in 1797, butter was reduced because 'the people would not purchase it' but also because 'some of them began to be riotous', the distinction in real terms between boycott and riot became even more tenuous. The *Bristol Gazette* would not countenance disorder, but remained convinced that a reduction had been 'very prudent'.[74] *Felix Farley's* supported the 'fair prices' agreed by boycott committees in 1801, but was sharply critical of the prices demanded by crowds and imposed by Taunton magistrates on Somerset farmers. 'The impropriety . . . is too obvious to require elucidation, for it is a measure which cannot possibly be generally complied with.' Yet, boycotting, like rioting, exploited collective strength to impose a 'just' price over the rights of individual retailers. Its organization was a clear infringement of the free market Bristol Corporation had pledged itself to protect; its legitimacy rested with the dominance of bourgeois class prejudice about *forms* of social action and economic freedom. A tradesman who witnessed the city's 1801 food riots put it this way:

> The magistrates, it is true, are not authorised by law to compel the farmer or butcher to sell at a certain price; but the purchaser has a clear right to determine what he will give, as the seller has to fix what he will ask—But it would be of no avail for any individual to stand out and pretend to fix the price of the market. No, that must be the work of many.[75]

A vestry meeting in St John's parish a week later condemned the 'ill-judged conduct of purchasers . . . in giving whatever price has been asked', and drew up fair-price restrictions on all meat, potatoes and dairy products in the market by agreement with 'nearly every housekeeper in the parish'. The effect of such a

---

73 *Felix Farley's Bristol Journal*, 15 and 22 January 1757, 7 August 1784 and 20 October 1810; *Bath Chronicle*, 25 June 1772 and 23 September 1773; *Bristol Mercury*, 19 January 1795.

74 *Felix Farley's Bristol Journal*, 27 June 1772, 15 August 1801; *Bristol Gazette*, 1 June 1797; *Bristol Mercury*, 25 January 1796. A butter boycott agreed by householders at Godalming, Surrey, in 1800, led directly to rioting there and at Midhurst when the printed agreement was read out like a proclamation by market-place crowds: Public Record Office, Home Office Papers 42/52, Milford to Portland, 8 October 1800.

75 *Felix Farley's Bristol Journal*, 11 April 1801.

radical document was only curtailed by a delegate meeting of all city vestries which resolved simply to give 'preference' to lower-price traders but to protect the freedom of the market.[76]

VI

This case study has discussed the relative success of measures taken in one urban community to preserve stability, continuity and order despite sweeping fluctuations in the market. Bristol's favourable position as a port, its wealthy patronage and an unusually inclusive polity were particularly conducive to oligarchic enterprise. Indeed, it was largely the city's well-developed sense of self-respect and economic independence that oiled the wheels of relief. In making clear their unequivocal rejection of 'fair price' agreements, the magistrates developed a paternalistic strategy in which they and their business associates exercised pivotal control, rather than invite conflict between themselves, producers and retailers. This distanced Bristolian practice from the aquiescence of corporate bodies in Somerset, South Wales, Oxford, Nottingham and elsewhere.[77] Above all else, as the chaotic debacle of 1753 had shown, popular unrest was terminally bad for business. Displays of military strength (rather than military action) were the scaffolding upon which commercial stability was fashioned and provision shortfalls rectified: failures in military discipline could critically upset the balance. It is not, to use Bohstedt's terminology, that shifting 'horizontal' and 'vertical' relationships forced a change in the nature of riot at Bristol. Rather, community polity tended against crowd action altogether.[78]

The paternalistic nature of Bristol's civic tradition did not suddenly collapse before the remorseless advance of nineteenth-century political economy at the close of the French wars. Yet certain trajectories of change are clearly identifiable at this point. First, rocketing post-war poor rates hardened middling-class attitudes against Speenhamland solutions, moral economy and what the Soup Kitchen Committee of 1816 referred to as 'indiscriminate donations' which 'pamper vice and engender idleness'. Soup servings were reduced so that 'the poor will value more what is not made too common', while other charities offered relief by visitation to discourage crowds and published lists of applicants 'to prevent imposture'. The soup kitchen, which would become an annually recurring institution during the 1820s, set its face against both cheap bread schemes and the prosecution of monopolists and forestallers who 'unwittingly rendered the poor an essential service' by conserving stocks.

---

76 *Felix Farley's Bristol Journal*, 18 and 25 April 1801, 15 August 1801, 30 January 1802.
77 For government's irritation with authorities which 'surrendered' to the crowd, see Wells, *Wretched Faces*, pp. 238–39.
78 Bohstedt, *Riots and Community Politics*, pp. 3–4.

Harassment merely exposed magisterial ignorance about 'the important science of political economy'. By 1821, *Felix Farley's* had assimilated enough Malthusian wisdom to praise speculators for raising prices to levels which 'discourage consumption' and 'encourage thrift and good management' among the poor.[79] Second, middling-class consumer boycotts lost support as the virtues of free trade found greater acceptability. Increasingly, the 'unjust' prices of retailing cartels were met by competition from gentlemen's cooperatives and joint-stock provision companies in nineteenth-century Bristol. These had their origins in the Corporation-backed Flour and Bread Concern of 1800 which, by mid-century, faced mounting criticism for being 'the head of a monopoly', dictating artificially high bread prices and reaping enormous profits for its shareholders. Nevertheless, the Corporation's early encouragement of this 'modern' business structure is significant; a similar venture at Bath was scrapped for want of Corporation support. A rival Bristolian Bread Concern, established in 1829 by the political reformer, James Acland, attracted some four thousand members through a populist campaign against the Company of Bakers and a mass march through the city.[80] This was a peaceful enough crowd, however. No attempt was made to forcibly regulate prices despite much hooting outside the shops of unpopular bakers. Indeed, the riot of 1812 was Bristol's last, despite price-fixing outbreaks in Somerset a few miles to the south in 1816, 1847 and 1867. The introduction of a professional police force in 1836 finally freed the Corporation from many of its concerns about disorder and provided a catalyst for the abandonment of welfare pragmatism. When a lone radical councillor urged his fellow members to lobby Parliament against the Corn Laws with the arrival of 'famine prices' in 1839, his proposal was met with universal derision. 'Public questions' of this nature, it was pointed out to him, were simply not the business of the Council.[81]

Eighteenth century Bristol was no 'town of strangers'. Outsiders, as we have seen, remained a constructed 'other' until well into the 1790s, while insiders

79 *Bath and Cheltenham Gazette*, 11 and 18 December 1816, 15 January 1818; *Felix Farley's Bristol Journal*, 23 and 30 November 1816, 14 December 1816, 22 September 1821; *Bristol Mirror*, 14 June 1817.
80 *Felix Farley's Bristol Journal*, 6 and 20 September 1800, 1 and 8 December 1821, 10 July 1847; Bristol Record Office, Corporation Letter Book, Mayor of Bristol to Edward Protheroe MP, 14 May 1813; Bristol Public Library, Abstract of the Articles of Agreement of the Bristol Flour and Bread Concern (1801). The rise and fall of the Bristolian Bread Concern is charted in James Acland's newspaper *The Bristolian* between 28 August 1829 and 13 October 1830 (particularly Acland's series of letters 'To the Bread Eaters of Bristol'). For later cooperative ventures at Bristol, see *Bristol Times and Mirror*, 6 November 1867 and *Warminster Herald*, 7 December 1867. Bath Corporation's insistence that financial assistance for cooperative projects was a responsibility of central government is complained of in Public Record Office, Home Office Records 42/52, Caulfield Lennon to Portland, 5 October 1800.
81 *Felix Farley's Bristol Journal*, 9 February 1839. The reaction was partly political, the Tories having taken control of the Council in 1836.

were encouraged to recognize the transcendant qualities of common heritage over their alienation from local government. This was a factor which, despite mounting public dissatisfaction with the unaccountability of the Corporation, preserved power relations through a mutual acceptance of paternalism and without the 'feeble or disorderly' nihilism of Bohstedt's Manchester. Authorities in such rapidly expanding but politically excluded and unincorporated industrial towns wielded little influence in Whitehall and may have seen no practical alternative but 'impersonally' and 'mechanically' to discipline their citizens with cavalry and soup kitchens.[82] Charitable relief may, in fact, have been equally impersonal at Bristol, but this is precisely why the 'common interest' conjured by its paternal civic tradition was so important. In Bristol, a need to maintain a dynamic tension between market freedom and control beyond the simple containment and suppression of protest was effectively recognized. Yet it remained the case that 'quick fix' solutions to scarcity were not always in the gift of the elite. Well-stocked and busy markets sometimes lent Bristol an appearance of abundance that obscured the bigger picture of shortages beyond its gates. Given largely uninterrupted networks of supply, the seemingly unresponsive rate of price reduction did not always match popular expectation. The accessibility of forums for public debate and opinion, of which a flourishing and independent local press was both cause and effect, permitted the constant teasing of popular frustrations over prices and scarcity. Ultimately, neither elite management nor bristling displays of military strength could be expected wholly to erase the threat of disorder before the advent of the nineteenth century. In concentrating on the activities of the elite, this essay has attempted to open new avenues of debate for historians of scarcity and disorder. Strong lines of demarcation, drawn between rural/moral and urban/political economies, are, it is suggested, unhelpfully cumbersome and simplistic. Comparative studies in a similar vein should further define and contextualize differences *within* the urban community politics of the eighteenth century.

82 Bohstedt, *Riots and Community Politics*, pp. 69, 95–97.

Chapter 6

THE MORAL ECONOMY OF THE ENGLISH MIDDLING SORT IN THE EIGHTEENTH CENTURY: THE CASE OF NORWICH IN 1766 AND 1767[1]

SIMON RENTON

INTRODUCTION

John Seed has recently remarked upon the tendency of social historians of the nineteenth century '. . . whose attention has been concentrated upon the working class, or to a lesser extent, the landed aristocracy and gentry', to produce a distorted image of the prevailing class structure, due to the absence of a middle class.[2] The same has been even more true of social historians of the eighteenth century. Where middling people do appear, it is rarely as the figures of power and influence upon which the structures for the administration of the local state were based, nor as the local arbiters of approved behaviour, morals and values. There is a tendency to underestimate the influence, power and political importance of the middling sort at a local level and to oversimplify and misconstrue their characteristic social and political attitudes. They appear as prototypes for the consumerism of a later middle class or, in work on the moral economy, most often as stage villains who serve as theatrical props against which moral economist proletarians and paternalist gentry may demonstrate their value systems, either in conflict or in agreement with each other. The case of the Norwich food riots of 1766 and their aftermath shows the middling sort of the city behaving very differently.

At the start of the eighteenth century, Norwich was the largest town in England, London excepted, and was half as large again as Bristol, its nearest rival. By 1750 Bristol had outgrown it, and by the end of the century at least six

1 Earlier versions of this piece were given to the 'British History in the Long Eighteenth Century' and 'Labour and Working-class History' seminars of the Institute of Historical Research of the University of London and to the 'Social Protest and Community Change' seminar at the Department of Geography of the University of Liverpool. I would like to thank those who commented upon earlier versions, and the staff of the libraries of University College London and Middlesex University and of the Norfolk Record Office.
2 J. Seed, 'Capital and class formation in early industrial England', *Social History*, Vol. 81, No. 1, January 1993, p. 17.

provincial centres were larger.[3] Although it did not really become any smaller, in the course of the century Norwich slipped from being the most important urban, provincial, manufacturing centre in England to being just one among several such towns as its worsted manufacture became less important nationally.[4] The effect which the relative decline of Norwich as a manufacturing centre had upon the regional grain market of East Anglia is difficult to assess. However, as early as the 1720s Defoe maintained that 'This whole Kingdom, as well the people, as the Land, and even the Sea, in every Part of it, are employed to furnish Something, and I may add, the best of every Thing, to supply the City of London with Provisions'.[5] Even if this is an exaggeration, the tendency in the development of the grain market was towards the realization of such a situation and the capital was attractive enough to grain dealers to avoid the sort of subsistence crises which precipitated riotous episodes elsewhere.[6] The importance of London to the workings of the grain markets of the provinces became increasingly marked, and those areas, like Norwich, without a dynamic industrial base found their ability to hold locally-produced grain diminished in competition with export to or through London.

The ideology of the ruling class of eighteenth-century England contained the obligations of traditional paternalists to care for the poor and embodied many of the beliefs, attitudes and prejudices which made up the pro-regulatory, collectivist ideology of offending crowds. This ideology, which underpinned class and industrial relations, settlement, poor relief and the right of gentry to govern, relied upon the belief that everyone had a community somewhere, their place of settlement, which had an obligation to feed, clothe, house and care for them. Although such a belief was false in many cases, this falsity became apparent only through local elites' inability to regulate markets during dearth.

Although the members of the Norwich municipal elite were drawn from the large bourgeoisie, they were obliged by the ideology of patronage and deference which legitimized their political, economic and judicial power to behave in the paternalistic manner which they attributed to their predecessors. The law relating to the management and regulation of food marketing was the product of this old paternalist social model. Although much of the law on these matters was not enforced except in time of dearth, justices were able, when a shortage was

3   P. J. Corfield, *The Impact of English Towns 1700–1800* (Oxford, Oxford University Press, 1982), pp. 11–15; Corfield stresses the impact upon the civic standing of the city, which was '. . . much the largest place . . . to experience the onset of relative eclipse through industrial change in the eighteenth century . . .' (p. 28).

4   P. J. Corfield, 'The Social and Economic History of Norwich, 1650–1850: A Study in Urban Growth' (unpublished PhD Thesis, University of London, 1976), *passim*.

5   Quoted by Corfield, *The Impact of English Towns*, p. 70; but she suggests that this is an exaggerated claim on Defoe's part.

6   Corfield points to the development of a London-centred national market during the century and how this led to the diversion of grain supplies to London. *The Impact of English Towns*, p. 70.

apparent or feared, to invoke the old regulations in order to demonstrate their care, to placate the poor and to deflect any threatened popular unrest.

Because the moral economy was an ideology which described and justified a traditional view of the existing reality of market relations in eighteenth-century England, it was part of the belief system of a community which included many in addition to the labouring poor. The case of Norwich shows that belief in the ethical marketing practices sanctioned by law, scripture and custom, which served to protect the labouring poor and their provincial communities from the worst effects of the free flow of foodstuffs during dearth, was held by many of the middling sort of the city.[7] The purpose of this essay is to show how the response of the middling sort of Norwich to the food riots of 1766 demonstrates the need to reassess the nature of their ideological culture and to restore them to an active role within the politics of rights and entitlements which made up the moral economy.

The county of the city of Norwich presents an interesting case study in which to observe the middling sort and their social attitudes since the political structures of the city rendered such attitudes unusually transparent. The political power of the poor and middling freemen of the city prevented the extinction of the traditional rights and privileges which allowed for their representation within the structures of municipal government and the criminal justice system of the city.

It is not easy to define with much precision who the middling sort were in the eighteenth-century. Nick Rogers has suggested that 'Contemporaries tended to use the term impressionistically . . . the social boundaries of the middling sort were essentially indeterminate . . .' and 'At its uppermost level it could include the merchant princes and wealthy bankers . . . who sometimes married into county families . . . At its lowest it could encompass the yeoman farmer and master craftsman, whose social horizons and tastes were vastly different.'[8] In the context of Norwich, it is unclear how useful a category the 'middling sort' may be unless it can be disaggregated in some way so as to split off, at least, the most genteel fraction. The situation which prevailed, in the Norwich of the

---

7 E. P. Thompson flagged the general failure of the twentieth-century imagination to take such ideas seriously as part of a viable ideological structure. 'The moral economy of the English crowd in the eighteenth century', *Past & Present*, Vol. 50, February 1971, *passim*.

8 N. Rogers, 'The middling sort in eighteenth-century politics' in *The Middling Sort of People: Culture and Politics in England, 1500–1800*, ed. J. Barry and C. Brooks (London, Macmillan, 1994), pp. 160–62; S. d'Cruze provides the suggestion that the term 'middling sort' 'as a "catch all" to include all occupational groups between the gentry and the labouring poor . . .' may be less than useful. She proposes that the middling might be disaggregated so that narrower and more meaningful class categories might be arrived at. S. d'Cruze, 'The middling sort in eighteenth-century Colchester: independence, social relations and the community broker' in *The Middling Sort of People: Culture and Politics in England, 1500–1800*, ed. J. Barry and C. Brooks (London, Macmillan, 1994), pp. 184 and 186.

1760s, was one in which archetypal landed gentry were almost completely absent from the governance and administration of the city. The gentlemen and esquires who peopled the Court of Aldermen and the bench were generally merchants, merchant manufacturers and manufacturers. There is little evidence that their adoption of the role of an urban gentry prevented them from continuing their previous commercial activities, and it certainly did nothing to inhibit the businesses of their families. It is reasonable to accept the class categories which were in use at the time and to accept that when merchants or manufacturers were referred to as 'gent' or 'esquire', this denoted a significant shift in their status, which their contemporaries recognized. Thus, those who were recognized in the eighteenth century as being gentry are treated as such here, and throughout this essay the term 'middling sort' is used to mean the middling and lower fractions of the middling.

THE CASE OF NORWICH IN 1766

A short outline of some of the peculiar characteristics of the municipal constitution of Norwich may be useful here, as these peculiarities served to preserve the empowerment of the middling sort of the city even in situations of their conflict with their rulers. Although it was the county town of Norfolk, the city with a small hinterland was a county in its own right. Its administration was controlled by a bicameral assembly of a Common Council and a Court of Mayor and Aldermen. Local ordinances required the approval of both houses. The members of both bodies were elected by the freemen of the city who also enjoyed the Parliamentary franchise. Freedom of the county of the city might be acquired in a number of ways. The most common were by birth and apprenticeship. Sons inherited it from free fathers and those who served their apprenticeships in the city or its county obtained it. Occasionally the freedom was purchased or given by the Corporation. Even very poor freemen were not excluded from the franchise, and being an inmate of the workhouse or of the gaol was not a bar to voting.[9] It has been estimated that, in the mid-seventeenth century, the electorate of Norwich was half as large as that of London, although its population was only one-twentieth the size. Norwich had the most democratic franchise in England, with the possible exception of Westminster.[10]

The city was divided into four Great Wards, and each of these into three sub-wards, for administrative purposes. The freemen of each of the four Great

---

9 S. and B. Webb, *English Local Government, Vol. 2: The Manor and the Borough*, Part 2 (first published London, Longman, 1908; repr. London, Cass, 1963) p. 531, n. 2: 'Democracy in Norwich was carried to an extreme. Even the freemen who were in prison were allowed to vote . . . and those in the Hospitals or in the Workhouse . . .'.

10 J. T. Evans, *Seventeenth Century Norwich: Politics, Religion and Government 1620–1690* (Oxford, Oxford University Press, 1979), p. 29.

Wards elected six aldermen for life. Generally, the most senior alderman who had not yet served was selected as mayor, but some persons held the office a number of times.

The common councillors were elected annually by the freemen of the Great Ward for which they sat. Wymer had 20 members; Mancroft 16; Northern and Conesford only 12 each. While this may have been an equitable distribution, based upon population distribution in the 1400s, it is difficult to imagine that its continuation despite considerable redistribution of population was not motivated by blatant political bias. By the eighteenth century, the more respectable wards were vastly over-represented compared with those wards with the least respectable and most radical populations.[11]

The conflict between the two chambers over the distribution of patronage was avoided by its formal division between the aldermen and the commons. Thus, both aldermen and common councillors were entitled to share in the benefits of 'old corruption' and the political rewards of the patronage networks which characterized eighteenth-century politics at all levels. Each sub-ward had two constables, one elected by the Common Council, the other appointed by the aldermen. Each year both the aldermen and the freemen elected a sheriff each, to serve concurrently. Other appointments preserved the division of power between the aldermen and the commons.[12]

There were limits to the autonomous political power of the poor and middling freemen, beyond the skewed distribution of municipal representation. Property qualifications within the structure of the municipal constitution served to keep them in check. Aldermen were subject to a property qualification of £10,000 so the Court of Aldermen could not fall into the hands of the poor. Since only aldermen who had served as both sheriff and mayor (both expensive offices to hold) became magistrates, the bench was the clear preserve of the propertied.

The justices of Norwich held exclusive jurisdiction within the county of the city.[13] All aldermen who had been mayor were justices and the mayor was the senior justice. He was available at the City Hall, beside the market place, Monday to Saturday for at least part of the day, and was often joined by one or

---

11 Evans, *Seventeenth Century Norwich*, p. 34. While Evans suggests that the distribution of seats may have been equitable in the 1400s, he shows that by the seventeenth century Mancroft Great Ward was considerably over-represented and the Northern Great Ward was much under-represented. P. J. Corfield, *Social and Economic History of Norwich*, p. 509, shows that the trend continued and that by 1786 the population of the Great Ward of Mancroft was less than half that of the Northern Great Ward which was the heartland of the freemen weavers. Thus, the respectable parts of the city became increasingly over-represented compared with the least respectable and most radical parts.

12 *Municipal Corporations (England and Wales). Commissioners' First Report, (John Blackburne) 1835 (116) XXIII, Appendix*, Part IV, pp. 2460–62.

13 Except in cases of disputes with Norfolk over settlement. In these cases, the Norfolk bench was empowered to overrule the city's justices.

more other justices who chose to attend. The mayor also presided over Quarter Sessions in the company of some of his colleagues, but the presence of either the recorder or his deputy, the steward, who were barristers of seven years' standing, was required to transact some business.

The inhabitants of Norwich did not share the difficulties experienced by many elsewhere in finding justices of the peace who lived nearby and who were willing to act as justices. Norwich was awash with justices because residence in the county of the city was a condition of their office and at least one was routinely available to act. The small size of the county of Norwich ensured that no resident could live beyond walking distance from the market place in Mancroft ward, where the mayor could be found. In addition to its ready supply, the magistracy of Norwich was also unusual in its elective nature. The magistracy and the controlling elite were obliged to take some account of the feelings of the poor freemen as the latter might injure them politically if provoked. The Municipal Commissioners believed that the political involvement and power of the poor freemen affected the treatment of the poor, employment practices of manufacturers and the ability of the wealthy to run the city as they wished.[14] The riots of 1766 and the response of the middling sort to them must be viewed against this judicial and administrative background.

The Norwich situation should also be seen against the backdrop of the national spate of disorders in response to the subsistence crisis of 1766. Contemporaries seem to have believed that the system of food distribution had become prone to crisis by the mid-eighteenth century. Arthur Young's opinion was that improved transport facilities were to blame. He thought that in 1769 '. . . all sensible people attributed the dearness of their country to the turnpike roads; and reason speaks the truth of their opinion . . . make but a turnpike road through their county and all the cheapness vanishes at once'.[15] In reality, transport improvement was one factor among a number which in conjunction precipitated the 1766 riots. D. E. Williams suggests that factors including '. . . cattle murrain, crop failure, extraordinary foreign demand and government inactivity ensured that the commodities which comprised the provision trade were expensive and/or in short supply'.[16] To describe the administration's behaviour as 'government inactivity' rather understates the baneful influence of central government upon the grain trade in 1766. The combination, which characterized all eighteenth-century administrations, of

---

14 *Municipal Corporations*, p. 2498.

15 Arthur Young quoted by J. Stevenson, *Popular Disturbances in England 1700–1870* (London, Longman, 1979), pp. 94–95.

16 D. E. Williams, 'The geography of food riots 1585–1847, section 3.6 1766' in *An Atlas of Rural Protest in Britain 1548–1900*, ed. A. Charlesworth (London, Croom Helm, 1983), p. 89. For a more detailed account of the circumstances which gave rise to the riots, see D. E. Williams, *English Hunger Riots in 1766* (Wales, PhD Thesis, 1978), especially pp. 52–71.

contemptuous indifference towards the labouring poor and extreme solicitous-ness towards the landed elite whose prosperity was enhanced by high grain prices, contributed greatly to the crisis. Ian Gilmour remarks upon the crass handling of the situation by both Rockingham and Chatham administrations and raises the possibility of a class-based conspiracy to make middling dealers bear the odium which was due to the landed elite. 'On the face of it, the government's performance in 1766 was so maladroit as to raise the suspicion that it intended to direct violence away from the landed interest towards the middlemen.'[17] Naturally, Gilmour is able to conclude that no such explanation is tenable and that simple incompetence was to blame.

As early as January 1766, a few riotous incidents had occured in Hampshire and Dorset. The government responded to these by imposing a temporary embargo on grain export. This was due to expire in August, and even before that time dealers began to stockpile grain for export as soon as this should become legal and rewarded by a bounty. By early September, an increasing current of discontent and disorder was apparent. Central government res-ponded to this by the issue of a proclamation against forestalling, regrating and engrossing. The implication of this was clearly that the King and his ministers held corn dealers to be to blame for shortages. At the same time, Parliament was prorogued and was therefore unable to take any action to stem the flood of grain out of the country.[18]

Williams tells us that he does not consider it useful to think of riot spreading in waves in 1766: 'rather it would be true to say that it was brought about by a process akin to spontaneous combustion. It is also misleading to speak of waves of disturbances . . . In East Anglia, the Upper Thames and the Midlands, the level rose simultaneously from almost zero to their peak in the same space of time, just a week later.'[19]

The general pattern of the food rioting of the summer and autumn was that it started earliest and was most common and widespread in the West of England, followed by the Midlands and Upper Thames, and later and less impressively, by East Anglia. Norwich was the most important site of disorder in its region, but crowd actions also occurred at the ports of Yarmouth and Wells in the north of the county. Smaller episodes of price fixing and the prevention of the transportation of food out of the area took place in Norfolk, Suffolk and North Essex.[20]

The government was forced, by the level of disorder and the threat of it worsening, to take action to safeguard the grain supply. Petitions from the

17 I. Gilmour, *Riot, Risings and Revolution: Governance and Violence in Eighteenth-Century England* (London, Pimlico, 1993), p. 242.
18 Williams, 'The geography of food riots', pp. 89–90.
19 Williams, 'The geography of food riots', p. 90.
20 Williams, *English Hunger Riots*, pp. 60 and 258–65.

corporations of Norwich and King's Lynn, together with those of Bristol and London concerning the scarcity of corn in their several regions, may have had a significant effect in pressing the government, finally, to act.[21] Controls on the export of grain were reintroduced and the bounty payable on such exports resuspended, both coming into effect during the weekend of 27 and 28 September.[22] This brought an end to rioting, just too late to save the poor of Norwich, and elsewhere, from the need to risk the law's wrath in order to protest at shortages.

The judicial records arising from the prosecution of some of those who took part in the food rioting of the autumn of 1766 provide us with a description of the actions of the crowd in the city. These documents were drawn up to facilitate the process of prosecuting rioters and so may present the crowd in a less favourable light than others might have. However, since they appear to be the only extant description of the events of 27 and 28 September, we are forced to rely upon them.

A large crowd of both men and women gathered in the market place, and at about two o'clock began to overturn the peds of the country people at the lower end of the market. They proceeded to destroy provisions and throw butter about the market. The justices who were assembled at the Town Hall, overlooking the market, went in a body to the market to calm the crowd. They were unsuccessful and were driven back to the Hall by the crowd. Henry Nobbs, one of the rioters, demonstrated the crowd's contempt for the Corporation and its officers, by throwing a pint of butter which struck Charles Lay, the sword bearer.

As soon as the justices had left the market place, the crowd resumed its destruction with even greater ferocity, encouraged by one of its number who announced: 'Damn them I have an order from the Gentlemen to serve them all alike and to make no exceptions of none.' The crowd responded to this by moving on from the peds at the lower end of the market to attack the fixed stalls at the upper end.

At about three o'clock, the crowd went to the New Mills in West Wymer and began to demolish them. After about an hour, the mayor and justices arrived and attempted to read the proclamation in the Riot Act, but the hail of stones and brick-bats drove them away. The proclamation was read in the course of the afternoon and evening at a number of places where it met less opposition.

While the justices returned to the Hall to consider what to do, the crowd visited a number of bakers in the city and spent the evening from five till eleven or twelve damaging bakers' houses and furniture and collecting money and beer from their owners. At about midnight, they called at the White Horse alehouse

21 Williams, *English Hunger Riots*, pp. 68–70.
22 Williams, *English Hunger Riots*, p. 71.

in the Haymarket for a night cap. After destroying the furniture and any liquors which they could not drink, they went home for the night.

At midday the crowd was reassembled by horn-blowing and flag-waving. They set off towards the south of the city and arrived at Trowse Mill, which they intended to destroy. However, the miller's house and the mill were saved by the intervention of his neighbours '. . . who said that Mr Sayer was a good man to the poor . . .' unlike millers in general. After receiving gifts of beer from Sayer, the crowd left the county of the city to visit William Money's house in Trowse Newton. They stripped the house of its furniture and fittings, which were burned, and attempted to burn the house itself. Many items of personal property of the Money family were also taken. The reason that the crowd went so far to visit Mr Money when so many appropriate targets were available within the city would seem to be the personal reputation of William Money himself. When a passing cleric attempted to persuade the crowd not to attack Money's house but to return to the city, a rioter said: 'Damn You, what Business have you here. Did not the Old Rogue Whip the Gleaners off his Lands?' This served to remind the crowd that Money was a general offender against ethical food distribution and therefore a most suitable target.

On leaving Money's house, the crowd returned to the city. They destroyed two malt houses and unloaded a keel full of corn into the river en route, but spared a house where they were assured a labourer lived. Once back in Norwich they resumed their visits to bakers. One baker had his furniture destroyed and his house partially demolished, another suffered only slight damage. The house of a third had been partially dismantled when the constables and staffmen arrived and put a stop to the rioting.[23]

Unfortunately, the local press suppressed any description of the riots and confined comment to telling readers how shocking and wicked the riots had been.[24] However, the papers did make some effort to explain the inept handling of the early stages of the disorder by the justices. The failure to suppress the riot in the market place was said to be due to '. . . an unwillingness to involve Numbers in the severe Punishments which the Law inflicts on Rioters . . .'.[25]

By 11 October, about a dozen were imprisoned in the city on capital charges and a large number on lesser charges. The Corporation engaged in an orgy of

23 Norfolk Record Office, Press B, Case 6, h, Bundles 1 and 2, papers relating to the riots of 1766.
24 *Norwich Mercury*, 4 October 1766, explained that the justices had decided to prohibit publication of any details of the recent riots as that might encourage 'The wicked and profligate to follow in other places: it is thought sufficient to acquaint our readers, that from specious Pretences a great Number of the lowest People wantonly destroyed the Provisions in last Saturday's Market, and committed many other Outrages . . .'.
25 *Norwich Mercury*, 4 October 1766. In view of the outcome of two days of rioting, this is a bizarre line of reasoning on the part of the apologists for the justices.

self-congratulation for having quelled the disorders with special constables equipped only with staves and without the use of troops or firearms.[26]

In the following week the first signs of support, from outside the ranks of the labouring poor, for those being held for riotous offences were to be seen. The prisoners used the pages of the local press to thank an anonymous donor for a gift of a 2d. loaf, half a pound of cheese, a pint of beer and 5s. each.[27] This represented a very considerable expenditure, certainly beyond that which the labouring poor could be expected to support unless organized for the purpose. In the context of the prosecutions for riot, incitement and of accessories taking place at the time, any such association would have been the subject of attack in the press, if not of prosecution. No evidence is to be found of any such organizational activity. If these gifts to prisoners were not provided by any organization of the labouring poor, then the anonymous donor must have been an individual of some substance. A steady trickle of such anonymous donations continued into 1767.[28] The donation of cash and food to all prisoners, irrespective of the offence charged or of their family or trade connections, suggests that the gifts came not from relatives or workmates but from those not personally connected with the prisoners, who sympathized with the aims or activities for which they were gaoled.

John Clover, whose malt house had been destroyed by the crowd, appears to have accepted that the market beliefs of the moral economists had some validity. Soon after the riots, he wrote to the *Norwich Mercury*, one of the local papers, to deny that he was an engrosser, a forestaller or even a large-scale exporter of grain from the district, and blamed malicious rumour for the recent attacks upon his property.[29] This is a case of a respectable corn dealer and maltster using the pages of the local press to defend his reputation among his peers and business associates from allegations of unethical dealings in the grain market. This might imply that belief in the moral economy was to be found among persons like John Clover. However, it may be that his statement was a cynical ploy to divert the hostility of the crowd away from him and his property. The effect would appear the same from the point of view of the moral ecomomists. Such statements would be seen as evidence for the widespread support for the moral economy from outside the labouring poor. It is unlikely that Clover's statement would have seemed convincing to his contemporaries unless either he or other similar persons were known to genuinely hold such views. If maltsters, badgers and corn dealers are to be seen as upholders of the moral economy, as Clover seems to have been, at least some of the middling sort must

26 *Norwich Mercury*, 11 October 1766.
27 *Norwich Mercury*, 18 October 1766.
28 *Norwich Mercury*, 20 December 1766 and 3 January 1767.
29 *Norwich Mercury*, 18 October 1766.

be viewed as party to the discourse of rights which characterized the moral economists, and not as external to it and bound up in the ideology of the 'free' market applied to an unregulated grain market.[30]

Having been defeated on the streets of the city by the massed ranks of the staff-wielding respectable classes, led by the law officers of the Corporation, the discontented moral economists of Norwich resumed their attacks by way of another traditional medium of subversion, the anonymous letter. Letters were sent to John Patteson, the mayor, and to James Poole, a large-scale grocer and future mayor. The text of these letters was reproduced in the local press and a reward was offered for the apprehension of the villain or villains responsible.[31]

As usual, this served only to spread the message of the anonymous author. It is hard to believe that the authorities responsible for the publication of such letters in newspapers believed that this would contribute in any way to the deterrence or detection of their authors. It is more probable that those responsible set out to create or reinforce the state of anxiety or fear of the threatening poor, which the respectable classes experienced in times of crisis. The work of Jennifer Davis, Jason Ditton, Peter King and Geoffrey Pearson has shown very clearly the role of newspaper coverage in the creation of exaggerated fear of crime and moral panic and how such panics encourage the respectable to behave with disproportionate savagery towards offenders.[32] The creation of such a climate of fear or moral panic served to encourage cohesion between class fractions, which might otherwise have shown divergent ethical or political views and allowed more severe or indiscriminate punishment to be administered to examples of the threatening classes.

In response to the continuing discontent in the city, the Court of Mayoralty took up the sort of campaign against marketing offences which was customary after periods of food rioting. On 1 November the justices published notices

30 A. Randall, 'The shearmen and the Wiltshire outrages of 1802: trade unionism and industrial violence', *Social History*, Vol. 7, No. 3, October 1982, p. 300, and n. 30. Randall makes it clear that the motive for support of the riotous poor was not intimidation by the crowd but a genuine sympathy for the poor in their struggle against innovation which would harm the interests of both workers and small masters. Small-scale corn dealers and others in the food processing industries were similarly vulnerable to the same threat from larger capital, as were their poorer neighbours.

31 *Norwich Mercury*, 25 October 1766 and 15 November 1766.

32 J. Davis, 'The London garotting panic of 1862: a moral panic and the creation of a criminal class in mid-Victorian England' in *Crime and the Law: The Social History of Crime in Western Europe Since 1500*, ed. V. A. C. Gatrell, B. Lenman and G. Parker (London, Europa, 1980); J. Ditton, *Controlology: Beyond the New Criminology* (London, Macmillan, 1979); P. King, 'Newspaper reporting, prosecution practice and perceptions of urban crime: the Colchester crime wave of 1765', *Continuity and Change*, Vol. 2, No. 3, 1987; and G. Pearson, *Hooligan: A History of Respectable Fears* (London, Macmillan, 1983). All these provide case studies of the apparent creation of 'crime waves' by the increased incidence of prosecutorial activity arising from a spurious fear of rising real crime rates due to the moral panic inspired by press reporting. It is clear that crises lead to increased newspaper sales and that a heightened fear of crime has such an effect.

which defined forestalling, regrating and engrossing and threatened offenders
with the pillory, imprisonment and forfeiture of goods. The same notice was
repeated later.[33] Despite the notices and other warnings, or perhaps because of
them, there is no evidence of any prosecutions of offenders of this type in the
city until the following autumn, when four zealous constables presented six
persons for regrating veal. However, seven convictions for selling short-weight
bread occurred in the autumn and winter of 1766–67. Henry Shuter, a bread
seller, was convicted twice and fined £2:3s.9d. and John Spratt, another bread
seller, was fined 10s.6d. on one conviction on 24 October. The following day
Joseph Warner, a baker, was convicted three times and fined £1:15s.6d. and
bound in a recognizance of £100 to appear at the next Quarter Sessions to
answer charges of contempt for John Patteson, the mayor, in the exercise of his
office as magistrate. Perhaps more surprisingly, Richard Lubbock, one of the
bakers whose houses were attacked and partially demolished in September,
demonstrated that in his case at least the crowd had selected an appropriate
target by getting caught selling underweight bread. He was fined 5s.[34]
Unfortunately, we do not know whether the other bakers selected for attack
were similarly well chosen, but the case of Lubbock suggests that they were not
a random sample but were picked for their illegal and unethical marketing
practices.

On Monday 1 December, the Special Commission, with Sir Henry Gould
presiding, opened to deal with Norwich cases. He was joined upon the bench by
the mayor, recorder, steward and all the aldermen who were justices. All those
who were qualified to sit did so in a splendid demonstration of the solidarity of
the city's rulers in response to the threats of the riotous lower orders. The trials
started the next day and were complete by noon on Friday 5 December. Eight
men were capitally convicted, two of them twice. Two were acquitted on all
charges. One was acquitted on these charges but was ordered to remain in gaol
to await the next assize for the city, the following summer. Four were not
convicted of any offence before the Special Commission but were ordered to
remain committed to prison to await trial on lesser charges at the next Quarter
Sessions. One convicted of aiding and abetting was ordered to remain
committed to await the judges' opinion on whether his offence was capital or
not.

The *Norwich Mercury* said of the trial juries:

> The petty jury consisted of sixty of the principal Manufacturers and Tradesmen:
> Fifty-nine of whom appear'd in Court on Tuesday Morning. The Candid and
> Humane Treatment of the Prisoners reciev'd from the Court in the course of their
> Trials, the Attention and Circumspection of the juries, together with the generous

---

33 *Norwich Mercury*, 1 November 1766 and 15 November 1766.
34 Norfolk Record Office, Press C, Case 11, cxxi; Quarter Sessions Papers.

Concern express'd when Sentence of Death was pass'd on Eight unhappy Convicts, afford convincing Proofs of the Reluctance with which the citizens have been oblig'd to call for the Protection of the Laws, for the Preservation of their Lives and Properties: And it is hop'd will make a lasting Impression on the Minds of everyone.[35]

It has not been possible to find a list of the petty jurors who sat, but the report in the *Mercury* would suggest that the jurors selected to try these cases at the Special Commission were far from being a typical selection of those qualified to serve. Thus, if the *Mercury*'s description of the jurors and of their behaviour may be relied upon, even an unusually wealthy and respectable panel of jurors selected by the sheriffs were found to be sympathetic to the prisoners coming before them accused of riotous offences. If persons like these could not be relied upon to be hostile to food rioters and their ideology of moral economy, it is not easy to imagine who might be.

Tension remained high in the city despite the conclusion of the trials by the Special Commission. A large number of prisoners still awaited trial at the next Norwich Assize, at Quarter Sessions or, in the cases of 27 of the city's prisoners, at the next Norfolk Assize to be held at Thetford. Alderman Hancock received an anonymous letter threatening arson. A reward of £100 was offered for information leading to the apprehension of the offending correspondent in late December. A similar offer was made twice more in January. As usual, the advertisements served no purpose other than the heightening of the anxiety experienced by the respectable and the encouragement of their exaggerated fear of the wrath of the crowd.[36]

The authorities' response to the high price of corn and the continuing discontent which it encouraged among the poor, took three simultaneous forms: charity, a show of force, and a demonstration of mercy and lenity were all tried together during January 1767.

Edward Bacon Esq., the recorder, arranged for a large quantity of grain to be distributed to the poor at far below the prevailing market price, and about 1600 persons were said to have received some of this subsidized corn by the end of January.[37] A new subscription was started in mid-February to purchase further supplies in order to continue the supply of cheap food for the poor which undercut the prevailing price determined by the market.

The first of the riot-related hangings took place on the Castle Ditches on Saturday 10 January when John Hall and David Long were hanged for their part in the destruction of John Clover's malt house at Carrow in Norfolk. The

---

35 *Norwich Mercury*, 6 December 1766.
36 *Norwich Mercury*, 20 December 1766, 3 January 1767 and 10 January 1767. See note 32 above for comment on newspapers' tendency to cultivate moral panics.
37 *Norwich Mercury*, 3 January 1767, 31 January 1767 and 14 February 1767.

reports of the event say that both men were penitent and, in the approved manner, cautioned the onlookers against Sabbath breaking and similar misbehaviour which, they said, had set them on the path to their unhappy ends.[38]

Those still held in prison accused of riotous offences were treated very sympathetically. Elizabeth Parr and Susanna Soons, two women who were prosecuted for inciting others to attack bakers' houses, were sentenced to only three months' imprisonment in the first case and bound over to keep the peace in the second. Ten of the remaining prisoners were discharged from gaol on their own recognizance to keep the peace for twelve months, despite having behaved '. . . very illegally in the late tumults . . .'.[39]

By mid-July, shows of force had been abandoned by the authorities in the city, but subscriptions for grain to be sold below market prices continued and the treatment of those still imprisoned became increasingly lenient. Those capital convicts who remained in custody received pardons, either conditional on transportation or free. Even Henry Nobbs, who was noted for throwing butter at Charles Lay, the sword bearer, and who had been sentenced to death for other offences, received a free pardon.[40]

While the Recorder arranged for a large quantity of grain to be distributed at well below the market price to prevent a recurrence of the disorders, the supporters of the prisoners resumed their gifts to the incarcerated. On 27 December an unnamed donor received thanks for half a guinea and a large beef pie.[41] During December, January and February the prisoners regularly thanked their friends for their frequent gifts, including three-and-a-half stone of beef, thirty-four 3d. loaves and 30s. in early February and sixty 4d. loaves, 24s. worth of beef and 15s. worth of beer seven days later.[42]

THE RIVER PROSECUTION WAVE OF 1767

The support of the middling sort of the city for the rioters of the previous year was not confined to the giving of gifts to prisoners. The active system of Presentment Juries allowed them to demonstrate their disapproval of those responsible for the punishment of the rioters by presenting many of them for criminal nuisances. A presentment was very like an indictment but was for a misdemeanour rather than a felony. They might originate from a justice, a constable, a Grand Jury or, as in this case, from a Presentment or Nuisance Jury. Presentment Juries resembled Grand Juries, having more than 12 sitting

38 *Norwich Mercury*, 17 January 1767. It may be that abstaining from the destruction of malt houses on the Sabbath might have been sufficient to save them, without the need for too much moral reform.
39 *Norwich Mercury*, 31 October 1767.
40 Norfolk Record Office, Press B, Case 6, h, Bundle 2, Papers relating to the riots of 1766.
41 *Norwich Mercury*, 27 December 1766.
42 *Norwich Mercury*, 17 January 1767, 7 February 1767 and 14 February 1767.

upon them (15 seems to have been the customary number), but they differed markedly from Grand Juries in that their members were not nearly as socially elevated as were Grand Jurors. Presentment Juries in eighteenth-century Norwich were impeccably middling-sort bodies and might therefore be expected to reflect the attitudes, beliefs and ethical or moral views which were common to such persons. During the eighteenth century, all of the four Great Wards—Mancroft, Wymer, Conesford and Northern—maintained active Presentment Juries. They appeared at Quarter Sessions to report on the nuisances occurring in their respective wards, but did not normally deal with river nuisances. These matters were left to the River Committee of the Corporation which rarely had recourse to the courts to enforce its deliberations. When the juries of the wards which made these presentments are compared with the list of all persons qualified to serve as jurors for the county of the city compiled in 1764, it is possible to obtain a rough occupational profile of the men who presented, and thereby created, the Norwich river prosecution wave of 1767.[43]

Of the identifiable presentment jurors who sat on the juries for the Great Wards of Wymer, Conesford and Northern, the proportional occupational representations are shown in Table 1. Persons described as labourers do not appear on these juries even in the small numbers in which they appear on the lists of persons qualified to serve. The low incidence of worsted weavers might appear more puzzling. We may only assume that few of them were middling enough to make their way into this company. An occasional gentleman appeared on these juries but, while they may have been disproportionately influential in the deliberations of the jury, they are not numerically significant. The very high number of barbers appears bizarre, but is quite consistent across a number of juries of this type.

In respect of river nuisances 136 presentments were issued against 69 separate presentees or offenders: 49 arose from offences in the Northern ward, 44 in Conesford ward and 36 in Wymer ward. Five related to offences within the Cathedral Precincts and two arose from stretches of water which cannot be located. The Great Ward of Mancroft had no navigable waterways.

The 69 offenders include very few who cannot be identified. Of those who may be, at least four were 'grocers' or 'shopkeepers' and each was presented once, and four were 'widows' whose actual occupations are not given. Two surgeons and seven woolcombers, twisterers or dyers were together presented 12 times. One clerk was presented once and Norwich Corporation and the

---

43 Norfolk Record Office, Case 12, Shelf C, Box 1, Parcel of names of persons qualified to serve as jurors, 1764; and Press C, case 11, cxx, Quarter Sessions Papers. Those potential jurors who were not sworn have been excluded as they cannot have served, as have any where there was any doubt that the person appearing on the two lists was identical.

Table 1 *Occupational composition of presentment jurors who sat on the juries for the Great Wards of Wymer, Conesford and Northern*

Occupation	Percentage of jurors
Barber	20
Butcher	5
Carpenter	10
Cow keeper	5
Gardener	5
Gentleman	5
Plumber or glazier	5
Printer	5
Poulterer	5
Salesman	5
Shopkeeper	5
Taylor	5
Twisterer or dyer	10
Waterman	5
Worsted weaver	5
Total	100

Dean and Chapter of the Cathedral were presented seven times each. Four carpenters were presented six times. Two of these may have been exceptional in that one had been an important prosecution witness at the Special Commission and another was a relative and employer of another such witness whose evidence was held to be vital in putting the lives of a number of the accused at risk by placing them at riotous incidents.[44]

Of the 14 gentlemen and esquires presented, six were justices. Clement Ives Esq., a representative of one of the leading families of the city which regularly provided mayors and justices, was presented 20 times, for a total of 2,971 feet of mud and filth, a bridge, brick walls and banks of earth placed in the river, 12 square yards of hoves, 13 feet of dangerous wall and two unsafe stayths. Robert Harvey Esq., the head of another of the city's most influential families, an ex-mayor, justice and father of one of the sheriffs, was presented only twice. One was for a bad stayth and another, an irritating and probably symbolically important demand, that he remove his boghouse from the creek into which it

---

44 Norfolk Record Office, Press B, Case 6, h, Bundles 1 and 2, Papers relating to the riots of 1766.

was built, together with the ordure and filth derived from it. Altogether, the Presentment Juries called for the removal of nine boghouses.[45]

It might be expected that brewers, distillers, maltsters and corn dealers would be the object of popular hostility due to their role in the precipitation of subsistence crises. However, only nine were presented on this occasion. Eight of them shared 14 presentments between them. The ninth was William Money, who as noted above, had been a major object of the crowd's anger in the previous year and was far and away the most spectacular object of the wrath of the presentment jurors. Although his nuisances gave rise to only 16 presentments, these amounted to a total of 14,865 square feet of hoves, over 2,090 yards of defective river bank to be rectified and the removal of a bank of earth which he had built into the river.[46]

It is quite possible that some of those presented were not among the deliberate targets of the righteous and vengeful jurors. Others may have been caught together with those who had offended against the norms of the popular political culture of the city as it may have proved difficult to prosecute ethical offenders but to leave others untouched, even if their stretches of river were in very bad order. However, it is possible that many of those who appear to have had no connection with food marketing or with the punishment of rioters were connected indirectly as landlords or relatives of those who did, or that they have not been correctly identified here. The case of John Drinkwater Esq. of Brentford Butts in Middlesex is an example of one who was punished vicariously by the presentment jurors for the offence of another. Drinkwater was John Clover's landlord and the owner of the malt house, containing malt and barley awaiting export, which a crowd of about 20 demolished during the afternoon of Sunday 28 September, for which John Hall and David Long were hanged on 10 January 1767.[47]

The meaning of these presentments becomes clear when they are situated against the background of other middling-sort responses to the prosecution of

45 Norfolk Record Office, Press C, Case 11, cxx and cxxi, Quarter Sessions Papers. An entertaining excursion into the class significance of sewage disposal is provided by P. Linebaugh, '(Marxist) social history and (Conservative) legal history: a reply to Professor Langbein', *New York University Law Review*, Vol. 60, No. 2, May 1985. In the case of the condemned boghouses and many other complaints, it is impossible that the alleged nuisance was of very recent origin. The presentment jurors had decided to label as 'criminal' behaviour that which under normal circumstances was considered legal, if anti-social, behaviour.

46 Norfolk Record Office, Press C, Case 11, cxx and cxxi, Quarter Sessions Papers. As we have seen, Money was singled out not only for his activities in the grain market but also for his failure to tolerate customary gleaning on his land. The fact that he lived outside the county of the city might also have cast him in the role of outsider and thus rendered him more vulnerable to communitarian and collectivist hostility.

47 Norfolk Record Office, Press C, Case 11, cxx and cxxi, Quarter Sessions Papers; and Press B, Case 6, h, Bundle 1, Papers relating to the riots of 1766.

rioters. On 1 October 1766, the justices wrote to the church wardens and the overseers of each parish of the county of the city, asking that they be informed of anyone who had absented themselves since the recent disturbances. Many declined to reply and many of the replies that do exist contained little which could have been of any assistance to the justices in their search for the rioters. Some name no person at all, others name only those already known to be in custody, thus appearing to cooperate while being as obstructive as possible. The most extreme example is that of St Peter Permountergate in Conesford Great Ward. This went beyond the failure to incriminate any residents of the parish, which was common. It set out to maintain the innocence of one who was already being held for his part in the rioting:

> We the Officers of this Parish cannot find that any one Man is Absent or that any one was Gilty of Rioting & we are sorry that our Neighbour por Sam¹ Houghton is Confined because we believe him Inosent & hope your Worships will set him at Liberty.[48]

As the riotous attack upon the house of the baker, Robert Elwin, took place within their parish, it seems improbable that the parish officers did not know of it. Certainly, the justices believed that they had clear evidence of Houghton's involvement with the rioting on Saturday 27 September and thought him to have been active again on the following day when Elwin's house was attacked. It is clear that two competing concepts of innocence are in evidence here and that they arise from very different views as to the culpability of riotous behaviour in support of the moral economy.

The river prosecution wave, taken together with the gifts of food, drink and money to those imprisoned, accused of riotous offences, and the clear reluctance of parish officers to take part in the process of identifying and punishing those involved, clearly shows the hostility of the middling sort to these prosecutions. The justices and the prosecutors of the rioters either failed to notice this lack of enthusiasm on the part of the middling men of the city or chose to ignore it and blunder on as if there was no problem.

One of the most salient characteristics of the theatre of the criminal law, as performed in eighteenth-century England, was the prominence of its symbolic aspects over its functional performance.[49] The presenting jurors could not have believed that their presentments would be acted upon and their complaints pursued through to enforcement. In fact, one of them against John Drinkwater slipped through. The mass of the others not only threatened to swamp the

---

48 Norfolk Record Office, Press B, Case 6, h, Bundle 1, Papers relating to the riots of 1766.
49 W. G. Carson, 'Symbolic and instrumental dimensions of early factory legislation: a case study in the social origins of the criminal law' in *Crime, Criminality and Public Policy*, ed. R. Hood (London, Heineman, 1974), *passim*.

workings of the judicial system of the city, they also served as a threat to the powerful that an ethical line existed which they overstepped at their peril.

It is difficult to imagine a more expressive gesture than to publicly reprimand Alderman Harvey for the public nuisance of his defecating onto his poorer neighbours, or at least into their creek. Thus the theatre of the criminal law might be used not only by the powerful against their social inferiors but also by those who, while not among the most powerful locally, were yet not socially or politically impotent enough to be safely denied access to some of the levers of power within the criminal justice system. As long as the ideology of England's rulers required that access to the law be perceived by the governed as a multi-use right, this was a governing strategy which was not without risk. The period of the river prosecution wave of 1767 was one occasion on which the powerful were forced to pay for the benefits of the system which accrued to them at other times.

There can be no doubt that William Money was singled out to be pilloried for his bad-neighbourliness, in addition to the very real threat of very substantial financial loss and possible ruin in the event of the bills against him being found true and enforced. It would appear that the presentment jurors had chanced upon a perfect stick with which to bludgeon their superiors. However, the river prosecution wave of 1767 was a one-off. This type of prosecutorial activity was not attempted at any other time during our period. It may be that the trouble required to mount the campaign was too great or that nuisance prosecution was thought to be dangerously two-edged. However, it may be that middling men of the city, as represented by and acting through the Presentment Juries, believed that the lesson which they set out to teach had been thoroughly learned by the city's rulers.

CONCLUSION

The case of Norwich in 1766 and 1767 demonstrates the need to disaggregate the middling sort so that the attitudes of small shopkeepers and corn dealers and those of substantial dealers to a free corn market may be distinguished. Far from being uniformly hostile to ideas of moral economy, many and probably most of the middling sort of Norwich subscribed to the political culture of rights and entitlements which motivated the eighteenth-century's food rioters. This suggests that the majority of middling people saw their self-interest as best served by pooling their political influence with that of their poorer neighbours in their opposition to the engrossers of the national market. This is consistent with the situation which has been shown to have prevailed elsewhere. Where a large, stable and self-conscious body of working people were able to develop and maintain an autonomous political culture, they were able to draw many of their middling neighbours out of the orbit of respectable opinion and into that of a popular radicalism which revolved around a moral economy.

   In the West of England clothing districts and in Manchester, middling people
have been shown to have retained a belief in the moral economy to the end of
the eighteenth century and beyond. The attitudes of many of the middling sort
of Norwich to the moral economy are analogous to those which Adrian Randall
has found among small- and medium-scale clothiers in Wiltshire at the end of
the century. While the deregulation of the cloth trade disadvantaged smaller
manufacturers by increasing clothiers' capital requirements, it also offended
their sense of ethical and proper behaviour towards the labouring poor.[50] The
deregulation of the food market affected those who dealt in food in the same
mixture of ways. While a few who operated in a national and even international
market stood to benefit from changes which reduced control over their
activities, many more who dealt on a smaller, local scale did not. Like Randall's
manufacturers, those who were being disadvantaged relative to their more
capitalized competitors lived among the labouring poor and were active
members of the communities which suffered the consequences of the free
market. In all three cases, in Norwich, Wiltshire and Manchester, we see
middling people whom a twentieth-century observer might expect to be the
natural supporters of *laissez faire*, actively opposing it.
   The ideological structure of the moral economy which supported the
Norwich presentment jurors, overseers and supporters of prisoners in confrontation with their rulers must have been about more than the 'just price' alone.
The support for rioters shown by middling people would have rendered them
liable to elite retaliation. A deep commitment to a world view structured by a
discourse of rights and entitlements, in which communities had obligations to
protect their weaker and poorer members from the ill-effects of both natural
and man-made disasters, was required to make them behave in this way. This
sort of commitment to an all-encompassing moral economy was grounded upon
a deep appreciation of the material conditions which determined the economic
well-being of manufacturing districts and the subsistence of their poorest
residents. The response of the middling sort of Norwich to the food rioting of
1766 suggests that they shared many of the beliefs and ideological underpin-
nings of the moral economy with the labouring poor. The threat of severe
retribution which they placed before those they held to be responsible for the
excessive punishment of those who were convicted of such offences is an even
clearer sign of their hostility to the new unregulated market and to those who
attempted to police its operation.

---

50 A. Randall, 'The shearmen', p. 300 and n. 30. That a similar situation prevailed in Manchester in the
   early nineteenth century, where the city fathers still thought it advisable to regulate food marketing
   rather than trust to the invisible hand of unfettered market forces, is shown by A. Charlesworth,
   'From the moral economy of Devon to the political economy of Manchester, 1790–1812', *Social
   History*, Vol. 18, No. 12, May 1993, *passim*. Also see note 30 above.

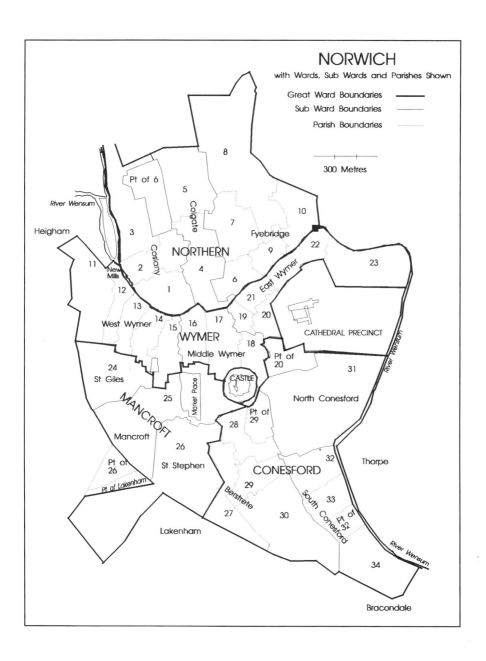

KEY TO GREAT WARDS, SUB-WARDS AND PARISHES

Great Ward	Sub-Ward	Parish
Northern or Over the Water	Coslany	1 St Michael Coslany
		2 St Mary Coslany
		3 St Martin at Oak
	Colgate	4 St George Colgate
		5 St Augustine
	Fyebridge	6 St Clement
		7 St Saviour
		8 St Paul
		9 St Edmond
		10 St James
Wymer Great Ward	West Wymer	11 St Benedict
		12 St Swithin
		13 St Margaret
		14 St Lawrence
		15 St Gregory
	Middle Wymer	16 St John Maddermarket
		17 St Andrew
		18 St Michael at Plea
	East Wymer	19 St Peter Hungate
		20 St George Tombland
		21 Ss Simon and Jude
		22 St Martin at Palace
		23 St Helen
Mancroft Great Ward	St Giles	24 St Giles
	Mancroft	25 St Peter Mancroft
	St Stephen	26 St Stephen
Conesford Great Ward	Berstrete	27 All Saints
		28 St John Timberhill
		29 St Michael at Thorn
		30 St John Sepulchre
	North Conesford	31 St Peter Permountergate or Parmentergate
	South Conesford	32 St Julian
		33 St Etheldred or Etheldreda
		34 St Peter Southgate

Chapter 7

OXFORD FOOD RIOTS:
A COMMUNITY AND ITS MARKETS

WENDY THWAITES

Many factors determined the incidence and character of eighteenth-century food riots. Most obviously, dearth, with its accompanying high prices and supply breakdowns, almost inevitably underlay outbreaks of food-related disturbances.[1] Oxford's food riots certainly took place in the context of scarcity which not only produced straightforward effects on prices but also distorted normal patterns of marketing and trade.[2] However, it is the aim of this paper to concentrate on three interconnected themes which ran through the Oxford disturbances and which together help to explain both why the city should have been prone to riot and the way in which rioters and authorities responded to crisis. The first theme is the clash between the food needs and expectations of the local community and the demands made on local supplies by distant and perhaps more attractive markets. The second is the long tradition of market regulation in Oxford which provided both the crowd and the authorities with an accessible and intelligible set of ideas about how marketing and trade should operate to which both could refer in dearth. The behaviour of the Oxford rioters provides support for E. P. Thompson's view that there was a 'moral economy' of the crowd, which involved a restatement of the paternalist tradition of market regulation and questioned free market values.[3] It will also be suggested that Oxford's tradition of market regulation may have helped in the formulation of the ideas, which can be encompassed within the term 'moral economy'. The third theme is the unusual nature of Oxford society. John Bohstedt, in his examination of the relationship between riot and community politics, includes Oxford in a list of towns which he sees as the natural home of traditional, successful food rioting.[4] Oxford certainly shared characteristics

1 One Oxfordshire food riot, at Burford in 1713, is less clearly in this context. W. Thwaites, 'The marketing of agricultural produce in eighteenth century Oxfordshire' (unpublished PhD Thesis, University of Birmingham, 1980), pp. 470–71.

2 This point is discussed in W. Thwaites, 'Dearth and the marketing of agricultural produce: Oxfordshire c. 1750–1800', *Agricultural History Review*, Vol. XXXIII, 1985, pp. 122–24.

3 E. P. Thompson, 'The moral economy of the English crowd in the eighteenth century' and 'The moral economy reviewed' in E. P. Thompson, *Customs in Common* (London, Merlin, 1991), pp. 185–351.

4 J. Bohstedt, *Riots and Community Politics in England and Wales 1790–1810* (Cambridge, Mass., Harvard University Press, 1983), p. 203.

with other major riot centres. However, it will be seen that riots and the response to them also reflected an individual world in which, for example, authority was divided between university and city and the crowd often had links to the wider world which trade itself had opened up to it.

I

By the mid-eighteenth century, Oxford had long been incorporated into the wider trading world. The River Thames, which was navigable into Oxford from 1635, enabled the city to forward malt and grain to London, the barges returning with sea-coal and foodstuffs.[5] An advertisement for the Oxford Company's barges in 1770 referred to them carrying barley, malt, timber and stone.[6] When local food supplies were secure, the river could be a vital lifeline for the local economy and the all-too-frequent problems with its navigation a source of intense hardship for the bargemen and farmers.[7] While heavy, bulky goods were consigned to the capital by river, waggons were leaving the Oxford area for London laden with perishable items. Thus, in June 1754, it was reported that the Oxford waggon had overturned on its way to Newgate market with veal and butter.[8] Oxford market might be chosen as the collection point for produce for London. For example, an advertisement in 1762 suggested that poulterers who were engaged to supply Westminster with poultry and wild fowl would be opening a country poultry warehouse at Oxford market.[9] Collecting and processing foodstuffs for the capital and moving them to it were a visible and well-known aspect of city life, as well as the source of many employment opportunities.

While Oxford was firmly within the orbit of the London market, it was also an important market centre in its own right. Oxford was a county town and, as Peter Clark and Paul Slack indicate, 'Most county towns served as a focus for a web of major trade routes, while their hinterland was both more extensive and diverse than that of a market town: often it embraced or overlapped with the market areas of smaller places'.[10] In other words, as London was a magnet to

---

5 M. L. Prior, 'Fisher Row—The Oxford community of fishermen and bargemen, 1500–1800' (unpublished DPhil thesis, University of Oxford, 1976), p. 154; A. Crossley (ed.), *The Victoria History of the County of Oxford, IV: The City of Oxford* (Oxford, Oxford University Press, 1979), p. 208.

6 *Jackson's Oxford Journal*, 10 November 1770.

7 For example, Anthony Wood recorded the problems caused by drought in 1666. A. Clark (ed.), *The Life and Times of Anthony Wood, Antiquary of Oxford, 1632–95, II: 1664–1681*, Oxford Historical Society, Vol. XXI, 1892, pp. 82, 86.

8 *Jackson's Oxford Journal*, 8 June 1754.

9 *Jackson's Oxford Journal*, 13 November 1762.

10 P. Clark and P. Slack, *English Towns in Transition 1500–1700* (Oxford, Oxford University Press, 1976), p. 26. Oxford is mentioned in the subsequent discussion.

Oxford, so Oxford itself could expect to be an important and attractive market centre in its own locality.

The city offered a range, albeit not a full range, of market facilities. The corn market has been discussed fully elsewhere.[11] Here it is simply necessary to reiterate that in spite of uneven fortunes and structural changes, it did survive into the nineteenth century. Throughout the period, Oxford possessed a successful provisions market, with meat, fish, poultry, herbs, roots, garden stuff, fruit, butter and eggs largely sold in the streets until 1773, when they began to be brought into a new covered market.[12] All attempts to establish a general livestock market seem to have enjoyed only short-lived success, although there is evidence to suggest that a pig market may have been held more continuously.[13] University opposition, based partly on the existence of alternative markets at Thame and Abingdon, defeated a city petition for a livestock market in 1684.[14] As this suggests, even tradesmen from a successful market town would almost certainly have attended other local markets for some of their business dealings. They would also have patronized the region's specialist fairs.[15]

Oxford market was a community market, serving and linking the city and the villages and smaller towns around. Although the city's own tradesmen provided many of the vendors of malt, meat and other provisions, their numbers were augmented by a range of outside suppliers. Malt was brought in from the surrounding villages and, while the evidence on the corn market is not extensive, wheat, barley, oats and beans would seem to have been supplied by the local farming community. Almost all identified corn vendors came from within 10 miles of the city, with a statistically significant proportion from the villages of East and West Hanney in the fertile, but deeply conservative, Vale of the White Horse.[16] As this suggests, agricultural specialization had an influence

---

11 W. Thwaites, 'The corn market and economic change: Oxford in the eighteenth century', *Midland History*, Vol. XVI, 1991, pp. 103–25.

12 Thwaites, 'Marketing', pp. 118–19; L. L. Shadwell (ed.), *Enactments in Parliament specially concerning the Universities of Oxford and Cambridge . . . II, I George I–II George IV*, Oxford Historical Society, Vol. LIX, 1912, p. 124. The Act of Parliament establishing the covered market allowed fishmongers and poulterers to continue selling in their own shops and houses.

13 Thwaites, 'Marketing', pp. 28–32; A. Clark (ed.), *Survey of the Antiquities of the City of Oxford, composed in 1661–6, by Anthony Wood, I, The City and Suburbs*, Oxford Historical Society, Vol. XV, 1889, p. 479.

14 F. H. Blackburne Daniell and F. Bickley (eds), *Calendar of State Papers Domestic Series, October 1, 1683–April 30, 1684* (London, HMSO, 1938), pp. 310–11.

15 For an example of this, see Committee of the Oxford Historical Society (ed.), *Remarks and Collections of Thomas Hearne, VIII (Sept. 23 1722–Aug. 9 1725)*, Oxford Historical Society, Vol. L, 1907, p. 267.

16 Thwaites, 'Marketing', pp. 180–81, 199. Names of both sellers and buyers of corn are drawn very largely from 'The assize of bread 1692–1700', Bodleian Library, Ms Top Oxon f 18: 'Corn books of the clerks of the market 1733–1822', Oxford University Archives MR 3/5/1–MR 3/5/6; 'Corn returns 1795–1800', Oxford University Archives MR 3/5/7–MR 3/5/8. All material from the University Archives is quoted by kind permission of the Keeper. W. Page and P. H. Ditchfield (eds), *The Victoria History of the County of Berkshire, IV* (London, The St Catherine Press, 1924),

on supply patterns.[17] Among the established suppliers of meat and garden produce, inhabitants of villages within 10 miles of the city were, again represented.[18] Some of the suppliers of the provisions market were higglers, dealers in products like butter, cheese, eggs and poultry, for whom Oxford would have been one, and perhaps the most important, of a circuit of towns visited.[19] Others were casual suppliers of often small amounts. Thus, in 1775 the market committee determined that only one halfpenny be taken for a standing with a parcel of goods not exceeding a peck in quantity.[20] Like the formal suppliers, these casual vendors might attend the market regularly over many years.[21]

Records of corn buyers show that the dominant purchasers were food processors, bakers, millers, brewers and maltsters from Oxford itself. However, there were also purchasers from other towns and villages, the majority from within 10 miles of Oxford, but with a handful coming from farther afield.[22] Members of the city hierarchy were among the buyers. Of the members of the Corporation in 1800 whose occupation is known, the four bakers, two brewers and an innholder bought corn, wheat, barley, malt and oats in the market in the course of pursuing their occupations.[23] The provisions market seems to have served the whole community. Thus, in November 1773, when the Vice-Chancellor and the mayor announced their intention to suppress Sunday trading, they suggested that masters should pay their handicraftsmen and labouring people with at least a part of their wages sufficiently early on Saturday as to enable them to go to market.[24] Again, in December 1772, it was announced that the Oxford colleges had decided not to contract with particular butchers but deal at large for ready money, and that butchers bringing good meat to market would receive encouragement.[25]

---

p. 285; W. Mavor, *General View of the Agriculture of Berkshire* . . . (London, Sherwood, Neely and Jones, 1809), p. 505.

17 Anthony Wood showed the influence of agricultural specialization on supply patterns as early as the 1660s. Clark, *Survey*, pp. 52–53.

18 For a table showing places of origin of, in particular, stallholders in the new market, see Thwaites, 'Marketing', p. 370. For the sources from which information in this table is drawn, see note 41.

19 In 1753, five higglers were presented for dealing in Oxford on a regular basis without being licensed. Quarter Sessions Bundles, Trinity 1753, Oxfordshire Record Office.

20 'Book of the Oxford market committee, 1771–1835', Oxford City Archives, FF 2. 1a, fol. 73.

21 For an example of this, see W. N. Hargraves-Mawdsley (ed.), *Woodforde at Oxford 1759–1776*, Oxford Historical Society, Vol. XXI, 1969, p. 34.

22 Thwaites, 'Marketing', pp. 183–88.

23 The names are listed in M. G. Hobson (ed.), *Oxford Council Acts, 1752–1801*, Oxford Historical Society, New Series (NS), Vol. XV, 1962, pp. 278–80. Occupations have been identified using *The Poll of the Freemen of the City of Oxford taken 25–27 May 1796*. Seventy-three out of 105 have been identified using this source.

24 *Jackson's Oxford Journal*, 20 November 1773.

25 *Jackson's Oxford Journal*, 26 December 1772.

Even without other factors, Oxford can be seen to have provided an environment in which food riot was both a possibility and could be an intelligible form of protest. On the one hand, the trade with London could easily turn from advantage to threat in conditions of dearth. On the other, Oxford was the focus for a large community, which expected it to be able to satisfy its food requirements. Again, the city's market was an open world, in which farmers, higglers and food processors were known figures, to the authorities and to the crowd, and therefore accessible targets for rioters. Finally, the constant coming and going of visitors to the city and tradesmen from it would have facilitated a flow of information about crops, prices and supply availability as well, no doubt, as tolls and regulations in a variety of markets, providing the crowd with material on which to have based its perceptions of crises.

II

However, Oxford was not simply a county town on a trade route to London. It was also a university town, with the university a powerful determinant of the economic, social and political life of the city.[26] Employment in the town was shaped to a considerable extent by the requirements of the gown. Nathaniel Spencer wrote in 1771: 'It is not to be expected that trade can be carried on in Oxford, nor would it be prudent to suffer it, where there are so many young gentlemen residing for the benefit of their education'.[27] Mary Prior, writing on the early nineteenth century, presents a less complacent picture: 'The economy of Oxford was hopelessly dependent on the university, expanding and contracting with its season'.[28] The Corporation of the City of Oxford consisted of a mayor, four or five aldermen, eight assistants, two bailiffs, former bailiffs and chamberlains and a common council consisting of 24 members.[29] An analysis of the occupations of the Corporation in the important riot year 1800 reveals clearly the lack of an industrial base in the city and the preponderance of occupations in the service sector, food and drink, clothing, building and transportation.[30]

Over the centuries, the need to protect the university's food supplies and to ensure that its members were not exploited as consumers had had a very significant effect on the operation and regulation of marketing in the city.

---

26 P. J. Corfield draws attention to a range of distinctive towns in the eighteenth century, among which she identified university towns. P. J. Corfield, *The Impact of English Towns 1700–1800* (Oxford, Oxford University Press, 1982), pp. 15–16.

27 N. Spencer, *The Complete English Traveller . . .* (London, J. Cooke, 1771), p. 339.

28 M. Prior, *Fisher Row: Fishermen, Bargemen and Canal Boatmen in Oxford, 1500–1900* (Oxford, Oxford University Press, 1982), p. 195.

29 Crossley, *Victoria History*, p. 130.

30 See note 23.

In the 1660s, Anthony Wood recorded that the university possessed the privilege of forcing all the country within five miles of Oxford to supply it with provisions.[31] This right seems to have been exercised as late as the seventeenth century. Thus, 'Orders of c.1575 reserved to Oxford market the sale of all grain from within five miles of the town . . . Similar proclamations were made in 1591, between 1591 and 1603 and in 1606 . . .'.[32] These proclamations seem to have been separate from the enforcement of 'the emergency measures in time of scarcity whose operation, in the years between 1580 and 1630, were codified in the *Book of Orders*' and which had allowed magistrates to require the surrounding countryside to supply the market. However, these regulations, which Thompson felt to be part of the tradition to which the 'moral economy' referred back, seem also to have been enforced by university officials.[33] According to R. B. Outhwaite, 'the *Book of Orders* for the relief of dearth was issued in December 1622', and W. F. Lloyd records the existence of a table 'dated 1623, and signed with the initials of the Vice-Chancellor and the clerks of the market, containing the names of about eighty persons . . . with the quantity of corn they were severally required to bring to market weekly set down opposite to each name'.[34]

The right to command supplies from the surrounding countryside was only one of a range of privileges the university had gained in relation to marketing. After the massacre of St Scholastica's Day in 1355, the wide-ranging rights of the university had been clarified and included responsibility for the assize of bread, beer and wine and weights and measures, for the quality of provisions and for amercing forestallers and regrators.[35]

As late as 1681, the Vice-Chancellor could still be found fixing the prices for a wide range of products including butter, cheese, eggs, poultry, rabbits, pigs, mutton, lamb, bacon, candles as well as fodder at the inns.[36] The forms used were printed with the prices added in, and Anthony Wood saw them stuck up in public places.[37] There is also evidence that the assize of ale, 'a mechanism for

31 Clark, *Survey*, p. 53.
32 Crossley, *Victoria History*, p. 309.
33 Thompson, *Customs in Common*, pp. 224–26.
34 R. B. Outhwaite, 'Dearth and government intervention in English grain markets, 1590–1700', *Economic History Review*, Second Series, Vol. XXXIV, 1981, p. 391; W. F. Lloyd, *Prices of Corn in Oxford in the Beginning of the 14th Century. Also from the year 1583 to the Present . . .* (Oxford, Oxford University Press, 1830), pp. 21–22. The Vice-Chancellor also took measures to lessen the number of maltsters. See also Prior, *Fisher Row: Fishermen*, pp. 170–71.
35 T. Salmon, *The Present State of the Universities and of the Five Adjacent Counties of Cambridge, Huntingdon, Bedford, Buckingham and Oxford* (London, J. Roberts, 1744), pp. 117, 305–06; Sir J. Peshall, *The Antient and Present State of the City of Oxford* (London, J. and F. Rivington, 1773), p. 334.
36 O. Ogle, 'The Oxford market' in M. Burrows (ed.), *Collecteana II*, Oxford Historical Society, Vol. XVI, 1890, pp. 127–28.
37 Clark, *Life and Times*, II, p. 520.

relating the price of beer to that of malt', was being set until 1701.[38] While these regulations appear not to have survived beyond the opening of the eighteenth century, the assize of bread, the mechanism whereby the price of bread was related to that of wheat, continued to be set by university officials throughout the period.[39] Moreover, there is evidence of periodic checks on weights and measures during the early eighteenth century and of seizures of short weight butter in the last decades of the century.[40] Checks on both weights and measures and the weight of butter were still taking place in the nineteenth century.[41]

The day-to-day checking on the quality and weight of goods was the work of the university-appointed clerks of the market.[42] A report in Thomas Hearne's diary for 1725 concerning a fight between one of the clerks and a poulterer who had forestalled the market may suggest that the clerks also watched regularly for this type of abuse, although no other references of this type have been found.[43] The Vice-Chancellor intervened in this case, and it was the Vice-Chancellor who was technically the chief officer of the market, with the clerks subject to his authority. He could issue regulations in his own right. Thus, Sir John Peshall recorded that, in 1772, the Vice-Chancellor, Dr Wetherall, had, in his own name, called for the enforcement of the laws against forestallers.[44]

However, while university officials were responsible for enforcing many market regulations designed to protect themselves and others as consumers, in one respect they were on the other side of the marketing divide. By *18 Elizabeth c VI(1575–6)* it was enacted that one-third of the rents of Oxford college properties should be reserved in wheat and malt or determined according to the highest prices for wheat and malt on the market day preceding the day upon which the rents were due.[45] According to Arthur Young, writing in 1813, 'The university of Oxford is supposed to possess the property in whole or in part, of

38 Thwaites, 'Corn market', p. 106. There are also suggestions of an assize of fish. Ogle, 'Oxford market', pp. 128–30.

39 W. Thwaites, 'The assize of bread in 18th century Oxford', *Oxoniensia*, Vol. LI, 1986, pp. 171–81.

40 Thwaites, 'Marketing', pp. 388, 411–14. The checks on weights and measures are detailed in 'Miscellaneous market regulations c. 1664–1732', Oxford University Archives, NEP Supra 14.

41 'Perambulations of the clerks of the market, 1808–1828', Bodleian Library, Ms Top Oxon f2; 'Bliss papers—Oxford market, 1828–1848', Bodleian Library, Ms Top Oxon d 71; 'Papers relating to the clerks of the market and their work, 1821–1851', Bodleian Library, Ms Top Oxon e 98.

42 S. Lewis, *A Topographical Dictionary of England . . .* (4 vols, London, S. Lewis and Co., 1831), Vol. III, p. 474. This shows from whom the clerks were drawn.

43 H. E. Salter (ed.), *Remarks and Collections of Thomas Hearne, IX, Aug. 10 1725–Mar. 26 1728)*, Oxford Historical Society, Vol. LXV, 1914, p. 48.

44 Peshall, *Antient and Present State*, p. 334.

45 L. L. Shadwell (ed.), *Enactments in Parliament specially concerning the Universities of Oxford and Cambridge...I, 37 Edward III–13 Anne*, Oxford Historical Society, Vol. LVIII, 1912, pp. 190–91.

one sixth of the county' of Oxfordshire.[46] As considerable landowners, in receipt of corn rents, the colleges might therefore appear to have gained as much from high corn prices as the farmers.[47]

Given the considerable control of marketing by the university, it is easy to lose sight of the fact that Oxford was also a corporate town. Ogle suggested that rivalry between town and gown over the government of Oxford market was continuous between the reigns of Edward III and George III, although it would seem that by the eighteenth century the rivalry was manifested in relatively trivial bickering over issues like the placing of stallholders.[48] However, the competition between university and city had almost certainly helped to preserve a high level of market regulation in Oxford as both town and gown saw the exercise of their privileges as a means of asserting supremacy over the other. As such, it had a part to play in providing the background to Oxford's food riots even if the rivalry was rarely evident in the response of university and city officials to the disturbances.

One of the university's rights was to grant 'privileged' status to, for example, 'members of certain occupations regarded as of special university concern', and this might enable non-freemen to practise a trade in the city.[49] However, except for these privileged persons, only freemen were permitted to carry on a trade or craft in Oxford, and much of the regulatory action taken by the town leaders seems to have been designed to minimize 'foreign' competition in the market place. The records of two of the trading companies which survived into the eighteenth century contain references to moves against 'interlopers' and payments for 'annoying Hawkers', and the Corporation backed this stand with the regular harrying of unapprenticed or unfree tradesmen and periodic attempts to suppress hawking.[50] Regulations, which on the face of it were designed to keep trading open, like those against forestalling, engrossing and regrating, seem to have been employed more to determine the boundaries of certain occupations, for example, whether grocers could sell bread, or to

46 A. Young, *General View of the Agriculture of the County of Oxfordshire* (London, Sheerwood, Neely and Jones, 1813; repr. Newton Abbot, David and Charles, 1969), p. 39. Estates were, of course, also possessed in other parts of the country.
47 Corn rents could be used by landowners and magistrates as a threat against farmers who refused to ameliorate price demands in dearth periods. *Jackson's Oxford Journal*, 18 October 1800.
48 Ogle, 'Oxford market', p. 3; M. G. Hobson, *Oxford Council Acts, 1701–1752*, Oxford Historical Society, NS, Vol. X, 1954, p. xviii.
49 Crossley, *Victoria History*, p. 161.
50 'The company of the butchers and poulterers', Bodleian Library, Ms Morrell 19, fol. 11; 'The company of the mercers and grocers', Bodleian Library, Ms Morrell 1, fols 3, 4. Cases under the Elizabethan Statute of Artificers can be found in the Oxford City Quarter Sessions (QS) minutes, for example, 'QS minutes, 1791–1807', Oxford City Archives, 0.2.11, fols 4, 19; Thwaites, 'Marketing', pp. 116–18.

suppress very small traders.[51] Thus it seems likely that the large number of indictments for forestalling and regrating at the Oxford city sessions in the early eighteenth century may have targeted a group below even Thompson's 'local wide-boys or market-men', whom he saw as the principal targets of exemplary prosecutions in dearth.[52] The great majority were those automatic outsiders, women.[53] Moreover, there is some suggestion of people who engaged in other marginal activities, like selling ale without licence.[54] Within the market place itself, free tradesmen enjoyed extra privileges. Thus, non-freemen were restricted to selling their wares on the two general market days of Wednesday and Saturday, whereas, for example, free butchers were able to keep market on other weekdays.[55]

These restrictions on competition were probably not entirely in the interests of the poorer sections of society. Thus, the suppression of hawking may have denied the poor not only a source of cheap goods in small quantities, but also an opportunity of employment.[56] Few of the regulatory actions taken by the city authorities between the 1680s and the mid-eighteenth-century disturbances seem to fit into a wider and less self-interested framework. However, following the proclamation of the laws concerning middlemen in 1698, a number of forestalling and engrossing cases involving those occupied in the corn trade were tried at the city Quarter Sessions.[57]

Oxford's food rioters therefore had a very wide tradition of market regulation on which to draw, even if it is important to recognize that it was often the self-interest of both town and gown which had helped to create that tradition and keep it alive.

III

In three important respects, Oxford's mid-century food riots can be located very closely in the local environment described above. First, in both 1757 and

---

51 A number of engrossing and regrating cases in the late seventeenth century seem to have involved the question of whether grocers and chandlers could resell bread. 'Oxford city sessions rolls, 1679–1712', Oxford City Archives, O.5.12, fols 11, 22; Thwaites, 'Marketing', pp. 439–41.

52 Thompson, *Customs in Common*, p. 209.

53 These cases are discussed in W. Thwaites, 'Women in the market place: Oxfordshire c. 1690–1800', *Midland History*, Vol. IX, 1984, pp. 30–31.

54 One of those indicted for regrating garden stuff or fruit in 1712 was indicted for selling ale without licence in 1730, and in 1731 was accused of keeping a bawdy house. 'QS minutes, 1726–1734', Oxford City Archives, 0.2.6., fols 89, 112.

55 Ogle, 'Oxford market', p. 37; Crossley, *Victoria History*, pp. 306–07.

56 J. Houghton, *Husbandry and Trade Improv'd—Being a Collection . . . Revised . . . by Richard Bradley* (4 vols, London, 1727), Vol. III, pp. 7, 77. Houghton provided a cogent defence of hawking. For the suggestion of hawking as an employment opportunity, see Thwaites, 'Women', pp. 28–29.

57 Thwaites, 'Corn market', p. 114.

1766, the riots arose within the context of the trade with London and formed part of a wider pattern of disturbance in the Thames Valley. Thus, in 1757 rioting in Oxford followed disturbances at Abingdon, the first town down river from the city, and on both riot days, 15 and 16 June, wheat was seized from the Folly Bridge river wharf.[58] Again, in 1766, the Oxford riots took place in the context of the price-fixing activities of the 'regulators' in the Thames Valley and involved not only the selling of roll butter seized from a London waggoner at four pence per pound, whereas butter brought into Oxford market was sold at six pence, but also a threat to stop all kinds of provisions being moved to London.[59]

However, it is important to appreciate that the crowd was not merely objecting to the normal trade with London or, necessarily, to regular marketing practices, but was alert to the distortion of standard practices brought about by dearth conditions. There is clear evidence of unusual developments. For example, by the mid-eighteenth century, Oxford's Wednesday corn market had long been moribund, trade being confined almost entirely to Saturday.[60] However, it was reported that, on Wednesday 15 June 1757, great quantities of corn had been brought to Oxford market where it was snapped up by 'Locusts', almost certainly dealers for London, preventing Oxford's bakers obtaining supplies.[61] Rioting began in the city that day. Again, the evidence suggests that, in 1766, there may have been speculative hoarding of wheat. Thus, although a writer from Oxford reported that all the old wheat, that is the remains of the 1765 crop, had been sent down to London by 3 September, as late as 13 June 1767, *Jackson's Oxford Journal* was recording prices for new and old wheat, indicating that not all of the 1765 crop had yet been marketed.[62]

Not only did the crowd react to the irregular but its members were also alert to longer-term marketing changes which were undermining the open market ideal, for example the growth of sample selling and the use of inns for business dealings.[63] The 1750s and 1760s were decades both of transition in market organization and of adjustment, as demand for British corn began to outstrip

---

58 *Jackson's Oxford Journal*, 18 June 1757; Thwaites, 'Marketing', pp. 474–76.

59 A full account of the 1766 food riots in the Upper Thames Valley can be found in D. E. Williams, 'English hunger riots in 1766' (unpublished PhD thesis, University of Wales, 1978), pp. 226–53. See also Thwaites, 'Marketing', pp. 477–80; *Jackson's Oxford Journal*, 27 September 1766.

60 Thwaites, 'Corn market', p. 106.

61 *Jackson's Oxford Journal*, 18 June 1757. Although we may note that, on 11 June, when the dealers were also said to have dominated the market, the only two named purchasers were almost certainly Oxford bakers. 'Corn book of the clerks of the market, 1751–1767', Oxford University Archives, MR 3/5/2.

62 Williams, 'English hunger riots', p. 231; *Jackson's Oxford Journal*, 13 June 1767.

63 The riot of 1757 started when the crowd alleged that a waggon of wheat had been bought by sample. *Jackson's Oxford Journal*, 18 June 1757. For a discussion of rioters focusing on inns, see Thwaites, 'Dearth', pp. 120–21.

supply and the population centres widened their net for food. The behaviour of the rioters illustrated the changing context.[64]

The second respect in which the riots reflect the world described above is that the crowd couched much of its response to the crisis of 1766 in terms of the regulatory framework of the past. The riots opened on 23 September with the stopping of a waggon with flour going at night from Holywell Mill, while the following day flour was taken from the mill and distributed. On 25 September systematic price-fixing commenced when wheat from Osney Mill and wheat and flour found at the city's inns and elsewhere were sold at five shillings per bushel, the poor being supplied first, followed by the bakers who had to agree to sell 12 pounds of household bread for one shilling. The crowd then compelled the dealers in groceries to reduce the prices of bacon, butter, cheese, candles and soap and, on 26 September, after the selling of the London waggoner's butter, the price of ducks and chickens was fixed and freshwater fish was sold off at a low price. Finally, and clearly demonstrating the crowd's awareness of the flows of trade into and out of the city, it awaited the return of cheese waggons from Burford fair and forced the owners to sell the cheese at two pence halfpenny per pound.[65]

It would seem likely that the crowd was influenced in such comprehensive price-setting by the wide-ranging price regulation which had been and, over the assize of bread, still was such a feature of the university-controlled market. It is certainly possible that the formal lists noting the commodity prices fixed by the Vice-Chancellor could still be seen in the city. Viscount Torrington commented on the Vice-Chancellor's list for '1680' on a visit to Oxford during his tour of 1785.[66] Moreover, while this may be coincidence, both perhaps reflecting customary prices, the prices fixed by the crowd for butter, bacon and chickens were those set by the Vice-Chancellor in 1681.[67]

The third point concerns the nature of the crowd. The extreme orderliness of the price-fixing in 1766 suggests restraint, care, complex motivation, that is the desire to punish appropriately as well as to obtain cheaper food, and a thorough knowledge of the working of the paternal model. Moreover, *Jackson's Oxford Journal* recorded that men, women and children visited Holywell Mill in 1766, indicating perhaps a popular community movement.[68] However, those

---

64 For a fuller discussion of the points raised here, see Thwaites, 'Dearth', pp. 119–31, and 'Corn market', pp. 103–25.

65 *Jackson's Oxford Journal*, 27 September 1766.

66 C. Bruyn Andrews (ed.), *The Torrington Diaries. Containing the Tours through England and Wales of the Honourable John Byng* (4 vols, London, Eyre and Spottiswoode, 1934), Vol. I, p. 209. It was probably the 1681 list.

67 In the Vice-Chancellor's lists, these were the prices for best butter and chickens and rib bacon. Soap and fish were not on the Vice-Chancellor's lists of provisions.

68 *Jackson's Oxford Journal*, 27 September 1766.

identified by the riot victims and the authorities as the riot leaders in both 1757 and 1766 seem to have been members of a distinctive group, with a reputation for disorderly conduct.

On 16 June 1757, some of the rioters at the wharf were seized and examined by the Vice-Chancellor. William Best gave evidence against 28 others but, together with one Ward, was rescued and disappeared.[69] The arrest of John Green (alias Gunston) for being one of the leaders of the riots led to threats against one of the city bailiffs, but Green and another rioter, James Carter, were taken to be tried at the Berkshire summer assizes at Abingdon.[70] There, both were found guilty of feloniously stealing wheat from the granary of Sarah Panting, spinster, and sentenced to transportation for seven years.[71] At the trial, evidence appeared against 'two more of the Carters, one Scraggy Parker, Bossom, two or more of the Bests', among others. *Jackson's Oxford Journal* had as little sympathy with the supposed perpetrators of the riots as with the corn dealers who were carrying on the prosecutions. While it complained that the poor 'might be artfully seduced by those abandoned wretches who have long been the Pest of Society', it still suggested that the named rioters might be wise enough to abscond.[72] From the fact that Charles Bossom, a bargeman, was apprehended in London, it would appear that this is what they did.[73] At the Berkshire Lent assizes in 1758, he was found not guilty of stealing wheat.[74]

At the time of the riots, William Best, James Carter and John Green were each described as 'horse-takers', a term used widely in *Jackson's Oxford Journal* in the 1750s and 1760s to describe members of a group associated with or blamed for a variety of anti-social activities in and around Oxford.[75] John Green had been acquitted of horse stealing earlier in 1757 and James Carter had been mentioned in 1755 when, after an execution, a dispute over the body led to a fight between him and a bargeman.[76] Several references exist to the Bests. For example, John Best, the younger, was indicted for taking horses in 1751 and for

---

69 *Jackson's Oxford Journal*, 18 June 1757.

70 *Jackson's Oxford Journal*, 25 June 1757; 16 July 1757.

71 *Jackson's Oxford Journal*, 23 July 1757; 'Berkshire summer Assizes 1757', Public Record Office, Assizes 5: 77/2. The prosecutions were instigated by the three mealmen whose wheat had been stored at the wharf.

72 *Jackson's Oxford Journal*, 23 July 1757.

73 *Jackson's Oxford Journal*, 11 February 1758.

74 'Berkshire Lent Assizes 1758', Public Record Office, Assizes 5: 78/1; *Jackson's Oxford Journal*, 4 March 1758. Bossom, like Green and Carter, was described in the assizes papers as from St Aldate's parish. However, this may reflect the location of the riots. Bossom, at least, seems to have been from St Thomas's. Prior, *Fisher Row: Fishermen*, p. 262.

75 *Jackson's Oxford Journal*, 18 June 1757; 16 July 1757.

76 *Jackson's Oxford Journal*, 2 April 1757; 3 May 1755. It is assumed these are the same John Green and James Carter.

being involved in an attack on the house of a Roman Catholic at Chipping Norton during the notorious 1754 election campaign.[77]

Two of the three named rioters in 1766 seem also to have been associated with general lawlessness, although they were not referred to as 'horse-takers'. In November 1766, an attempt was made to arrest Henry Brown and Samuel Faulkner, described as 'two of the late Rioters here', for stealing wet linen. A description of Brown recorded that he had generally worked in malting and brewing, both in Oxford and London.[78] Arrested in London, Brown was branded for this offence.[79] He was arrested again in 1769 for stealing fowls and sentenced to transportation to America, from where, in 1772, he was reported to be well.[80] The third named rioter, William Morris, provides an example of continuity between the 1757 and 1766 riots. *Jackson's Oxford Journal* commented that 'from his having lost one Hand, and being likewise Captain of the Rioters', he had acquired the nickname Young Gunstone, after John Green.[81]

The important point concerning the identified rioters is not their frequent criminality, which does not appear to have impinged directly on the food riots, but their connection with the Thames, through living in the riverside parish of St Thomas's and/or working in trades which linked Oxford and London, like transport or malting. The liberating effect which the Thames had on Oxford's economic life may have been mirrored in the apparent freedom of the riverside community from the restraints of the tightly regulated, formal world of university and city.[82] Moreover, their knowledge of the storage and movement of corn meant they were well placed to direct the crowd.

IV

In spite of Oxford's tradition of market regulation, the authorities, both university and city, failed conspicuously to take a proactive role in the crises of 1757 and 1766. Everything they did was essentially a response to the crowd. This is typified by their reaction to the riots of 1766. While rioting commenced

77 'QS minutes 1750–1761', Oxford City Archives, O.2.9., fol. 5; *Jackson's Oxford Journal*, 16 March 1754. At the trial of another Best, Joseph, a former bargeman, for murder in 1756, it was suggested that he had led the riot at Chipping Norton. *Jackson's Oxford Journal*, 25 September 1756; 2 October 1756. Prior, *Fisher Row: Fishermen*, p. 173.

78 *Jackson's Oxford Journal*, 15 November 1766.

79 *Jackson's Oxford Journal*, 21 February 1767; 21 March 1767.

80 *Jackson's Oxford Journal*, 23 September 1769; 7 October 1769; 5 December 1772; P. Babcock Gove, 'An Oxford convict in Maryland', *Maryland Historical Magazine*, Vol. XXXVII, 1942, p. 196. In November 1766 it had been concluded that Brown and Faulkner were part of a gang of poultry thieves.

81 *Jackson's Oxford Journal*, 23 April 1768; 7 May 1768.

82 We should note, however, that the Bossoms were freemen. Prior, *Fisher Row: Fishermen*, p. 269. For an important discussion of the bargemen and the community, see *ibid.*, pp. 170–76. I am indebted to Dr Prior for discussing with me the riots of 1757 and 1766.

on 23 September, it was not until three days later that the Vice-Chancellor, mayor and other members of the Corporation informed the crowd of the illegality of their proceedings, threatened them with the law if they continued to riot and, at the same time, committed themselves to tackling the crowd's grievances, which evidently meant attempting to prevent forestalling and other illegal marketing practices.[83]

However, it is possible that the Oxford authorities may have emerged from these decades of crisis and unrest more determined to regulate provisions marketing in the interests of the consumer. Thus, in December 1771, the gentlemen of the university and city announced their determination to pay for the prosecution of anyone forestalling, engrossing and regrating because these practices were held to be responsible for a rise in the price of meat and other provisions.[84] When the central government committed itself to free trade, with the repeal of the Tudor statutes for the regulation of middlemen in 1772, the Oxford authorities failed to follow its lead. In June 1787, the clerks of the market announced that persons forestalling and regrating in Oxford market would be prosecuted.[85]

Part of the reason for the apparent determination of the Oxford authorities to be seen to be acting in the consumer's interest may have been a concern at the continued possibility of riot. The threat did remain. Thus, between 16 and 17 April 1773, an inflammatory paper addressed to both the Vice-Chancellor and mayor was fixed to Carfax Conduit, 'subscribed' by 'One Hundred of the Oxford Lads' and requiring the price of provisions to be lowered.[86] Again, in September 1774, Edward Tawney and Thomas Burrows of Oxford felt obliged to deny a rumour that flour of theirs had been seized as they attempted to send it abroad.[87]

The changed approach by central government to the problem of dearth would inevitably affect local authorities during the late eighteenth-century crises. However, in Oxford two major developments also caused a significant change in the context in which crisis and disturbance occurred.

One of these, the construction of the Oxford canal, linking the city with Coventry and thereby with the West Midlands and North West, was considerably to increase the impact on Oxford of the government's free trade commitment. Proposed in 1768, it was opened to Banbury in 1778 and Oxford in 1790. The construction of the canal was widely supported and 'Oxford inhabitants, particularly members of the university, were prominent among the

---

83 *Jackson's Oxford Journal*, 27 September 1766. For a general discussion of regulation as a response to riot in Oxfordshire, see Thwaites, 'Marketing', pp. 522–26.

84 *Jackson's Oxford Journal*, 14 December 1771.

85 *Jackson's Oxford Journal*, 30 June 1787.

86 *Jackson's Oxford Journal*, 24 April 1773.

87 *Jackson's Oxford Journal*, 3 September 1774.

shareholders . . .'.[88] The principal attraction of the canal was the prospect of cheaper coal from the West Midlands to counter the city's chronic fuel shortage.[89] However, like the Thames, the canal brought pressures as well as advantages in that it encouraged the exportation of Oxfordshire corn to the growing urban and industrial centres of Warwickshire and Staffordshire. Thus, in 1795 an Oxfordshire farmer commented on the purchase of corn for the use of Birmingham and Staffordshire, 'more particularly since a communication has been opened by a canal to those countries'.[90] In dearth, Oxfordshire food supplies might now be under pressure from two major demand zones, London and the Midlands.[91]

The other development was a significant change in the organization and regulation of marketing in Oxford itself. The construction of the new covered provisions market under the terms of the Oxford Mileways and Improvement Act of 1771 heralded a number of changes.[92] First, as Ogle shows, it brought to an end centuries of rivalry between university and city as the Act made provision for a committee of management consisting of six members of convocation and six members of the city council.[93] Second, both the terms of the Act and the concentration of provisions dealing in one central place encouraged and facilitated the regulation of marketing. Thus, selling outside the market, with a few permitted exceptions, was an offence punishable by a fine of £5, and the authorities obviously made a determined effort to ensure that sellers were confined to the new market.[94] In spite of evasion of the regulations, the existence of legal sanctions against selling outside the market seems to have provided the authorities with a more efficient mechanism for preserving the open market than the old common law provisions against forestalling.[95] Third, perhaps because the construction and supervision of the new market required the city and university officials to think through their approach to market development, a rather less obviously self-interested approach to marketing

---

88 Crossley, *Victoria History*, p. 293. For the widespread support for the canal, see J. Phillips, *A General History of Inland Navigation* . . ., 5th edn (London, B. Crosby and Co., 1805; repr. Newton Abbot, David and Charles, 1970), pp. 200–06.

89 Spencer, *Complete English Traveller*, p. 339.

90 *A Reply to the Instructions given by the Common Council of Oxford, to F. Burton and A. Annesley, Esqrs, their Representatives in Parliament, on the Present Scarcity of Provisions . . . by an Oxfordshire Farmer* (London, 1795), p. 12.

91 This point was made in 1795. 'Mr. Curzon to Duke of Portland, 5 July 1795', Public Record Office, Home Office 42:35, fol. 95.

92 Shadwell, *Enactments in Parliament . . . II, I George I–II George IV*, pp. 102–34; Crossley, *Victoria History*, p. 307.

93 Ogle, 'Oxford Market', pp. 5, 91–92.

94 Shadwell, *Enactments in Parliament . . . II, I George I–II George IV*, pp. 123–24, 178–79. For a list of announcements ordering the enforcement of the Market Acts, confining trade to the covered market, see Thwaites, 'Marketing', pp. 119–20.

95 Thwaites, 'Marketing', pp. 120–21.

began to be expressed. Thus, when Mr Wenman was required to determine whether country butchers were acting unlawfully in taking orders for meat and then sending it in for their customers, he replied that they were liable to the penalties of the Act because their actions seemed to defeat the purpose of a market, notably having provisions in a public place where they could be inspected by the clerks of the market and would be likely to be cheaper.[96] Meanwhile, an increase in the number of general market days gradually eroded the privileges of city tradesmen.[97]

During the crisis of 1795, the market committee could be found drawing on all its powers to threaten tradesmen. On 7 May it complained that traders were forestalling, engrossing and regrating, selling meat on Sunday and other provisions out of the market, all of which were either offences under common law or the terms of the Market Acts. At the meeting on 2 July, it was asserted that the regrating, particularly of meat, was continuing and a determination to put the law into execution against offenders was expressed. The stated motivation behind this crackdown was mixed. Thus the committee expressed concern that offences were injurious to the market revenue, 'to the great grievance of the inhabitants', and that regrating did in fact lead to price rises.[98] While it is possible that the 1795 crackdown was partly influenced by the threat of disturbances in Oxford, the committee's efforts to control marketing did not cease with the end of the crisis. In November 1797, it ordered that those selling meat out of the market be proceeded against and requested butchers to reduce the price of meat which appeared considerably higher than in the neighbourhood.[99] Moreover, in both 1808 and 1824, the committee issued essentially the same order as that of May 1795.[100] The work of the market committee therefore helped to keep alive the city's tradition of market regulation, even of price-fixing, by periodic restatement in a more modern context.

V

As the mid-century riots had taken place in the context of the trade to London, so the riots at the end of the century took place firmly in the context of the canal trade to the West Midlands. The first recorded incident was on 22 April 1795, when a handbill, which stated that the high price of provisions was an unacceptable grievance, was found in Oxford. In response, the town clerk, Thomas Walker, under the pseudonym 'Civis', printed a paper which was

---

96 'Papers of the market committee, 1774–1824', Oxford City Archives, D. 3. 11 (2).
97 Thwaites, 'Marketing', pp. 23–24.
98 'Book of the Oxford market committee', fols 96–100. The decisions of the market committee were published in *Jackson's Oxford Journal*, 16 May 1795; 4 July 1795. Arrears of rent were a problem at this time and may have influenced concern over revenue.
99 'Book of the Oxford market committee', fols 108–10.
100 'Papers of the market committee, 1774–1824', Oxford City Archives, D. 3. 11 (13) and (26).

largely a defence of the canal and the trade in corn to Warwickshire, indicating that the canal may already have been the root of the problem.[101] On 3 July, John Wills, President of Wadham and Vice-Chancellor, wrote to Dr Durell, Chairman of the Committee of the Company of Canal Proprietors, indicating that it had been signified to him that much 'sourness' had arisen among the lower class over the trade in corn from the canal wharf.[102] On 15 July, discontent spilled over into riot. While W. E. Taunton recorded that the initial disturbance was the work of 'a few turbulent women' and that all the rioters had achieved was 'to get an apron or a hat-full of flour . . .', other sources make it clear that a part of the riot must have taken place at the canal wharf.[103] Thus, in separate trials, William Cutland was acquitted of stealing two pecks of flour, the property of Francis Joule, from the canal wharf on 15 July, and Susannah Gray, spinster, was convicted for assisting in a riot at the coal wharf in July 1795 and for assaulting William Marsh.[104] Moreover, a letter written by Dr Durell on 17 July referred to the way in which the disturbance on Wednesday evening had intimidated those who used to supply the neighbourhood of Birmingham and Dudley.[105]

The canal was less of a focus in the 1800 riot. However, on 15 September a crowd of from 200 to 300 assembled at the house of the corn dealer, William Brookes, breaking the windows. The mayor of Oxford, finding that the reason for the attack was a belief among the crowd that Brookes was storing flour at the canal wharf, intending to send it out of the county, accompanied them to the wharf where, finding the rumour to be incorrect, they dispersed.[106]

As the Oxford riots of 1757 and 1766 had occurred within the wider framework of opposition by the Thames Valley towns and villages to the trade with London, so the riots of 1795 formed part of a wider pattern of unrest inspired by the trade with the West Midlands and the general feeling that corn was being illegally exported via Liverpool. In 1795, both Deddington and

---

101 'A calm address to the people of Oxford' in 'Oxford miscellanies', Bodleian Library, Ms Top Oxon b 116, fol. 81; *The Birch*, Vol. I, 1 May 1795, p. 3; 'Oxford Patriotism', Bodleian Library, G. A. Oxon c232, fol. 1.

102 'The committee book of the Oxford canal company, 1787–1797', Public Record Office, RAIL 855:4, fol. 427.

103 *A Short Address to the People of Oxford occasioned by the late Riot*, 2nd. edn. (1795), pp. 2, 7. Public Record Office, Privy Council 1/33/A87.

104 *Jackson's Oxford Journal*, 17 October 1795; 16 January 1796; 'QS minutes, 1791–1807', Oxford City Archives, O.2.11., fols 58, 61.

105 'The committee book of the Oxford canal company, 1787–1797', Public Record Office, RAIL 855:4, fols 429–30.

106 'W. E. Taunton to J. King, 23 September 1800', Public Record Office, Home Office 48:9, fol. 264. D. Durell reported to Portland that the canal wharf had been entered for the purpose of searching for corn. 'Portland to D. Durell, 19 September 1800', Public Record Office, Home Office 43:12, fol. 144.

Banbury further up the canal experienced disturbances.[107] Moreover, in 1800, rioting at Oxford and Banbury linked directly when a crowd in Oxford rallied to the cry of 'a loaf for a shilling' and tried to rescue three prisoners being brought to the county gaol after disturbances at Banbury.[108]

Other parallels exist between the late eighteenth-century disturbances and those of 1757 and 1766. In 1800, as in 1766, the crowd fixed prices. Thus, on 2 September, handbills appeared in different parts of Oxford inciting the poor to lower the price of provisions, and on 6 September the crowd forced the butter sellers to lower the price of butter and compelled four butchers to sell their meat at five pence instead of seven pence per pound.[109] In addition, the crowd remained concerned with traditional market regulations, threatening fore-stallers and complaining about the way in which the university was setting the assize of bread.[110] However, again like the mid-century rioters, the crowd in 1800 combined its continued interest in traditional regulation with an intelligent awareness of the shift away from the open market. Thus, on 6 September, the crowd went to the Crown Inn where it roughly treated an Abingdon mealman, Thomas Jones, and bargained with him for a reduction in the price of his meal.[111]

Nevertheless, it was not all continuity. Thus, in spite of the role of the university in regulating marketing in Oxford, until 1800 university officials appear not to have been the victim of food rioters. However, on 8 October 1800, a crowd assembled at Corpus Christi College and, when President John Cooke, Pro Vice-Chancellor, arrived, lamps and windows were broken and someone threw a stone which knocked off Cooke's cap.[112]

On top of this, there also seems, for the first time, to have been a hostile interest in the colleges as landowners and recipients of corn rents. The precise meaning of an anonymous letter sent to the Duke of Portland, the Home Secretary, on 12 September is a little unclear. It attributed his having sent troops to Oxford to his desire to keep up the incomes of the canons of Christ

---

107 F. M. Eden, *The State of the Poor, II, Parochial Reports–England* (3 vols, London, 1797), pp. 587, 591.

108 'R. Bignell to Charles Butler, 16 September 1800', inclosure in 'George Isted to J. King, 17 September 1800', Public Record Office, Home Office 42:51, fols 229–30; 'D. Harris to J. King, 16 September 1800', Public Record Office, Home Office 48:9, fol. 234; 'Examinations and depositions of witnesses, October 1800', Public Record Office, Home Office 48:9, fols 238–60.

109 'David Hughes to Portland, 4 September 1800; 7 September 1800; 15 September 1800', Public Record Office, Home Office 42:51, fols 36, 59, 155.

110 'David Hughes to Portland, 7 September 1800', Public Record Office, Home Office 42:51, fols 59–60; 'The examination of Thomas Robinson', inclosure in 'Dr Marlow to Portland, 17 October 1800', Public Record Office, Home Office 42:52, fol. 84. The problems which arose over the assize of bread in Oxford during the crisis of 1800 are discussed in Thwaites, 'Assize', pp. 178–79.

111 'David Hughes to Portland, 7 September 1800', Public Record Office, Home Office 42:51, fol. 59.

112 'The examination of Thomas Robinson', Public Record Office, Home Office 42:52, fols. 84–85.

Church and other members of the university.[113] However, another anonymous letter, this time to the proprietors of the Sun Fire Insurance, was completely unequivocal. It warned against insuring college properties because of a conspiracy to burn down college farms. The author blamed a rise in prices on the dispatch of printed handbills by the Vice-Chancellor, prompted by Portland, to college tenants, promising to protect and justify them whatever price they asked for corn.[114]

A further extension in the crowd's activities involved a direct targeting of farms. Each night from 13 September, a crowd of between 50 and 200 people assembled in the middle of Oxford and went from there to neighbouring farms and mills, obtaining agreement that wheat and flour would be brought to Oxford market on 20 September and sold at £20 per load.[115] This form of crowd action was particularly successful and orderly, and was remarked upon as such by Sir Christopher Willoughby, the Chairman of the Quarter Sessions, and John Cooke.[116] Cooke, who attended the market on 20 September in an attempt to prevent open disturbances, wrote to Portland that the dealers in corn and butter were influenced in the prices they asked by the crowd's nocturnal excursions. There was even a suggestion that the farmers had been required to sign papers for the sale of their corn.[117] Some certainly obeyed the crowd. Over a period of three consecutive Saturdays, 33 sales of wheat took place in Oxford market at £20 per load or under.[118]

In 1800, therefore, the crowd not merely concerned itself with marketing through from farm to retail market but, in its systematic approach to local farmers, produced behaviour which was reminiscent of that of seventeenth-century university officials. This type of crowd action was not unique to Oxford. Within the county, there were similar excursions from Witney.[119] However, it is possible that the university's traditional right to call in produce from the

113 'Portland to David Hughes, 12 September 1800' in '3rd Duke of Portland, copies of private letters, July 1797–1801', University of Nottingham, PWV III.
114 'Anonymous letter to the proprietors of the Sun Fire Insurance Office, London', inclosure in 'Mr Watts to J. King, 1 November 1800', Public Record Office, Home Office 42:53, fol. 12.
115 'Sir Christopher Willoughby to Portland, 17 September 1800; 21 September 1800', Public Record Office, Home Office 42:51, fols 92, 338–40.
116 'Sir Christopher Willoughby to Portland, 21 September 1800', Public Record Office, Home Office 42:51, fol. 338; 'John Cooke to Portland, 21 September 1800', Public Record Office, Home Office 42:51, fol. 319. Joshua Harris mentioned that the crowd had a leader who, on its return to Carfax, ordered the crowd to disperse. 'The examination and deposition of Mr Joshua Harris', Public Record Office, Home Office 48:9, fol. 240.
117 'Portland to Duke of Marlborough, 22 September 1800', Public Record Office, Home Office 43:12, fol. 159; 'John Cooke to Portland, 21 September 1800', Public Record Office, Home Office 42:51, fol. 319.
118 All recorded sales on 20 September were at £20 per load. On 27 September 17 loads were sold at or under £20. 'Corn returns, 1797–1800', Oxford University Archives, MR 3/5/8.
119 'John Cobb to Portland, 26 September 1800', Public Record Office, Home Office 42:51, fol. 468.

neighbourhood was, like the *Book of Orders*, reinforcing the idea of a 'moral economy', both in the city and elsewhere.

The authorities in Oxford, denied the support of central government for any interference with the operation of free trade yet faced with months of crisis and smouldering discontent, produced more mixed and uncertain responses to the crises of 1795 and 1800 than they had shown during the mid-century crisis.

While the canal trade was apparently the principal cause of the 1795 disturbances, a response to it was perhaps the most difficult problem for the authorities. There was only one unexceptionable course of action over the canal trade, and that was to request information as to whether Oxfordshire corn was being exported because, with an export ban in force, legal sanctions existed against the practice. This was done.[120] A much more difficult issue concerned whether the normal trade with the West Midlands could be prevented. Reservations over this trade were widespread. Thus, no less a person than the Vice-Chancellor suggested to Dr Durell that, while he did not know whether the traffic in corn along the canal could be stopped, he did think it should be considered.[121] The subsequent enquiry from Durell to John King, Under Secretary of State, led to an unequivocal statement from government supporting the free circulation of provisions.[122] Though compelled to accept the concept of 'free circulation', neither city nor county magistrates seem to have felt obliged to exert themselves to further it. Thus, on 28 July 1795, a letter from Birmingham on the problems of obtaining corn commented that Mr Tabernor had reported that the mayor of Oxford had been applied to by a cornfactor for the protection of corn he had wished to move to Birmingham, but the mayor would not assure him of aid.[123] In 1800, the mayor of Oxford was openly criticized by Portland over the incident at the canal wharf, for failing to appreciate that it was his duty to protect the free progress of grain from one part of the country to the other.[124]

If there was widespread disquiet over the canal trade and the discontent it was causing, there were nevertheless individuals who were prepared to defend

120 'The committee book of the Oxford canal company, 1787–1797', Public Record Office, RAIL 855:4, fols 417–18; *Jackson's Oxford Journal*, 11 July 1795.
121 'The committee book of the Oxford canal company, 1787–1797', Public Record Office, RAIL 855:4, fols 427–28.
122 'The committee book of the Oxford canal company, 1787–1797', Public Record Office, RAIL 855:4, fols 429–30; 'J. King to Mr Durell, 21 July 1795', Public Record Office, Home Office 43:7, fol. 27.
123 'Mr Garbett to Mr Legge, 28 July 1795', Public Record Office, Privy Council 1/27/A56. Mr 'Tabberner' is recorded buying barley in Oxford in the 'Corn returns, 1795–1797', Oxford University Archives, MR 3/5/7. Several spellings of his name are given. For a discussion of his activities, see Thwaites, 'Marketing', pp. 280–81. For criticism of the county magistrates, 'Letter from Samuel Garbett, 4 August 1795', Public Record Office, Privy Council 1/29/A64.
124 'Portland to D. Durell, 19 September 1800', Public Record Office, Home Office 43:12, fol. 144.

it. However, while their defence may have reflected genuine beliefs in the justice of the trade, it is noticeable that they each possessed a vested interest in the canal's success and/or profitability. Thus Thomas Walker, who defended the canal trade in April 1795, had been town clerk of Oxford since 1756 and, in that capacity, had helped to prepare and solicit the canal bill.[125] Walker's paper was roundly condemned by the anonymous and unidentified 'Academicus' in his publication *The Birch*. 'Academicus' believed that the completion of the canal was indisputably keeping corn from Oxford market and raising prices.[126] Other criticisms of Walker by 'Academicus' followed, and he claimed some of the credit when Walker resigned as town clerk on 29 July 1795.[127] Walker's replacement was W. E. Taunton, who held the office of town clerk until 1825.[128] After the disturbance in July 1795, he wrote a homily to the crowd, rather more general than that by Walker, but with a not-dissimilar approach to the canal.[129] In 1770 he possessed five £100 shares in the canal company, and in 1793 had bought £2,000 of stock.[130]

If there was an equivocal element in the response of the authorities to the canal trade, in other respects their reaction to the crisis of 1795 seems to have been similar to their approach to the mid-century riots, although promises to regulate corn marketing seem to have been more an attempt to head off riot than a direct response to it. Thus on 8 July, before the major riot, the corporation determined that it would prosecute those forestalling, engrossing and regrating corn and recommended that farmers avoid selling to corn dealers and deal immediately with mealmen and bakers.[131] Once the riot had taken place on 15 July, the Corporation took a less sympathetic approach to the crowd's grievances and concentrated on the suppression of disturbance.[132]

However, as Oxford emerged from the 1795 riots and the problem of the crowd became less pressing, a change began to appear in the stated attitude of the city authorities. As the crisis of high prices continued into the autumn, they appear to have developed a growing sense of identity as urban, middle-class consumers. Thus, in an address to the two city Members of Parliament on 4

125 Crossley, *Victoria History*, pp. 184, 224–25; Phillips, *A General History*, p. 202.
126 *The Birch*, Vol. I, 1 May 1795, pp. 3–5.
127 'Academicus' criticized Walker for his close connection with the Duke of Marlborough. *The Birch*, Vol. III, 1 July 1795, p. 22; Vol. IV, 17 August 1795, pp. 27–28; Hobson, *Oxford Council Acts, 1752–1801*, p. 235.
128 Crossley, *Victoria History*, pp. 224–25. Taunton resigned as city solicitor when he took up his post as town clerk.
129 *A Short Address*, pp. 3–5.
130 'Oxford and Coventry canal navigation company minutes', Bodleian Library, Ms Top Oxon c 551, fols 91–92; 'Transfer book of Oxford canal company 1793–1800', Bodleian Library, Ms Top Oxon c 753, fol. 39.
131 *Jackson's Oxford Journal*, 11 July 1795; Hobson, *Oxford Council Acts 1752–1801*, p. 233.
132 *Jackson's Oxford Journal*, 18 July 1795; Hobson, *Oxford Council Acts, 1752–1801*, pp. 234–35.

November, they declared that the causes of the crisis appeared almost wholly artificial and waxed eloquent on the problems of the 'middling class', those living upon 'stated incomes, or by the profit of a small trade' and who were trapped between high prices and an increased poor's rate.[133] An Oxfordshire farmer was quick to point out the perhaps rather selfish motivation behind their address, commenting that most of them had formerly wielded the labouring oar and had risen by the same methods they condemned in the farmers.[134]

The growing consumer consciousness of the city authorities added a new dimension to the 1800 crisis. Dr David Hughes, fellow of Jesus College, who was a major source of Portland's information on the Oxford riots, felt that the city authorities bore a measure of responsibility for the 1800 disturbances. Thus, between 3 and 12 September the city leaders, through the council, a meeting of the inhabitants and a committee appointed by the latter, passed a series of resolutions on the crisis. They determined, among other things, that the high price of necessities was not justified, that subscriptions should be opened to pay for the prosecution of marketing offences, and that the inhabitants be recommended to abstain from the use of butter while the price was so high. The varied resolutions appeared in *Jackson's Oxford Journal* on 6 September or 13 September, and Hughes felt strongly that there was bound to be a disturbance on the latter date as a combination of Saturday night ale and the words of the mayor and his committee worked on the poor.[135] The fact that the crowd had fixed the price of butter on 6 September, the same day that the council's recommendation of a boycott had appeared in the paper, may suggest that Hughes' fears were not unreasonable. However, as the first resolution of the council on the crisis, on 3 September, followed the appearance of the handbills calling on the poor to regulate the markets, it is possible that the authorities may themselves have been responding to crowd pressure.

Ultimately, the problem of determining the exact relationship between crowd and city authorities would seem to reflect the widespread dissatisfaction with high prices in 1800. The grievances of the crowd and city authorities were similar and the distinction between them perhaps not absolute. Thus, five members of the city council were among those to purchase the cheap wheat which the crowd had insisted be brought to market. Between them they benefited from 19 of the 33 low-price transactions.[136] When the bakers in Abingdon also refused to give more than £20 per load for wheat, the town's

133 *Jackson's Oxford Journal*, 7 November 1795.

134 *A Reply to the Instructions*, p. 10.

135 Hobson, *Oxford Council Acts, 1752–1801*, pp. 276–77; *Jackson's Oxford Journal*, 6 September 1800; 13 September 1800; 'David Hughes to Portland, 15 September 1800', Public Record Office, Home Office 42:51, fol. 154.

136 Hobson, *Oxford Council Acts, 1752–1801*, pp. 278–80; 'Corn returns, 1797–1800', Oxford University Archives, MR 3/5/8.

mayor blamed the problem on the inadequate conduct of the Oxford magistrates.[137] The Oxford Armed Association of Loyal Volunteers, in which a large section of the city population was involved and which had been founded in April 1798 with the brief to help in the suppression of riots and disorder, was suspect in 1800.[138] Thus, Hughes expressed the opinion that the city volunteers would be unlikely to exert themselves against a crowd who wished to lower provisions prices, and it seemed as though his fears were justified when one of those seen unloading butter from a cart was a member of the city association.[139] However, we should not go on from this to conclude that the city leaders were actively involved in riot. Thus, around 1805, when there were approximately 900 volunteers, 42 were apprentices and 14 labourers, very much the people one might expect to find in the crowd.[140]

Definite faces in the crowd tend not to emerge in 1800. The only named rioter was one 'Dunn', present at but not responsible for the attack on John Cooke. All that is known about him is that he had a large family.[141] General accounts suggest that the rioters were apprentices, journeymen and small tradesmen. Thus, on 6 September, a notice invited journeymen carpenters to make a guillotine for the destruction of mealmen, farmers and higglers, and David Hughes found one of his own tradesmen among the rioters.[142]

Given Hughes' persistent condemnation of the city leaders and the first hints of threats to university figures and college properties, it is perhaps tempting to postulate a split between university and city in 1800. However, the evidence points to serious criticism of the city authorities and their interpretation of the crisis from Hughes alone, and this may be partly explicable in terms of his own experience and position. Thus, unlike the other university figures principally concerned with the disturbances, the Vice-Chancellor and John Cooke, Hughes appears not to have been involved in the regulation of marketing. On the other hand, he was a small farmer at Bessels Leigh, where he was rector, and aware of the deficiency of his own crops.[143] Not only were Cooke, who had

137 'G. Knapp to Portland, 29 September 1800', Public Record Office, Home Office 42:52, fols 514, 523.
138 *Jackson's Oxford Journal*, 14 April 1798; 12 May 1798.
139 'David Hughes to Portland, 4 September 1800; 7 September 1800', Public Record Office, Home Office 42:51, fols 36, 59. David Hughes appears to have been the chairman of the general committee regulating the volunteer corps in the university in 1798. 'Oxford Patriotism', Bodleian Library, G. A. Oxon c 232, fol. 3. J. Bohstedt discusses the involvement of the volunteers in Devon riots. Bohstedt, *Riots and Community Politics*, pp. 49–51.
140 *Pamphlets: OLV* (c 1805), Bodleian Library, G. A. Oxon 8⁰ 161 (14).
141 'Dr Marlow to Portland, 17 October 1800', Public Record Office, Home Office 42:52, fols 86–87.
142 'David Hughes to Portland, 7 September 1800', Public Record Office, Home Office 42:51, fols 59–60.
143 'David Hughes to Portland, 14 September 1800', Public Record Office, Home Office 42:51, fol. 140.

been Vice-Chancellor and was a member of the market committee, and Michael Marlow, the Vice-Chancellor, accustomed to the regulation of marketing, but they were both county magistrates with a responsibility to keep order in Oxfordshire.[144] There seems to have been a recognition that this involved tackling the crowd's grievances as well as condemning the riots. Thus on 16 October, a meeting of county magistrates, at which Cooke, Marlow and also Dr Durell were present, passed a series of resolutions which may have included a condemnation of riots but otherwise failed to reflect the beliefs on marketing of central government. They called on Parliament to suppress jobbing, forestalling, engrossing and regrating, and suggested that an act to enforce the sale of grain in bulk in the open market would be expedient.[145]

However, if it would be false to portray city and university as representing opposite viewpoints, there is no doubt that the city authorities found themselves in conflict with central government, both for their overt continued espousal of traditional market regulations and for their apparently relaxed attitude to the riots. Thus W. E. Taunton, who, in a letter to the War Office, dismissed the significance of the crowd's fixing of the price of butter, was severely rebuked by Portland, who saw the incident as an unjustifiable attack on property.[146] Again, the supposed failure of the city authorities to prevent the rioting at the gaol led Portland to contemplate proceeding against the mayor 'by indictment or information' for neglect of his duty.[147] The investigation was very thorough, and it was not until November that the Lord Chancellor was able to declare that there were insufficient grounds to prosecute the mayor.[148]

Nevertheless, while it is tempting to stress the deep clash of philosophical and practical attitudes between central government and city authorities, it is possible that the reality of the conflict can be exaggerated. First, government's approach to the problems of Oxford was determined, to some extent, by its sources of information, and some reporting was definitely misleading. Thus, Portland's shock over the attack on the gaol was partly explicable on the basis of an exaggerated report written by Richard Bignell, which referred to a crowd of 3,000 trying to rescue the prisoners and the mob being determined to pull down

---

144 It was Cooke who, as a member of the market committee in 1797, had pressed for every week day to be a general market day for the sale of meat. 'Book of the Oxford market committee', fols 111–12.

145 *Jackson's Oxford Journal*, 18 October 1800.

146 'W. E. Taunton to War Office, 6 September 1800', Public Record Office, War Office 40:17; J. King to W. E. Taunton, 8 September 1800', Public Record Office, Home Office 43:12, fols 106–07.

147 'J. Mitford and W. Grant to Portland, 30 October 1800', Public Record Office, Home Office 48:9, fol. 228.

148 Public Record Office, Home Office 48:9, fol. 226.

the gaol.[149] A much more realistic appreciation of the nature of the riot at the gaol comes from the realization that the total cost of the damage was £6:14s.6d., of which £2:16s.8d. was for crockery and a watch belonging to the porter.[150] Second, there was, in fact, no reliable alternative power source in Oxford, partly because the riots occurred in the long vacation when the university officials were frequently absent.[151] Third, a combination of inertia and local political loyalties meant there was little backing for a concerted attack on the city authorities. Thus Portland, who was angered by the approach of W. E. Taunton, the town clerk, to the crisis of 1800, pointed out to the Duke of Marlborough, the *custodes rotulorum*, that Taunton could be dismissed as clerk of the peace, a post he had held since 1781, on the representation of the magistrates to Marlborough.[152] However, Cyril Jackson, the immensely influential Dean of Christ Church, confided that Marlborough shrank from business.[153] Moreover, Taunton, like Walker before him, was a prominent lawyer and closely connected with Marlborough.[154] Portland's suggestion fell on deaf ears. Taunton went on to be knighted in 1814 and T. H. Taunton, his son, whose activities as secretary of the committee of inhabitants in September 1800 were commented upon unfavourably to Portland by Hughes, succeeded him as clerk of the peace.[155] It is perhaps ultimately not surprising that city authorities and central government both made concessions and avoided a final, and perhaps mutually damaging, showdown.[156]

During the summer of 1801, the Reverend Robert Trotman Coates was on his perambulations of the Corpus Christi college estates and corresponded with the president, John Cooke. With Coates was the solicitor W. E. Taunton. At Cullompton there was a dispute over a copyhold, and Coates, reporting on the

---

149 'R. Bignell to Charles Butler, 16 September 1800', inclosure in 'George Isted to J. King, 17 September 1800', Public Record Office, Home Office 42:51, fols 229–30. Bignell was the canal company's solicitor. 'The committee book of the Oxford canal company, 1787–1797', Public Record Office, RAIL 855:4, fol. 417.

150 'Quarter Sessions Bundles, Epiphany 1801', Oxfordshire Record Office.

151 On 14 September, David Hughes wrote from Bessels Leigh, the following day from Nettlebed and on 19 September from Marlow. 'David Hughes to Portland, 14, 15 and 19 September', Public Record Office, Home Office 42:51, fols 140, 154, 222.

152 'Portland to Duke of Marlborough, 29 September 1800', Public Record Office, Home Office 43:12, fol. 204. Crossley, *Victoria History*, p. 224; *Jackson's Oxford Journal*, 29 December 1781.

153 'Letter from Cyril Jackson, 21 October 1800', Public Record Office, Home Office 42:52, fol. 201.

154 Crossley, *Victoria History*, p. 224.

155 *The Tauntons of Oxford by One of Them* (London, Elliot Stock, 1902), pp. 4, 6, 54; 'David Hughes to Portland, 14 September 1800', Public Record Office, Home Office 42:51, fol. 140.

156 Neither side backed down philosophically, but the city council adopted a more conciliatory attitude to the use of troops while central government decided that the prosecution of a magistrate, the mayor, was something to be avoided. 'W. E. Taunton to J. King, 16 September 1800', Public Record Office, Home Office 42:51, fol. 183; 'J. Mitford to J. King, 31 October 1800', Public Record Office, Home Office 48:9, fol. 263.

failure to secure agreement, commented that he did not think it in the interests of the college to abate one sixpence. Mr Taunton sent his compliments to John Cooke.[157] The riots were over and life had returned to normal, and normal life in Oxford meant a college wishing to profit from its estates, while its president was simultaneously regulating marketing in the consumer's interest. It meant, too, Taunton holding stock in the canal while, as clerk to the market committee, continuing to put his signature to documents condemning forestalling.[158] It involved, moreover, Taunton, whom government held blameworthy in the Oxford riots, on amicable terms with the riot victim, Cooke. Neither rioters nor central government had fundamentally altered Oxford society.

In dearth, conflict between the food needs of the city and those of the major population centres was almost inevitable. With the construction of the canal, the problems were exacerbated. At the same time, Oxford not merely possessed a strong tradition of market regulation in the consumer's interest but had seen a major restatement of that position when the covered market was constructed. The crowd reacted strongly to the pressures of the market economy, while drawing strength and arguments from the framework of regulation. The authorities, perhaps not even aware of the ambivalence in their own attitudes, and well versed in the tradition of regulation, reacted to the crowd in a way that suggested riot was still an intelligible and successful form of protest.

---

157 'Bundle of correspondence of President Cooke, 1801', Corpus Christi College Archives.
158 He had been delegated by the city to be a member of the committee but had resigned to become clerk. 'Book of the Oxford market committee', fol. 5.

Chapter 8

THE IRISH FAMINE OF 1799–1801: MARKET CULTURE, MORAL ECONOMIES AND SOCIAL PROTEST

ROGER WELLS

In Ireland, as in Britain, market forces exercised a powerful influence over the later eighteenth-century agrarian economy. Local marketing systems, with the numerous modest market towns drawing foodstuffs from limited hinterlands, were themselves subsumed in a national marketing system which embraced most of the country, with perhaps the partial exception of the remotest parts of Connacht. Dublin demand for food exercised a pervasive influence over the country, roughly paralleled by London's predominance on the mainland. However, in Ireland, a countervailing force derived from the much larger British market, which sucked in exports of oats, oatmeal, wheat, meat and dairy products from Ireland. Capitalism was central to Irish agricultural production, distribution, manufacture, retail, and export. Whatever the difference of scale, these similarities between food-marketing systems in Britain and Ireland have not generated much comparative study of responses to food shortages, dearth, and even famine in the two countries. In Britain, E. P. Thompson's critical concept of the moral economy, notably the key role of the various forms of food rioting, has been widely debated. Curiously, Irish experiences and evidence have been largely excluded. Irish evidence is important in its own right, though it is vital that it should be firmly located within an Irish context. The food supply to the Irish was affected by its colonial status, and in the immediate aftermath of the rebellion of 1798, by further complications deriving from the political situation as the authorities struggled to extinguish the residues of that rebellion. The famine of 1799–1801 nevertheless revealed various confrontations between moral and market economies and provoked government intervention. These are of importance in themselves, and of significance for subsequent dearths, including the Great Famine commencing in the mid-1840s. Their study also adds key comparative details about market culture, moral-economic precepts and the nature of social protest in both countries.

I

The 1799–1801 famine's causal factors were the identical weather conditions responsible for the devastating mainland situation.[1] The extraordinarily cold summer of 1799, and prolonged precipitation from May until the late autumn, delayed harvesting and badly reduced cereal yields. The rains caused extensive flooding and seriously compromised potatoes by rotting proportions of the unharvestable main crop in the ground. In later November, rain-drenched oats remained in Co. Wexford fields while frost gave the *coup de grâce* to potatoes in Co. Meath.[2]

In contrast, the 1800 deficiencies derived principally from the prolonged drought over almost the entire summer. Drought wrecked early potatoes, while the heavy rains which fell in late August were too late for the main potato crop. Although there were regional variations, with the Connacht crop being 'tolerably good', other considerable areas reported decimations, notably Co. Kerry. Cereal crops varied widely. Good ones were reported from the south-west, where all grains, especially wheat, looked 'remarkably well' considering the drought. Ulster barley was reputedly 'abundant' and 'excellent', but that province's critical oat crops were mixed; in parts they were 'abundant', elsewhere but 'tolerable'.[3] Once again, in Ireland as in Britain, the 1801 harvest produced a bumper crop of all cereals. As much more Irish land was devoted to potatoes than normal, the unprecedented but common claim was made that their 'abundance will far exceed the usual consumption'. The prolific 1801 harvest terminated the crisis.[4]

---

1 R. Wells, *Wretched Faces: Famine in Wartime England, 1793–1801* (Gloucester, Alan Sutton, 1989), pp. 37–39.

2 Steward Wainright to Earl Fitzwilliam, 21 November 1799, Sheffield City Library, Wentworth Woodhouse Muniments, F89, f. 229. 'Minutes of a Conversation of a Meeting Assembled . . . to consider the Supply of Corn . . . & the best means of preventing a Scarcity', 9 November 1799; Mayor of Cork, to Castlereagh, and Postmaster, Kells, to J. Lees, 2 and 23 November 1799, National Archives of Ireland, OP, Series II, 72/6; State of the Country Papers, I, 1018/20. *Belfast Newsletter*, 31 May, 20 August, 24 September and 19 November 1799, and 3 January 1801.

3 William Gregory, Coole, Co. Galway, to Marsden, 7 September 1800; J. Hassard, to Castlereagh, 19 August 1800; J. Hancock, Lisburn, to Littlehales, 17 October; Sir F. Flood, near Wexford, and Sir G. Hill, Belfast, to Cooke, 8 September and 2 December 1800; Lord Altamont, Bulinasloe, to Marsden, 23 October 1800; Archbishop of Cashel, to Cornwallis, 26 August 1800; J. Collins, Tipperary, to J. Lees, 19 August 1800, National Archives of Ireland, 620 [Rebellion papers] 620/49/72; 620/57/52, 62, 64, 107, 124, 146, 148. Slane Flour Mill manager's letters (hence Jebb letter book), 15 July, 12 August, 10 September, 11 and 25 November, and 9 December 1800, National Library of Ireland, Ms. 11,877. *Cork Advertiser*, 4 and 20 September and 18 November 1800.

4 Bishop of Killala, to Marsden, 22 April 1801; Lt Craig, Wicklow, and W. Parker, Cork, to C. Abbot, 1 and 19 September 1801, National Archives of Ireland, State of the Country Papers, I, 1020/28; II, 115/15: 620/59/17. *Cork Advertiser*, 13 June, 3 September and 20 October 1801. Jebb letter book, 7 October 1801, National Library of Ireland, Ms. 11,877. John Tydd, Humbertstown, Co. Limerick, to Pelham, 2 September 1801, British Library Add. Mss. 33107, ff. 407–08.

In some senses, the two consecutive famine seasons were 'potato-led'. As potatoes rarely figured in the export trade, the supply was perennially fragile and the entire crop was consumed indigenously whatever its yield from year to year.[5] If contemporaries united in the view that potatoes constituted the 'general support of the labouring part' of the population, quantitative estimations of the degree of dependency varied at the turn of the century. One authority asserted that 'at least' half of the people 'use potatoes as their principal food', while another concluded that 90 per cent derived three-quarters of their food from the root. Dependency was greatest among smaller farmers, including dual-occupationists, and the rural 'labouring Poor', the cottiers and agricultural labourers customarily dependent 'on their Potatoe Garden for their Sustenance', supplemented principally by oatmeal purchased to tide them over between the exhaustion of their potato stocks in the spring and the new harvest in the late summer.[6] But potatoes were a primary staple of working-class diets everywhere, including the towns. Deficient potato yields dictated that producers consumed their own stocks much earlier in the season, while those dependent on market supplies faced hugely inflated prices, exemplified by the December 1800 Belfast cost of 42d. for a bushel normally fetching 8d. Potatoes dug in 1799 lasted until February 1800, instead of the usual early summer period, and identical calculations were made for the 1800–01 season, except for parts of Connacht, where drought had been less intense. Rural labourers usually commanded 'little work in the early part of the Spring', and were forced into reliance on 'ready Money' to purchase food in a 'Public Market' at the very season when cash was the problem.[7] Additional problems concerned seed potatoes, as small farmers, cottiers and labourers with gardens tended in exigencies to consume stocks normally reserved for seed, thereby driving up seed-potato prices.[8] Those usually dependent on potatoes were forced to

5 R. Griffith, Dublin, to Cornwallis, 16 January and 7 February 1801, National Archives of Ireland, OP, 115/12.
6 J. Collins, Tipperary, to J. Lees, and J. Galbraith, Barons Co., to Littlehales, 8 and 19 August 1800; T. Ellis, Castlebar, to Cooke, 18 February 1801; R. Griffith, Dublin, and R. Baggs, Carlingford, to Cornwallis, 16 January and 7 February 1801, National Archives of Ireland, 620/57/64, 123; OP, II, 115/11-2, 16. *Cork Advertiser*, 4 and 20 September 1800. Cf. P. M. A. Bourke, 'The use of the potato crop in pre-Famine Ireland', *Journal of the Statistical and Social Inquiry Society of Ireland*, Vol. XXI, No. 6, 1967–68, pp. 74–77, 80–83. E. M. Crawford, 'Dearth, diet and disease in Ireland: a case study of nutritional deficiency', *Medical History*, Vol. XXVIII, 1984, p. 152 and note 6. J. Archer, *Statistical Survey of the County Dublin* (Dublin, Dublin Society, 1802), pp. 43–44. R. Fraser, *A General View of the Agriculture . . . of the County Wicklow* (Dublin, Dublin Society, 1801), pp. 54, 102.
7 R. Griffith, Dublin, and R. Baggs, Carlingford, to Cornwallis, 16 January and 7 February 1801, L. M. Cullen, *An Economic History of Ireland since 1660* (London, Batsford, 1972), p. 70.
8 Cornwallis to Portland, 28 July 1800; Commissary General, Ireland, Colonel Handfield, to Cornwallis, December 1800, Public Record Office, Home Office Papers 100/94, ff. 122–23, 263–68. *Ennis Chronicle*, 29 January 1801. Hill to Cooke, 2 December 1800, National Archives of Ireland, 620/49/72.

compensate by consuming 'Corn of various descriptions' over a much longer part of the season than normal.[9]

If cereal deficiencies were universal and serious only in 1799, the potato shortage injected fierce inflationary pressures into the market for corn. The complete exhaustion of the 1799 cereal crop by the time of the 1800 harvest meant that the usual 'carry over' residue was absent in 1800–01, thus negating any positive effect from the somewhat better crops in 1800. Normal surpluses of oats and wheat were eradicated, and only partially compensated by consumers switching to barley, customarily used for malting and distilling. Wheat price trends traditionally led the entire cereal market and these duly rocketed, partly in response to internal conditions but also in reflection of the achievement of record mainland cereal prices.[10] Ironically, Irish cereal prices were driven to levels which triggered automatic banning of exports under the Corn Laws from mid-1799 to January 1802. But the scale of cereal price inflation ensured that most customers, including significant sectors of the middle class, experienced a rapid erosion of their living standards. The situation of all working-class consumers was seriously jeopardized, whether they were principally dependent on potatoes and seasonal oat supplementation over most rural regions, or the greater relative users of oatmeal notably in the four 'proto-industrial counties' of north-eastern Ulster. Higher-paid urban artisans, particularly numerous in Dublin and Cork, who subsisted partially on cheaper grades of wheaten-flour, were identically situated. The 'poorest of the People', namely those with the heaviest dependency on potatoes—in one calculation an eighth of the five million population—would be unable 'to purchase Corn, [and] are likely to perish thro' famine'.[11]

Several critical considerations should caution against orthodox historical claims that pre-1845 famines were local or regional and were exclusively 'potato led'. First, potatoes were less difficult to transport than often assumed. They passed through local marketing systems to the ports. In 1799, for example, in addition to the huge but unquantified stocks coming down the canals and overland to Dublin, the metropolis received 8,567 tons of potatoes up to the end of October from no less than 16 ports. These were dominated by Kinsale (4,550.5) and Baltimore (1,630) in Co. Cork, and Strangford in Co. Down with 902, but among the more minor sources was the 20 tons from Killybegs in Co.

---

9 Cornwallis to Portland, 3 December 1800, Public Record Office, Home Office Papers 100/94, ff. 256–60.
10 Jebb letter book, 11 November 1800, National Library of Ireland, Ms. 11,877. *Belfast Newsletter*, 27 June 1800.
11 *Cork Advertiser*, 3 January, 26 June and 4 August 1801. 'Minutes of Conversation . . .', 9 November 1799, National Archives of Ireland, OP, II.72/6. J. M'Evoy, *Statistical Account of the County of Tyrone* (Dublin, Dublin Society, 1802), p. 39.

Donegal.[12] If acute shortages drove up potato prices everywhere, a rough parity in this inflation derived from the embryonic national market.

The national market was far more developed in cereals. Wheat was critical, and its centrality in part derived from Foster's 1784 Act which aimed through the provision of bounties to stabilize wheaten flour supplies to Dublin. It had effects way beyond legislators' anticipations. While it deliberately accelerated the increases in acreages set to wheat by capitalist farmers, its profound impact in enhanced investment in corn-milling comprised 'an industrial revolution in milling' which was less foreseeable.[13] So too was the genesis of a commercial interdependency linking capitalist farmers, provincial millers, Dublin flour factors, bakers and metropolitan consumers. In 1800, Dublin merchant McGuere informed Lord Lieutenant Cornwallis that:

> When a Mill is erected, the Flour Factor agrees to take all the Flour manufactured at the Mill to be delivered in such portions as he may in future order. The Miller in consequence engages to take all the Grain within his District and the Farmer is induced to agree as he will deliver it without Expense of atten[din]g Markets or going distant from his residence . . . that the [Dublin flour] Market should not be overstocked the Factors . . . agree among themselves not to bring more than will preserve . . . their accustomed profitts.

This national infrastructure created semi-incestuous characteristics. 'The Scene of Mercantile Transactions . . . is . . . confined, and the Communication between the Corn Factors in Dublin and the Millers in every Part of the Country . . . [is] closely kept up.'[14] Thirdly, this system and the stimulus to capitalist agrarian production also facilitated the growth of the export trade in cereals. Although some big wheat millers, including Jebb and Co. at Slane, also dealt in oats, less is known about the more ubiquitous merchants and mealmen who specialized in oat distribution and oatmeal production. The scale of exports in both commodities is a certain indicator of sophisticated commercial structures, operated by those with considerable investment capital.

While famine conditions generated greater aggregate dependency on the market, the erosion of working-class real incomes led to reduced demand for basic manufactured goods, notably textiles. The different branches of that major Irish industry were also affected by a parallel situation in British markets and further disruptions of overseas markets owing to the war. As food prices

---

12 Dublin potato supply, 1 January 1798 to 6 November 1799, National Archives of Ireland, OP, II, 72/6. Cf. Bourke, 'The use of the potato crop', p. 88.

13 L. M. Cullen, 'Eighteenth-century flour milling in Ireland', *Irish Economic and Social History*, Vol. IV, 1977. L. M. Cullen, *An Economic History of Ireland*, pp. 92–93. J. Barry, 'The Duke of Devonshire's Irish estates, 1794–7', *Analecta Hibernica*, Vol. 22, 1960, p. 279.

14 McGuere, 'Observations with respect to the Scarcity of Corn', 20 November 1799, National Archives of Ireland, OP, II, 72/6. Commissary-general's report, enclosed Cornwallis to Portland, 3 December 1800, Public Record Office, Home Office Papers 100/94, ff. 263–68.

also struck at non-agrarian middle-class domestic economies, service industries, including building, were adversely affected, too. Industrial and especially urban employment prospects worsened throughout the crises. Dublin artisans were unable to secure 'Employment in their Respective Trades' during the winter of 1799–1800. The problem recurred on a broader scale during 1800–01. In January 1801, hundreds of skilled men were unemployed in Cork, together with almost all stuff weavers in Limerick City. Both the linen and cotton manufactures in the Drogheda district stagnated. The most spectacular industrial failure, that of the Sadleir brothers' massive cotton enterprise near Cork, saw 4,000 employees thrown out of work in 1801. Adverse conditions caused by severe food shortages and hugely inflated prices were immeasurably aggravated by widespread and intensifying under- and unemployment, notably, though not exclusively, in urban locations.[15]

II

Extreme poverty existed in normal times on a scale in Ireland unknown in England. The absence of a statutory Irish poor law was the primary cause of this stark contrast. The 1799–1801 period witnessed a vast increase in begging, many reports of desperation, choked workhouses and infirmaries, together with outbreaks of disease attributed to malnutrition, notably in the towns. These phenomena suggest that a not inconsiderable proportion of the most vulnerable of rural inhabitants migrated to urban localities. As famine conditions existed for at least 20 consecutive months, the cumulative pressures on the poor were very severe.

As early as September 1799, the Belfast press reviewed the poverty problem visible in the 'filth and wretchedness which many lanes, entries and by-ways in this town abounds'; the 'numerous, affecting troublesome, nay sometimes disgusting applications for alms, we daily experience in our streets and at our houses', were denounced, while 'objects incapable of labour, crawling to pick-up a precarious sustenance', received an iota of sympathy. In January 1801, Cork journalists reported that 'so many are pining in secret', especially 'those numerous and wretched families who depend often on the labour of a single person, and yet are ashamed to solicit charity on our streets'. Desperation drove them out; subsequent reports referred to people 'fainting in our streets from absolute want', and in March 1801 it was claimed that 'particularly . . . women . . . crowd the streets as beggars'. When Reginald Cocks arrived in Dublin in

---

15 W. Evans, Dublin, to Littlehales, 9 January 1800; B. Tandy, Drogheda, to Castlereagh, 8 December 1800, National Archives of Ireland, 620/49/23; 620/57/97. C. O'Gråda, 'Industry and communications' in W. G. Vaughan (ed.), *A New History of Ireland*, Vol. 5, (Oxford, Clarendon Press, 1989), p. 139. *Belfast Newsletter*, 12 August 1800. *Saunders's . . . Daily Advertiser*, 5 September 1800. *Cork Advertiser*, 17 January and 5 February 1801.

July 1801 to take up a Castle posting, he was shocked by 'Beggars (especially female) abound[ing] in every street', and he added that 'the house of industry is full, though the inhabitants are . . . very poorly supplied with food'. Parallel scenes occurred in the countryside. Near Listowel, a witness reported 'a swarm of poor starved . . . people', mostly shoeless, 'Eating dry potatoes'. The Inspector-General of Prisons 'encountered Famished children . . . pulling the unripened Stalks of Potatoes to devour the Crude diminutive Roots' in King's and the 'Adjacent Counties' in June 1800. He 'feared that Dysentries will succeed this auspicatious Dearth'.[16]

Serious outbreaks of disease struck Cork in the early summer of 1800. The following December, the 'Chief Magistrate' of Drogheda reported the

> very deplorable situation of our Tradesmen and Labouring poor, some of whom within the last six Months died thro' actual want, many, very many indeed, at this moment are in a starving condition, and to add to this calamity a slow infectious fever rages among them, which where it falls upon a constitution debilitated by famine, seldom fails of putting an end to the sufferings of the . . . victim.

Over the 1800–01 winter, the Dublin House of Industry received £2,000 from government to build a five-ward 'Fever Hospital' where the 'victims are immediately admitted without any Recommendation' from a subscriber in the normal way, together with a mortuary 'for the Reception of the Dead who are immediately removed from the Wards and . . . Interr'd in the Evening'.[17]

It is provisionally estimated that the excess death rate in 1800–01 was about 40,000. More extensive parish register analysis could double this figure. The seriousness of demographic disturbance is also testified by steep declines in baptismal rates, exemplified by that of about 25 per cent among Catholics in eight North Leinster parishes.[18] Other factors prevented a greater catastrophe. Emigration, much of it directly attributed to 'scarcity', was particularly pronounced from Ulster and on a scale sufficient to rattle the Castle. Cornwallis claimed that it revealed inadequate policing by customs and ordered rigid enforcement of the laws against 'Artificers, Manufacturers, and others' illegally departing for 'foreign Countries', including the USA, the main destination of these people.[19] More importantly, governmental and mercantile action to secure imports of customary subsistence cereals and substitutes,

16 *Belfast Newsletter*, 24 September 1799. *Cork Advertiser*, 7 and 21 March 1801. Cocks to R. Pole-Carew, 6 August 1801, Cornwall County Record Office, Carew Mss., CC/L/33. T. Hartnet, and F. Archer to Cornwallis, 5 April and 16 July 1800, National Archives of Ireland, 620/57/45, 133.
17 *Cork Advertiser*, 2 September 1800. Tandy to Castlereagh, 8 December 1800: Memorial, Dublin House of Industry, to Cornwallis, 8 June 1801, National Archives of Ireland, 620/49/73: OP, II, 100/5.
18 D. Dickson, 'A gap in famines: a useful myth' in E. M. Crawford (ed.), *Famine: The Irish Experience 900–1900* (Edinburgh, John Donald, 1989), pp. 103, 107.
19 Cornwallis to Customs, and Portland, 22 and 30 April; General Gardener, Loughall, to Alridge, 4 May 1801, Public Record Office, Home Office Papers 100/103, f. 149; 100/105, ff. 209, 211.

together with charitable initiatives, especially in the towns, but also in the countryside, were crucial to the prevention of greater mortality.

III

Four major reasons stimulated speedy action by the Lord Lieutenant in the autumn of 1799. First, very adverse weather conditions visibly presaged a defective harvest. Second, the British government was identically motivated, though it had the additional spur of the 1794–96 crisis which had not badly affected Ireland. Third, Cornwallis could not afford serious subsistence problems to complicate the difficult task of securing the passage of the Irish Act of Union through the Dublin Parliament, nor fourth, compromise his public order campaign hinging on suppressing the last major vestiges of revolt, notably banditry. He was particularly concerned that the large and volatile working class in Dublin should be adequately fed. He had already decided that government should clandestinely buy some stocks.[20] This was concealed from the 'most considerable Merchants' and other experts including revenue officers, who convened at the Castle on 9 November to fully investigate ways of averting serious scarcities. A prolonged debate followed. If there was no question over the certainty of shortages, both their seriousness and, more importantly, how to combat them, generated contradictory proposals. While there was agreement that imports were essential and insistence that Irish merchants could not compete with their British counterparts in overseas markets, some merchants argued that traders would not speculate if government intervened. Others asserted that government was too ill-equipped to import significantly. Debate also raged over the identity of foreign markets, the volumes which might be obtained at what prices, and whether merchants would speculate without the payment of government bounties on imports. Furthermore, what levels of bounties were appropriate on cargoes from different sources? Exchanges followed over potential substitutes, primarily maize and rice. Could savings be anticipated by activating legislation preventing the production of fine wheaten bread in favour of the supposedly more economical brown variant, Standard Wheaten Bread? Could more affluent consumers be cajoled into abstaining from luxury articles, like pastries, to reduce demand for wheat and stop or cut potato consumption to preserve stocks for the poor—a British precedent, also briefly adopted in Ireland in 1796? Further argument developed over the hoary question of distilling. Prohibition would hit the revenues and so massively increase illicit distilling as to negate any potential saving of grain for food. Conversely, if no restrictions were imposed on the distillers, their continued operations might provoke a savage public backlash.[21]

20 Annesley to Marsden, 8 November 1799, National Archives of Ireland, OP. II, 72/6.
21 'Minutes of Conversation . . .', 9 November 1799.

Within two days, Cornwallis publicly announced that, although exports were stopped under the Corn Laws, they were banned and imports permitted duty free until 25 September 1800 as precautionary measures. The first 40,000 barrels of wheat or flour imported and sold on the open market were to command ten shilling bounties, reduced to five shillings on the following 25,000. Cornwallis was aware that this might lead to a 'war of bounties between the two Kingdoms', because they became payable in Britain under that country's emergency legislation, but as the Irish bounties were inapplicable to stocks coming via British ports and Irish aggregate demand would be too small to affect mainland supplies, he was sure he had got the balance right. As yet, he adhered to the view that prohibiting distilling would be counter-productive, but he issued the order preventing bakers from producing bread finer than Standard Wheaten.[22]

Prices continued their inexorable rise into the winter in both countries. The Westminster Parliament commenced recurrent investigations and Cornwallis asked for documentation, including that promoting economy by charity-run soup kitchens, prior to bringing the issue before the Irish Parliament in February 1800. Its select committee confirmed deficiencies and reported that, in the event, Irish bounties had not enabled her merchants to compete with the British. The solution lay in banning malting and distilling, and securing maize and rice imports by spending the funds available for bounties on those commodities imported by the only people able to do so, namely Irish merchants. The committee concluded, with optimistic pragmatism, 'that there is not such a deficiency of grain as to cause real alarm, if proper pains be taken to husband it with strict economy', facilitated by imported substitutes. The report was circulated to the entire magistracy, who were also enjoined vigilantly to enforce the malting and distilling bans and to take 'such measures as shall appear best calculated to economize the consumption of provisions'. Finally, and quite critically, justices were instructed 'to impress upon . . . the People the importance of . . . the free circulation of provisions', as the 'worst consequences must follow, if the removal of provisions from any particular place is impeded'. In the event of infringements, the Bench was to use 'every exertion' against those responsible, 'as nothing could more discourage the Merchant than that the Market for the Importer should be confined to' the ports themselves.[23]

22 The Cabinet was clearly displeased by Cornwallis' initiative, and it was at Whitehall's insistence that cereals re-exported from the mainland were ineligible; Pitt also insisted that bounties were not to be renewed in the 1800–01 season. Cornwallis to Portland, 30 October, 11 and 20 November, and reply 14 November 1799; Marsden to King, 9 November 1799, Public Record Office, Home Office Papers 100/89, ff. 268–80; 100/92, ff. 252–54. Contractor Annesley to Marsden, 8 November 1799, National Archives of Ireland, OP. II, 72/76. *Belfast Newsletter*, 19 November 1799.
23 Very few letters from the Castle to local authorities have survived; exceptions categorically stated that interruptions would generate a 'total Famine' in 'many Districts . . . while others would enjoy an unnecessary superfluity'; Cooke to the Sovereign of Belfast, n.d., and the Mayor of Limerick, 8

The select committee's confidence in Irish mercantile capacity to import substitutes was torpedoed by the extension of British bounties to maize and rice. Cornwallis arbitrarily decided to import these articles on governmental account, later adding American wheat- and rye-flour, using a handful of experienced merchants paid on commission.[24] There is relatively little information on these imports. They were principally directed to Dublin and Cork, with the remainder sent to provincial seaports to counter cereal price rises and reports of severe shortages. Maize stocks were definitely consumed in their hinterlands. Government shipments continued throughout the duration of the crisis, and were still arriving during the harvesting of the prodigious 1801 crop, despite new mainland price guarantees for merchants being extended to Ireland early in 1801.[25] Government bought imported cereals, had them ground surrogately by five substantial provincial millers, and tried to dampen price rises by strategic sales. Neither this covert operation, nor the much-advertised imports of rice and maize, appear to have ostensibly compromised merchants importing in 1800–01 under the so-called price guarantees. Malting and distilling bans continued until October 1801 and January 1802 respectively. Some traders believed that they had contributed to mitigate price rises.[26] The economizing appeal was well publicized in 1800, and reiterated to those 'not in the lower classes of life' with greater force early in 1801. Millers' sales figures suggested that it worked, particularly in Ulster, though in places it was 'but little attended to'. As on the mainland, bakers exploited the Standard Wheaten order, by mixing in inferior flour and excess bran.[27] Finally, as the second

December 1800, National Archives of Ireland, 620/57/1: Public Record Office, Home Office Papers 100/98, ff. 151–52. House of Commons, Ireland, *Journal*, 1800, pp. 54, 82, 89, 92, 99. *Belfast Newsletter*, 18 March 1800.

24 Cornwallis to Portland, and reply, 19 and 27 February 1800, Public Record Office, Home Office Papers 100/97, ff. 118, 141.

25 Capt. Skinner, Holyhead (Anglesea), to Irish Adjutant-General, and Handfield to Marsden, 19 May and 16 June 1800; Contractor F. Geale to Marsden, 24 September 1800; A. Ferguson, Derry, to Castlereagh, 14 December 1800: Mayor of Waterford, and Sir J. Newport, to Littlehales, 29 November 1800; Geale to Cooke, and Griffith to Cornwallis, 15 and 16 January 1801; Harvey and Co., Cork, to Cooke, 4 April 1801, National Archives of Ireland, 620/49/77; 620/57/125, 140: OP, II 100/3/1; 115/12, 15, 18. Marsden to Castlereagh, 25 August 1800, Public Record Office, Home Office Papers 100/97, f. 142. Jebb letter book, 7 and 14 July 1801, National Library of Ireland, Ms. 11,877. *Cork Advertiser*, 3 March 1801.

26 *Cork Advertiser*, 2 September 1800. Jebb letter book, 11 March 1800 and 4 January 1801, National Library of Ireland, Ms. 11,877. Littlehales to Marsden, 23 August 1800; Hardwicke to Pelham, 20 September and 31 December, and reply (no day) October 1801, Public Record Office, Home Office Papers 100/98, ff. 128–29; 100/107, ff. 62–68, 117, 253. Draft proclamation, 19 October 1801, National Archives of Ireland, Privy Council Office, carton 3.

27 *Belfast Newsletter*, 18 March and 4 April 1800. *Cork Advertiser*, 17 January 1801. Jebb letter book, 3 July 1801, National Library of Ireland, Ms. 11,877. Sovereign of Kinsale, to Castlereagh, 11 November 1800, National Archives of Ireland, 620/58/37. Barnett, Mullingar, report 2 February 1801, Public Record Office, Home Office Papers 100/103, f. 49.

season of famine peaked in the spring of 1801, Dublin Castle announced that it would pay a sum equal to one-third of totals raised by subscription charities since the start of that year.[28]

IV

In conformity with official encouragement, and precedents dating back to 1740, a subscription-funded soup kitchen opened in Belfast in November 1799, initially supplying gruel to the 'badged begging poor', and to 'poor house keepers' nominated by subscribers. Thereafter its activities broadened notably into the supply of free and cut-price oatmeal to a growing avalanche of claimants, necessitating repeated appeals for further funding. In mid-August it was decided that the kitchens would have to keep going throughout the summer and into the following season.[29] By then, soup kitchens were established in numerous towns including Dublin, Cork, Lisburn, Antrim, Drogheda and Slane. Other identically funded exigency charities preferred to secure stocks of oatmeal, maize and rice. Meal made from maize readily substituted for oatmeal in stirabout, but popular 'prejudice' against rice, in part derived from culinary ignorance, required 'great pains' to overcome.[30] Significantly, it became increasingly fashionable, following the example at Carmavy, to exclude 'strolling beggars' to concentrate on residents.[31]

As in Belfast, urban efforts intensified in the spring and early summer of 1800, and were expanded further throughout the remainder of the crisis. The Castle had already clandestinely pumped funds into some Dublin relief schemes prior to the autumn of 1800.[32] The spring 1801 announcement that government funds were available to supplement existing programmes proved crucial to the maintenance of flagging charitable efforts until the summer, though total expenditure under this head is unavailable.[33] Problems, and not

28 *Cork Advertiser*, 12 March 1801. *Ennis Chronicle*, 26 March 1801.
29 *Belfast Newsletter*, 24 September, 20, 24 and 31 December 1799, 23 January, 11 April, 23 May, 12 and 15 August 1800. M. Drake, 'The Irish demographic crisis of 1740–1' in T. W. Moody (ed.), *Historical Studies*, Vol. VI, 1968, p. 115.
30 J. Hancock, Lisburn, to Littlehales, and Sir G. Hill, Belfast, to Cooke, 17 October and 2 December 1800, National Archives of Ireland, 620/49/72; 620/57/148. *Cork Advertiser*, 16 December 1800.
31 *Belfast Newsletter*, 29 November and 21 December 1799, 8 April and 23 May 1800. *Cork Advertiser*, 19 April, 31 May, 10 and 19 June, 16 October, 23 and 27 December 1800, 1 and 17 January, and 19 February 1801. Jebb letter book, 14 January and 5 February 1800, National Library of Ireland, Ms. 11,877. Evans, Dublin, to Littlehales, 9 January; F. Geale, Dublin, to Marsden, 24 September 1800, National Archives of Ireland, 620/57/97, 125.
32 Handfield to Marsden, 16 June 1800; accounts, government expenditure on Dublin soup kitchens, 15 April to 11 August 1800, National Archives of Ireland, 620/57/140: OP, II, 77/5.
33 Secretary, Dublin House of Industry, to Castlereagh, 4 August 1800: Fingall to Castlereagh, 19 April 1801; chairmen, relief committees, Cork, Newry, Mountrath, and Caher, to Cooke, respectively, 18 and 27 April, 26 July, and 6 October 1801; Coolock vestry to Cornwallis, 17 January 1801; School St Committee, Dublin, accounts, 19 May 1801, National Archives of Ireland, 100/3/1-9: 106/10.

just of the perennial financial variety, were not surprisingly encountered. The sour atmosphere generated by squabbles over residual funds available to Drogheda soup kitchen was aggravated by Lord Conyham's refusal to subscribe as a punishment for those who had cut down trees on his estate, presumably for fuel.[34]

There is no reason to doubt the orthodox view that the residence of a principal proprietor, or his vigorous agent, was usually critical to whether rural localities received assistance. In the Barony of Ballinaboy in the westernmost reaches of Co. Galway, the only remotely affluent resident led a fund to buy in foodstuffs and 'wrote to several strangers who had properties', but secured a paltry £40 which was soon exhausted. Philanthropic efforts varied in scale from the Tullamore innkeeper and 'extensive farmer' who supplied food to his conacre tenants once their potatoes ran out, to the 'several thousand' pounds expended by Lord Londonderry in subsidizing his numerous tenants' subsistence so that famine prices 'have been little felt . . . in comparison'. Self-preservation motivated others, including John Pollock near Navan, whose supplies of cheap oatmeal succeeded in 'purchasing Peace and the power of sleeping in my house reasonably freed from the apprehension of Hunger forcing my doors at Midnight'. Others had to be cajoled, as represented by the threatening letter received by the 'Gentlemen farmers' of Portarlington, which gave 'notice' that, unless they 'subscribed to the support of the poor of the Parish and give employment', their premises would be fired.[35]

The Irish government's responses comprised a mixture of free trade and regulation, with a combination of experiences and exigencies dictating increased resort to the latter. If there was no public fracture of free-trade principles respecting the internal provision trade, the provision of bounties and then direct importation of food-grains constitute important governmental interventions in overseas trade. These were clearly critical in both containing prices and supplementing available stocks. If increasing supplies directly facilitated charitable initiatives notably in the ports, and indirectly across a broader terrain, this also reveals the state's own dependency on subscription and other charities. The clandestine pumping of Castle funds into Dublin organizations testified to the limits of public philanthropy where poverty and

---

34 J. Anderson, Cork, to Marsden, with enclosure, 19 October 1800, National Archives of Ireland, 620/57/51. *Cork Advertiser*, 18 October 1800. Jebb letter book, 27 January 1801, National Library of Ireland, Ms. 11,877.

35 Jebb letter book, 11 February 1800, National Library of Ireland, Ms. 11,877. Pollock to Littlehales, and Gregory to Marsden, 16 and 20 August 1800; Gregory to Marsden, 7 September 1800: R. Dovedale, Portarlington, to Aldridge, with enclosure, 27 February 1801: J. Fitzsimmons, Castlewood, to Castlereagh, 16 July 1800, Public Record Office, Home Office Papers 100/97, ff. 132–37: National Archives of Ireland, 620/57/122, 124; State of the Country Papers, I, 1020/47; II, 411. *Belfast Newsletter*, 5 August 1800.

indigency were concentrated, and provided a secret precedent when the government, faced with faltering charitable initiatives across a broader spectrum, could respond only with further subsidies. It constituted another form of intervention in response to experienced rather than anticipated problems.

V

Unusual market conditions derived from the combination of harvest failures and remedial measures piloted by government. In addition to inflated prices, their usual seasonal pattern was distorted, most significantly with peaks in midsummer rather than the late spring. These distortions forced adaptations by all involved in the trade—producers, merchants, manufacturers and retailers—to maintain profit levels while endeavouring to improve them. The evidence suggests that experiences during the 1799–1800 season proved educational, with lessons learned being exploited during 1800–01. Moreover, those who benefited in the first season of dearth, notably the more affluent farmers, invested inflated profits into operations during the second famine year.

The unusual survival of the letter book of major Slane miller, Jebb and Co., reveals that the conflicts of interest between capitalist farmers, merchants, millers, flour factors and bakers were both aggravated by famine conditions and rather more complicated than assumed by most contemporary commentators. Farmers who in normal times may have been content with long-term contracts at fixed prices, were concerned to attend exchanges when prices were rising. At Drogheda, Jebb's main source of supply, the firm's buyers had to contend with farmers recurrently 'very stiff in selling', thus intensifying competition between buyers. At times, Jebb's was unable to keep its stocks at safe levels without driving Drogheda prices higher still, thus compromising the firm's ability to make profits on flour sold in Dublin in competition with stocks milled from wheat purchased at lower prices elsewhere. Forced into a 'crippled situation', the firm sacrificed some customers, notably its 'Country' buyers, to preserve its substantial business with Dublin factors. Energies were absorbed in seeking imported stocks, new commercial contacts and attending auctions. Additional problems derived from qualitative differences between indigenous and imported wheat. Further experimentation was necessitated by meeting consumer demand for the cheapest grades of flour, including novel admixtures like pollard and oats. The firm made a number of loss-making decisions, ranging from simple miscalculations over anticipated price movements to antagonizing long-standing customers by trying to reduce normal credit facilities in an attempt to contain the extra running capital required to finance operations. Other problems included prolonged mill-stoppages owing to water shortages, and evading the attentions of food protestors.[36]

36 Jebb letter book, *passim*, National Library of Ireland, Mss. 11,877.

Further evidence suggesting broad exploitation of conditions during the 1800–01 season includes the 'very uncommon Proportion of . . . Ricks . . . thatching through the Country' in the autumn, 'apparently with an Intention of not threshing until Spring'. Some withholding was financed by the vast increase in paper currency, issued by an expanding provincial banking establishment. Market supplies fell off, exemplified by the complete absence of oats on sale at Clonmel market between October and December 1800.[37] In many districts, as the potato stocks of small farmers, cottiers and labourers disappeared, with serious implications for customary pig-rearing, their more affluent farming neighbours refused to sell locally except at 'extortionate' prices.[38] They speculated where possible by buying up cereals locally for future dispatch to distant markets.[39] Bankers at Waterford, Ross and Enniscorthy speculated directly through agents buying 'up all the Corn and Provisions . . . for sale in all the Neighbouring Counties', paid for in their notes, and were eventually denounced by the Co. Waterford Grand Jury. Parallel phenomena were reported even from Connacht, though here smaller producers, the 'Common People' in the Bishop of Killala's parlance, resisted offers, hoping to market surpluses themselves when they calculated prices peaking. However, famine conditions did not simply present an exploitable situation guaranteeing vastly inflated profits. Three of the speculative south-eastern banks stopped payment in the late spring of 1801. Some merchants who imported cereals also made losses.[40]

VI

Jebb's authoritative correspondence also detailed mercantile malpractice. An embryonic fall in Dublin flour prices in December 1799 was compromised 'by some interested Person' who maintained prices for the top quality article by releasing minimal stocks. In August 1800, one buyer at Drogheda bought a

---

37 Victualling Board memorandum, 18 November; Adjutant-General's report, enclosed Cornwallis to Portland, 3 December; Asgill, Clonmel, report, 11 December 1800, Captain Cornewall, Carlow Yeomanry, to General Derneker, 16 January 1801; D. Mahon, Wexford, to Cooke, 20 May 1801, Public Record Office, Home Office Papers 100/94, ff. 238–40, 263–68, 283–84; 100/103, ff. 57–58: National Archives of Ireland, 620/60/39. O'Grada, 'Industry and communications', p. 151.

38 Bastly Magnan in Co. Leitrim was charged 1s.1d. '& one Days Work of his Wife picking Flax' for a stone of potatoes; affidavit, 23 August 1800, National Archives of Ireland, 620/58/28.

39 J. Pollock, Navan, to Littlehales, 16 August 1800, Public Record Office, Home Office Papers 100/97, ff. 132–33. *Cork Advertiser*, 13 June 1801. Baggs to Cornwallis, 4 February 1801; T. Ellison, Castlebar, and Bishop of Killala to Cooke, 18 February and 20 May 1801, National Archives of Ireland, OP, II, 115/11: State of the Country Papers, I, 1020/28.

40 Handfield, report, *loc. cit.* R. O'Connor and R. Adams, merchants, Galway, memorandum, 14 November 1801: cf. S. Fulton, Dublin, petition to the Privy Council, 18 May 1801, National Archives of Ireland, 620/60/71: OP, II, 115/21. Accounts and Papers, House of Commons (95), 1812–13, Vol. XXII.

parcel of wheat at a price way above the going rate in order to maintain prices until his ship arrived with a cargo he aimed to sell at the engineered inflated price. Conversely, another key purchaser was duped into under-estimating the supply by farmers producing only 'pocket Samples' in order to aggravate supply deficiencies. In December 1801, two of Jebb's competitors made purchases adequate to arresting price falls, again calculating that this would maintain prices while they sold existing stocks.[41]

Rumours of such transactions were inevitable and helped to ensure that all subsistence crises unleashed populist perceptions of shortages being exploited by profiteers. These were fuelled by the press and especially by urban authorities. In May 1799, Dublin Corporation formally discussed traditional marketing offences. The Recorder's view, that only 'scrupulous vigilance' in market-policing could keep price levels commensurate with 'the plenty actually exising', underpinned recurrent, though not invariably successful, initiatives by successive mayors. Flour factors' price returns were challenged, and their practice of exaggerating supply deficiencies confronted. One mayor personally policed dockside potato sales, preventing dealings in excess of two stones to frustrate 'forestallers and huxters'. The Drogheda market inspector refused to enter suspect sales into his average price calculations. The new Leet Jury sworn in at Clonmel in October 1800 immediately drafted new regulations to combat traditional marketing offences:

> particularly the practice of sending and establishing agents on the different roads in
> the vicinity . . . in order to intercept and buy up the corn, potatoes, milk, or other
> articles of provision coming into the public market.[42]

If, in the main, the Irish press was less given to the excessive optimism over anticipated and actual harvest productivity which characterized its English counterpart, Irish newspapers recurrently mentioned profiteers and monopolists, though without elevating these people to the status of the architects of a *pacte de famine* as on the mainland. Nonetheless, it is significant that an 'exhaustive enquiry' was deemed necessary to contradict rumours that speculators dumped flour in the Liffey. The *Belfast Newsletter* reported in August 1800 that government stocks would be unloaded on to the market 'to frustrate the fraudulent intervention of monopolists', while *Saunders's Daily Advertiser* made vituperative remarks against all provision dealers, while recounting the Dublin streets were choked by their carts in September. Cork aldermen, several

---

41 Jebb letter book, 19 August 1800, 10 February and 8 December 1801, National Library of Ireland, Ms. 11,877.

42 *The Times*, 30 August 1799. Cooke to King, 13 December 1800, Public Record Office, Home Office Papers 100/98, f. 149. *Ennis Chronicle*, 8 January and 5 February 1801. Jebb letter book, 31 December 1799, 14 January and 22 April 1800, National Library of Ireland, Ms. 11,877. *Cork Advertiser*, 4 November 1800.

of whom were big merchants, specifically exonerated substantial middlemen from accusations of malpractices, with a diversionary official thrust at modest market-place retailers accused of using false weights and measures. Several were fined, their effigies 'gibbeted' by grateful consumers. Authorities at Waterford promptly followed suit. Considerable coverage was accorded to the autumn 1800 riots on the mainland, particularly those in London. The *Cork Advertiser* ruminated on the 'next to impossible task' of the city poor obtaining adequate 'sustenance for money' and how long they might 'be expected to remain quiet spectators of the luxury of the rich'. The press remained a source for moral-economic commentary throughout the prolonged crisis.[43]

The Castle's commitment to free internal trade, turning in the last resort on magisterial enthusiasm, found few determined supporters. The unusual justice who told people in his Lanesborough jurisdiction that they were not obliged to sell potatoes ' "unless they got their own demand be it ever so extravagant" ', was subjected to a barrage of wrath.[44] The magistrates acting jointly for Counties Leitrim and Longford were more representative. They responded to information that 'vast quantities of Oats, Meal & Potatoes' were sold 'by Millers & Country Farmers' to strangers for consumption elsewhere 'at an exhorbitant price', thereby causing 'Irreperable Injury to the Poor', with published instructions to constables to police roads and bridges. Constables were ordered to search 'Mills and farmers Houses' for 'stored up . . . Provision', which was to be 'seized . . . and lodged in the next Market place' for sale 'to the poor or such persons as have not provisions of their Own'. Enforced sale at prices stipulated by the Bench saw blows exchanged between officials and owners. When the Seneshal of Granard was remonstrated with, and given written evidence proving 'that Government did not countenance this interference', he retorted that he acted for the common good, riposting 'that the tempers of Juries' were such 'that he did not fear damages for striking a man, who refused to sell corn at the price he had fixed'.[45]

Many military commanders also articulated perceptions derived from moral-economic outlooks. General Duff spoke of 'many rich Individuals employed in the Monopoly of Grain' at Limerick. At Clonmel, C. O. Asgill said that 'farmers have entered into Combinations' to withhold, financed either by paper money,

---

43 *Cork Advertiser*, 19 June, 20 August, 30 September, 11 October, 1 and 6 November 1800. *Belfast Newsletter*, 5 and 12 August, 23 and 30 September 1800. *Saunders's . . . Daily Newsletter*, 9, 10, 13, 17, 19 and 24 September 1800.

44 J. Tigh, Lanesborough, to Lt Colonel Buchanan, Royal Artillery, Athlone, and Buchanan to Littlehales, 19 April and 2 May 1800, National Archives of Ireland, 620/57/14.

45 R. L. Edgeworth to Littlehales, June and 14 July, and to Marsden 15 September 1800; M. Monsey to Handfield, 16 March, with notice to all high and petty constables, signed Justices Watson and Nesbett, February 1800, sent by Justice Crawford, and forwarded to Littlehales, 15 and 19 March 1800, National Archives of Ireland, 620/57/99, 135.

or by advances 'from the Corn Buyers and their Emissaries'. They left the produce on the farms, until their agents organized its removal to 'receiving Houses . . . appointed in various Stations'. Asgill's counterpart at Ballina (Co. Tipperary) asserted that middlemen waived January 1801 rent demands on condition that their tenants 'shall not break Bulk or sell theirs till they rise to a particular price'. Asgill condemned the magistracy for failing to enforce the 'Laws against Forestallers and Regrators'. Subsequently, and not surprisingly, some interventionist magistrates claimed they were merely enforcing the army's orders. Moreover, magistrates and officers were commonly in a predicament, notably when neither the inhabitants nor the soldiers stationed in market towns were able to secure sufficient subsistence and joined forces 'under the necessity of going into the Country and forcing it from the People'.[46]

VII

There is something of a consensus among historians that the English, Scottish and Welsh traditions of food rioting were not paralleled in Ireland. They were 'almost unknown' according to one Irish authority. While Thompson believed there was adequate evidence, together with strong suggestions of under-reportage, to claim that 'classical' expressions were experienced, he also postulated that the absence of poor laws, and the rarity of a resident gentry, meant that there was neither statutory relief system nor paternalist presence to activate through mass mobilizations.[47] The range of evidential difficulties impresses. First, the rebellion was not completely suppressed when the crisis broke. This source of banditry was soon inflated by victims evading famine, and demarcating between their activities and social protest is problematic. Second, parts of the country remained under martial law. GOCs merely had to make

---

46 Duff to Littlehales, and Asgill's monthly report, both 1 December 1800, Public Record Office, Home Office Papers 100/94, ff. 261, 283–84. Informations, P. Gilman and M. Ruardan, and T. Galigan, all of Castle Connel, Co. Limerick, taken 10 March 1801; Major Maxwell, Carrick-on-Shannon, to Aldridge, with enclosures, 31 August 1800, State of the Country Papers, I, 1020/26; 620/58/28.

47 T. Bartlett, 'An end to moral economy: the Irish militia disturbances of 1793', Past and Present, 99, 1983, p. 43; E. P. Thompson, 'Moral economy reviewed' in E. P. Thompson, Customs in Common (London, Merlin, 1991), pp. 295–96. Cf. R. Gillespie, 'Grain crises in early seventeenth-century Ireland', Irish Economic and Social History, Vol. XI, 1984, pp. 11, 14–15, 17–18, who claims that while accusations of withholding by farmers and hoarding by urban-based speculators were common, 'Grain riots appear . . . rare in Ireland compared with England, and the administration seems to have maintained law and order even during the years of worst failure.' This remarkably naive assertion ignores evidential problems, surely more profound for the earlier than later modern period, and is based upon J. Walter and K. Wrightson, 'Dearth and the social order in early modern England', Past and Present, Vol. 71, 1976, which also omits evidential quality analysis, and ironically, aims to show that English food riots were also relatively uncommon. For a critique, see R. Wells, 'Counting riots in eighteenth-century England', Bulletin of the Society for the Study of Labour History, Vol. 38, 1978, pp. 68–72.

returns naming capital convicts. Extant court martial minutes only list summary proceedings.[48] Third, the destruction of virtually all legal records removes a source so central to events in Britain.[49] Fourth, the notorious absence of magistrates from numerous extensive districts was aggravated by the retreat of those resident to the towns after the rebellion. New recruits to the commission were hard to come by. Fifth, most justices had a propensity for 'Compromising felonies', and sixth, witnesses and victims were terrified into silence. Justice Winter of Aghern had, typically, 'heard of many Robberys of Potatoes & other Matters about the Neighbourhood . . . but I have received no Complaints of the Kind as a Magistrate'.[50] The press does not compensate. Editors simply did not have the space to catalogue multifarious 'outrage'. Reports of court proceedings were largely cursory.[51]

Despite the fact that the major, and a proportion of medium-ranking, towns had precisely that 'resident governing gentry' in their urban elites, which Thompson postulated as a critically absent factor, the documentation consulted for the 1799–1801 crisis failed to record one classic food riot in any such town, with the partial exceptions of Cork, Ennis, Limerick and Drogheda. They were nevertheless anticipated. In late September 1800, when flour supplies to Dublin were compromised by mill-water deficiencies at the same time that fierce disturbances in London were widely publicized, the Castle reported that:

> For a few days past there have been some appearances of a disposition among the Tradespeople to riot on account of the dearness of bread—they have had private meetings, but not appeared any where in bodies.

This discontent soon 'subsided' after government rice was speedily sold at low prices. One provision agent presumed in January 1801 that Cornwallis wanted 'to apply . . . Rice' under his superintendence at Cork, 'chiefly to Populous Towns as being the Places most liable to Tumult in Consequence of any Scarcity of Provisions'.[52]

48 Longueville, Cork, to C. B. Kippax, Dublin, and I. Cormack, Ferns Barracks, to Cornwallis, 7 October and 19 December 1799: Charles Abbot to Duff, and reply, 10 and 13 August 1801, National Archives of Ireland, State of the Country Papers, I, 1018/3, 31: 620/59/31, 33.

49 S. J. Connolly, 'Albion's fatal twigs: justice and the law in the eighteenth century' in R. Mitchison and P. Roebuck (eds), *Economy and Society in Scotland and Ireland 1500–1939* (Edinburgh, John Donald, 1988), p. 118.

50 A. Young, cited in L. Freeman, 'Land and people in c1841', in Vaughan, *A New History of Ireland*, p. 119. Cormack, and Lord Dillon, to Castlereagh, 19 November 1799 and 6 July 1800; John Fitzsimmons, Castlewood, to Castlereagh, 16 July 1800; Winter to General Barnet, and Roger Dalton JP, Dungannon, to Cornwallis, 4 and 6 April 1801, National Archives of Ireland, State of the Country Papers, I, 1018/31; 1019/1; 1020/35; II, 411: 620/49/98. Lord Redesdale to Wickham, 10 December 1802, British Library Add. Mss. 35737, ff. 139–40. See also K. Boyle, 'Police in Ireland before the Union', *Irish Jurist*, Vol. 7, 1972, pp. 131–34; Vol. 8, pp. 90–91.

51 *Cork Advertiser*, 23 August 1800, 4 April, 23 July and 6 October 1801.

52 Marsden to King, 24 and 27 September 1800, Public Record Office, Home Office Papers 100/93, ff. 169–70, 173. Geale to Cooke, 15 January 1801, National Archives of Ireland, OP, II, 115/15.

At Limerick on 1 December 1800, a 'very considerable' crowd angrily complained of starvation while wealthy traders monopolized available supplies for despatch to the east. The sympathetic General Duff achieved a dispersal by 'expostulation' with the protesters.[53] The collapse of food supplies to Cork in late February 1801 precipitated several 'partial risings' over at least three days, with people summoned by horns preceding attacks on warehouses holding mercantile stocks. A combination of factors, including sales at below cost price by these merchants and the fortuitous arrival of two trans-Atlantic ships, laden with maize purchased immediately by a mayoral relief committee, enabled food distributions adequate to 'tranquillize the city'.[54] The simultaneous Ennis disturbances followed the local press denunciation of 'Speculative Gentlemen who skulk in the Corn Market for . . . forestalling Oats', and price rises which were attributed 'to the unfeeling rapacity of a few interested individuals', together with farmers and gentry allegedly distilling from 'bread corns'. Tensions rose, and tempers broke after a merchant 'openly declared that he "would leave the people of Ennis to feed on Chaff" '. Warehouses were again attacked, together with mills still processing cereals. The contents were carted off, some left under military protection, the rest 'plundered . . . by a hungry multitude of men, women, and children'. Once again, these mobilizations stimulated a 'numerous' meeting of gentry and magistrates at the Court House and agreement to subscribe to subsidize food for the poor.[55]

Lastly, one short report, published by the *Ennis Chronicle* in the form of a letter from Drogheda, dated 17 March 1801, claimed that 'a numerous body of men and some women' had mobilized during most of the previous fortnight, broken into several warehouses to 'forcibly carry . . . away oatmeal and potatoes' brought to market. While the region's military authorities remained silent on these events and the press item appears to comprise the only extant evidence, Jebb's letter book, normally containing at least one weekly report, is silent for the period from 27 February to 3 April, suggesting that these actions seriously impeded and probably stopped all activities. It is not unlikely that many market towns, including the ports, experienced traditional food riots as the crisis intensified in the spring of 1801, which are obscured by evidential

---

53 The evidence comprises two thin reports in the *Cork Advertiser*, 26 and 28 February 1801, a report from Lord Shannon's agent, dated 24 February, and passed to Littlehales, and the Mayor to Cooke, penned on 18 March 1801, and only then to claim that the merchants' losses were a *de facto* subscription which should be included in the calculations, whereby the government contributed a sum equal to another third of all local charity exigency subscriptions during 1800–01. National Archives of Ireland, State of the Country Papers, OP, II, 100/3/3; State of the Country Papers, ser. II, 441.

54 *Cork Advertiser*, 27 December 1800, 24, 26 and 28 February 1801. Letter to Lord Shannon, from his agent, 24 February 1801, National Archives of Ireland, State of the Country Papers, II, 441.

55 *Ennis Chronicle*, 22 and 29 January, 2, 5, 16, 23 and 26 February 1801. *Cork Advertiser*, 3 February and 7 March 1801.

problems. The press, or sectors thereof, may have been more wary of even token coverage than certain British counterparts. The *Cork Advertiser* in March 1801 duly noted that Carrick-on-Suir 'corn buyers' stopped trading, 'in order that the inhabitants, meal sellers and bakers may be supplied at the lowest rate'. Fear of the threat or the reality of violence, rather than altruism, was the most probable cause of this 'example worthy of imitation'.[56]

Irish coasters in the provision trade used the larger ports and many others which were commonly mere hamlets with wharfs, where they were targeted by protesters who aimed to stop shipments. In January 1801 at North Ring, a hamlet two miles from Clonakilty, a crowd attacked a merchant's house and seized corn on a sloop moored at the jetty.[57] At Baltimore in Co. Cork, a vessel loaded with potatoes destined for Dublin was boarded by a crowd, backed by soldiers from the Cheshire Fencibles, and the cargo removed. The more substantial port of Youghal sent cereals to Dublin, and these were interrupted in December 1800, and in the following spring. Two mills belonging to one merchant, Reuben Fisher, were repeatedly targeted by well-organized crowds up to two hundred strong, armed with keys, who periodically carried off substantial volumes.[58] Parallel protests also occurred in river ports, including Killaloe, 12 miles up the Shannon from Limerick. Here, crowds mobilized to 'Swear . . . People not to sell their Potatoes out of the Parish, nor for a larger Price than Half a Guinea for Eight Bushels', and, when these injunctions were fractured, grouped again and smashed the boat sent to fetch a consignment. Overland shipments of foodstuffs destined for market and larger towns occurred in several locations, notably potatoes in Counties Cork, Tipperary, Kerry and Louth. Further evidential snippets deriving from these incidents reveal that the ship at Baltimore was 'provided with Arms', the Clonakilty protesters were supported by the 'middle order of People', while the principal concerns of the reporter from Killaloe were the participation of local yeomanry volunteers, violent attacks on farmers ignoring the crowd's orders, and threats to any doctor who attended the injured. Some magistrates formally banned

---

56 *Ennis Chronicle*, 26 March 1800. Jebb letter book, 27 February to 3 April 1801, National Library of Ireland, Ms. 11,877.

57 Part of the crowd was probably from Clonakilty, but the evidence derives exclusively from a bellicose JP who very unusually acted decisively and made arrests, on the premise that 'Mobs & risings, however insignificant in their beginning lead to such pernicious ends'. When he discovered that the issue of the prisoners spawned more mobilizations, he harangued a menacing crowd in Clonakilty itself, and brought in the army from Bandon 'to clear the streets'. Name undecipherable, Courtmachsherry, to 'my Lord', 20 January 1801, National Archives of Ireland, 620/49/86.

58 General Ross, Youghal, to Littlehales, and Aldridge, 3 January and 23 March 1801; J. Swayne, Youghal, 29 July 1801, to Cornwallis, with five depositions dated 21 to 23 July 1801; deposition of J. Day, W. Fleming and J. Downing of Killea, taken 23 March 1801; Public Record Office, Home Office Papers 100/98, f. 15: National Archives of Ireland, I, 1020/7; 620/60/88; 620/49/93.

potato sales outside a 10-mile radius, a rule imposed elsewhere by secret societies.[59]

These actions clearly reflect the effect of the devastation of the potato stocks of cottiers, labourers and the smallest farmers of rural Ireland who comprised the most vulnerable categories of famine victims. Labour, in reduced demand, remained their sole legal resort. In some locations, migrant labour seriously compromised indigenous workers. With no poor law, and often no paternalist initiative, these people's main protection came through the intervention of populist agrarian regulators whose actions during the famine reveal commercial moral-economic permutations.

Secret society, or terrorist, intervention aimed to protect the poorest strata from exploitation at the hands of their weathier neighbours, notably in Counties Tipperary, Limerick and eastern Kerry. In this extensive area, the intensification and then the continuation of the crisis after the 1800 harvest brought recent and indeed current agrarian changes into ever sharper relief. So much land had been converted to permanent pasture for cattle that there was 'little employment' for the poor, and then at 'very . . . low wages', a mere five- or sixpence per day, 'which bears no proportion' to present food prices. If employment was jeopardized further by the influxes of labourers from west Kerry, rents for 'Potatoe land let to the poor' were 'high' and rising. Consequently, 'the labouring People' were in a 'wretched state'. Protestors' 'Meetings are secret—it is impossible to infiltrate' their organizations or 'to procure Evidence'. Not surprisingly, 'the Farmers & Gentlemen are much intimidated'. While military commanders lobbied for 'the prompt exercise of Martial Law', Cornwallis' preferred option was paternalistic initiatives from the 'Few Gentry resident' so that 'the situation of the poor (could) be made more comfortable'.[60]

Injunctions were issued—in the name of Captain Slasher over parts of Munster—against sales to dealers or merchants from outside local communities, and prices were also fixed most commonly on potatoes, butter and milk, the latter being important for the stirabout made with oatmeal regularly substituted for potatoes.[61] Farmers were ordered, by groups who commonly broke into their houses at night, to sell specific volumes of foodstuffs at stipulated prices 'to the first four Men who should come for them in the morning', ensuring that

59 Letter to 'my Lord', *loc. cit.* J. Parker to the Bishop of Killaloe, 18 March 1800: Petition of Kinsale merchant John Heard, 17 June 1800, forwarded to Castlereagh, Public Record Office, Home Office Papers 100/93, ff. 196–98: National Archives of Ireland, 620/57/144. *Cork Advertiser*, 6 June and 12 August 1800, and 4 April 1801. *Saunders's . . . Daily Newsletter*, 3 June 1800. *Belfast Newsletter*, 15 April 1800.

60 Marsden to King, 23 October; Duff, and Asgill, to Littlehales, both 1 December 1800, Public Record Office, Home Office Papers 100/94, ff. 177–78, 227–30.

61 *Cork Advertiser*, 2, 9 and 11 September 1800, 27 June and 25 July 1801. *Belfast Newsletter*, 22 August and 2 September 1800. *Saunders's . . . Daily Advertiser*, 9 June 1800.

those specifically in want had priority. Action was also taken to force those who had already sold stocks at market prices to poor neighbours to return the difference between that and the stipulated price. On occasion, Slasher enjoined farmers against feeding potatoes to young pigs and prohibited the raising of calves, to preserve the root and milk for human consumption. In June he ordered milk supplied on credit until Michaelmas.[62] Those who refused were whipped and threatened with house burnings and, in the event of repeated reticence, death. A gang operating around Clonmel forced any number of their targets to swear to adhere to imposed prices, but flogged only some of their victims, among them a man whose son-in-law had commenced an unspecified legal action, and another for taking a farm over the long-term tenant's head some years previously. From March, 'Notices are daily posted . . . regulating the price at which Lands are to be let', and bands of 'rebels' up to two hundred strong enforced these stipulations.[63]

Slasher escalated the campaign immediately after the 1800 harvest. The first stage in October saw action against tithe proctors to preserve produce taken in kind, which otherwise would be sold at a distance on behalf of the clergy. Slasher also orchestrated the forcible 'Breaking up of Grass Ground . . . to reduce the price of Potato Ground', the prevention of west Kerry men working at less than stipulated daily wages, and used further 'force' to reduce milk prices. The second stage was clearly in response to the deepening crisis in April and early May 1801 when Slasher reactivated the campaign, on the authority of the 'Heads of the three Countys', 'To help and Relief the poor of not Stavering and reduce the price of provisions', according to many notices issued. Prices were then fixed on potatoes, wheat, barley, barley meal, oats, butter, veal, sour and fresh milk, and even three pigeons (1d.). These were to be observed until 1 August 1801, with the exception of fresh milk, to fall from three- to twopence per pottle from 1 May when dairy herds became more productive. The last order was underwritten by a prohibition on farmers with fewer than 10 cows raising more than a single calf. Those who resisited had their cattle houghed or killed. Again cardings—'with woollen Cards tore the flesh off their backs and Breasts'—and floggings were widespread, with new tenants taking land over existing tenants' heads, labourers who replaced discharged workers, and their employers taking the brunt. Many more affluent farmers were robbed, though

---

62 *Cork Advertiser*, 28 June 1800. Depositions of Thomas Long Snr and Jnr, and John Cane, Downbone Co. Tipperary, 27 June 1800; information of Cornelius Hozan, Clonmel, 19 July 1800; reply, 3 November 1800 to official enquiry into specific facets of rural economy, from Limerick, author and recipient's names excised, National Archives of Ireland, 620/57/49; 620/9/103/12.

63 Extract of a letter from Limerick, 29 March 1800, Public Record Office, Home Office Papers 100/93, ff. 245–46. Information of farmers James and Maygrath, Ballyboy, Co. Tipperary, 12 July 1800; Asgill, Clonmel, to Littlehales, 4 August 1800, enclosing depositions of Hozan, Joseph Dugan, both of Thory, and Connor Mecher, Clanmor, Co. Tipperary, all 19 July 1800, National Archives of Ireland, 20/57/36, 49.

the military authorities in their reports did not enlarge on whether the victims had infringed Slasher's moral code or not. He also insisted that 'none of the Inhabitants of the town is not to fore stall any of the above goods only what they want for their own Use'.[64]

Although a high proportion of the evidence of these forms of moral-economic additions to customary secret-society prescriptions relate principally to Munster, there are suggestions that parallel phenomena were common in Connacht and in parts of the North. In the most disturbed parts of the latter, the judiciary were even more hard pressed in trying to get statements from victims and witnesses to launch a judicial counter-offensive in districts not under martial law. But perhaps the scale of populist intervention, and its borrowings from commercial moral-economic litanies, were most eloquently symbolized in the addition to the formal proclamation promulgating martial law, namely 'that any person presuming to stop provisions of any kind, or fixing their prices, on being apprehended, would be punished as principally furthering the Rebellion'.[65]

Some peculiarly Irish—including sectarian—permutations accompanied this grafting of commercial to regular landed moral-economic precepts. Evidence of conspiracies, enforced by violence to refuse to sell provisions to the army or their provision contractors, derives from several locations. They seem to have been particularly effective against that small minority of troops stationed in the countryside at a distance from market towns, and in some places soldiers in billets and barracks in small towns.[66] Those who refused to sell often said they could not accept bank notes. Although Irish crises, including recurrent threatened French invasions, generated runs on the banks and many stored gold at home rather than use paper money or keep bank accounts,[67] these were politically-motivated and terrorist underwritten attempts to compromise what was essentially an army of occupation backing the Irish Militia. The issue was also juxtaposed with orthodox claims of profiteering. As the Catholic Andrew

64 Duff to Littlehales, 1 November 1800, and 21 May (enclosing Slasher notice, n.d.); Duff, and Asgill, to Lindsay, both 8 June 1801, Public Record Office, Home Office Papers 100/94, ff. 227–28; 100/103, ff. 183–85, 238, 242.

65 *Saunders's . . . Daily Advertiser*, 9 June 1800.

66 Dillon to Duff, and the Bishop of Killala to Marsden, 6 and 23 April 1801, National Archives of Ireland, 620/49/98; State of the Country Papers, I, 1020/30. *Saunders's . . . Daily Advertiser*, 9 June 1800. Cornwallis' policy of concentrating troops in towns, and avoiding wherever possible stationing detachments in the countryside, on strategic grounds, provoked hostile criticism. See especially Longueville, Cork, to Kippax, 4 November 1799, National Archives of Ireland, State of the Country Papers, I, 1018/4. Eventually, in late 1800, extra payments were made to officers 'deprived of the ordinary Means of Comfort', and 'harassed by constant Patrols' in districts 'without a Market'. Littlehales to W. Elliott, 2 October 1800, National Library of Ireland, Kilmainham Mss., Ms. 1,127, pp. 237–38.

67 *Cork Advertiser*, 30 August 1800 and 2 May 1801. *Belfast Newsletter*, 2 and 12 September 1800. R. Wells, *Insurrection: The British Experience, 1795–1803* (Gloucester, Alan Sutton, 1983), pp. 254–55.

M'Comas from near Carrick-on-Shannon deposed: 'the Scarcity in the Country was An Artificial one & was Fabricated by Design[in]g Monopolists for the Purpose of Harrassing & Distressing His Majesties Troops & the Languishing poor of the Country'. Connor Mecher, of Clonmore, Co. Tipperary, who was ordered to repay cash to consumers whom he had charged over 4s.4d. per barrel of potatoes, was told to give the money involved from an army agent to the parish priest.[68] Not surprisingly, troops so affected retaliated, usually in conformity with moral-economic norms. One of the few scraps of Connacht evidence reveals that hoarding was believed responsible for the complete cessation of potato supplies to the markets, and Castlebar inhabitants received none 'but what the Soldiers obtain from the Farmers by force'. Whatever the scale of soldiers visiting farmers in this cause, their intervention to stop potato supplies leaving the localities was seen as much more serious by both local and central authorities. On 23 February 1800, Cornwallis issued a circular to the troops, complaining that, despite 'the repeated orders . . . issued . . . several corps have dared to intercept potatoes on their way to market', in addition to 'some instances' of taking them from 'proprietor's . . . houses and grounds . . . pretending that the offer of what they deemed a fair price was a sufficient excuse'. Although Cornwallis threatened the perpetrators with 'the most rigorous example' and COs with being 'called . . . to a severe account', a further circular issued on 10 March reiterated the threats in response to the 'many instances' in which urban-bound supplies had again been stopped, thereby threatening especially the supply of potatoes overland and by canal to Dublin. General Dundas, responsible for the troops involved in Co. Kildare, responded by stressing difficulties experienced by soldiers in securing adequate provisions, pointedly noting, 'not so much on account of the Scarcity' but because the magistracy responsible for 'that part of the Canal' principally affected 'will not do their duty', implying that his men had no alternative but to seize food from barges along with civilian protesters. A solution was found in patrols by the local yeomanry, maintained until the summer of 1801.[69]

Cornwallis was particularly concerned at the political ramifications of this 'licentious outrage of . . . men who disgrace the name of soldier', and with typical eighteenth-century governmental parsimony offered to cover the cost only of the extra transport costs in implementing his order for quarter masters to scour their districts for stocks. Despite this and the instruction that the orders should be 'read to the men frequently on parade', the problem remained serious

68 Mecher's deposition, and M'Comas' affidavit, 19 July and 28 August 1800, National Archives of Ireland, 620/57/49; 620/58/28.

69 'E of L', Castlebar to Isaac Heron, 26 January 1801, National Archives of Ireland, State of the Country Papers, II, 115/6. Dundas' monthly report, 3 April 1800, Public Record Office, Home Office Papers 100/93, ff. 265–66. General Meadows to Littlehales, 20 June 1801, National Library of Ireland, Kilmainham Mss., Ms. 1,105, p. 312.

in the south-west, with the mayor and CO at Cork issuing and re-issuing injunctions against soldiers bastardizing their powers to impress vehicles by impounding those carrying potatoes and other provisions. Meanwhile, soldiers in Cork garrisons imitated their counterparts elsewhere with nightly parties going to dig potatoes in nearby fields. Some were executed for these actions, but the problem persisted across the 1800–01 season.[70] In Queen's County, members of the Protestant yeomanry, 'stiling themselves the Orange Club of Mountmelick':

> plundered all the industrious people . . . of their provisions not allowing them to be weighed nor offering any payment threatening death and destruction to any person who dare oppose them at the same time discriminating between Catholick & Protestant . . . And at going away with the plunder they generally play the Loyal tunes of the Protestant boys and Croppies lie down by way of Irritation.[71]

Clearly, the latter actions comprised some combination of sectarian-driven and legitimated looting and banditry, but evidence relating to banditry, not invariably with sectarian dimensions, derives from across Ireland during the 1799–1801 crisis. There are juxtapositions between those at the hands of political fugitives from the rebellion who retained nationalist aspirations, and those originating in famine-related desperation, spawning confusions shared by both local and central authorities. One magistrate who did make the distinction, Knighton of Mosstown, Co. Meath, reported that he knew of:

> nothing done by People stiling themselves Rebels, or Defenders, but there have been several Robberys . . . with many Petty thefts such as stealing in to the Poor peoples cabbins, and taking Bacon, Potatoes, Meal, Butter etc, And steal Potatoes of(f) the Land . . . stealing Sheep.

Major-General Barnet's précis of magistrates' reports from several Midland counties for which he was responsible confirmed that 'the very high price of Provisions and the serious distresses of the poor', aggravated by under-employment and 'very low wages . . . caused a variety of trifling Robberies for provisions', all of which he was 'confident proceeded from real want'. At Kilcock, 16 miles west of Dublin, it was said in the early spring of 1801 that 'deplorable Robberies of Every Species is hourly committed . . . on the Industrious Poor', and that, although the army's presence was adequate to arresting suspects, it was impossible to get witnesses to testify.[72]

There is little detailed evidence of this form of robbery, but John Keily, a

---

70 *Saunders's . . . Daily Advertiser*, 14 June 1800. *Belfast Newsletter*, 24 June 1800. *Cork Advertiser*, 15 April, 15 May, 10 June, 8 July, 26 August, 2 and 18 September 1800.

71 Copy of a letter, author's name excised, dated 19 March 1800, National Archives of Ireland, State of the Country Papers, I, 1019/7.

72 C. J. Welsh to Marsden, 2 March 1801; Knighton to Barnet, and Barnet to Aldridge, 9 and 16 April 1801, National Archives of Ireland, State of the Country Papers, I, 1020/54; II, 467.

member of a gang recurrently operative over the Cork–Waterford boundary, turned King's Evidence and made a revealing statement after they were surprised and arrested by a yeomanry patrol when setting out on another expedition. A nucleus of five or six members commonly swelled to around a dozen for different raids, but only one was armed—with 'a Pistol loaded with Powder and Slugs'—and the rest carried sticks. All blackened their faces with 'a Composition made of Soot and Grease'. The main targets comprised sheep, potatoes, meal and butter. Securing the latter three items involved entering farmers' houses. Cash was taken when found, but, of the three specimen raids detailed by Keily, only once did the confederacy physically beat the victim. If some localities appear to have escaped a significant upturn in such action, others experienced a crescendo in the spring of 1801, just before imported foodstuffs began to arrive in considerable bulk, which soon coincided with the early potato crop. The north, or at least significant parts thereof, appears to fall in the former category. As the Sheriff of County Derry asserted, following exhaustive consultations, it was untroubled by 'Rebels, Murderers or Robbers . . . More than is usually committed in the Most Peaceful Times'. The south-west was the most notable example of a region experiencing a peak, and there is some evidence that people—including the 'wealthy farmer' of Dungarvan, robbed of £1,000 in cash—'persist in hoarding the current coin . . . frequently became the victims of their own imprudence', in one journalist's estimation.[73]

Fugitive rebels from 1798 engaged in similar forms of robbery, but banditry committed by rebels—the most notorious was Dwyer, holed up in the Wicklow Mountains with 300 'deserters and ruffians'—tended to be more spectacular and ambitious. Mail coaches comprised a prime target. Even the presence of armed guards and military escorts did not preserve them from attacks, including that on the Dublin–Cork mail two miles from Carlow on 3 March 1801, when a cavalry detachment fled after a fierce interchange of gunfire with 40 bandits. Observers commonly attributed gang attacks on residences of the wealthy, seeking arms, horses and cash, as symbolic of rebel activity, correctly in many instances as with the raid on Colonel Dillon's mansion led by another veteran of 1798, Stephen Glynn in December 1799. He terrorized parts of Counties Galway and Roscommon prior to arrest in April 1801. Some gangs maintained a politically-motivated presence. In the Cashel district, 'Numbers of People going about the Country by Night Levying Contributions in Money to Support the Cause' were reported.[74] But again there were juxtapositions, including the

---

73 Keily, Carrigeew, Co. Cork, confession, taken 29 June 1801; Sheriff of Derry to Campbell, 15 May 1801, National Archives of Ireland, 620/59/66; State of the Country Papers, I, 1020/15. *Cork Advertiser*, 2 May 1801.

74 *The Times*, 12 March 1801. W. Dillon to Brigadier-General Scott, 30 April 1801, and other documentation re. Glynn, National Archives of Ireland, State of the Country Papers, I, 1020/38; cf. Asgill to Aldridge, 21 April 1801, *ibid.*, f. 42.

'unmerciful floggings' administered by people whom Duff did not know whether to designate 'armed Banditti', 'a numerous horde of nocturnal villains', a 'party of Rebels', or Slasher's people. Three magistrates from the same county wearily concluded there were 'so many' felonies 'they would be too tedious to mention'.[75]

VIII

Much of the evidence pertaining to internal Irish affairs derives from the Lord Lieutenant's reports to his political superior, the Secretary of State at the Home Office. Those reports reflect Cornwallis' principal objectives. Over the period of the famine, he was primarily concerned to eradicate vestiges of the rebellion, containing the upsurges in residual United Irishmen and Defender violence which accompanied recurrent invasion scares, and pursuing and capturing fugitive rebels subsisting by banditry. The Lord Lieutenant was also occupied in overseeing the Parliamentary progress of the Union and with initiatives to secure additional food supplies. Apart from these latter items, Cornwallis' outlook was that of a military supremo. From this perspective, his primary fears turned on organized revolutionary and insurrectionary plotting. In some contrast to Whitehall's perception of militant unrest in England,[76] he rarely revealed any concern that popular protest over famine could be transmuted into insurrectionary thrusts,[77] even in Munster where there was evidence of an overlap between agrarian and subsistence-oriented mobilizations and residual rebel organizations responsible for many murders. Cornwallis', and his senior officials', confidence in having smashed the United Irishmen through the suppression of the 1798 revolt, the ensuing trials and exile of the leaders, which pre-empted any capacity for renewed nationwide conspiracy, never wavered. The army, backed by martial law where necessary, could contain the situation. After the passage of the Act of Union through the Irish Parliament, Cornwallis stressed that the 'general tranquility', despite 'a few trivial exceptions . . . entirely precluded' troubling the Secretary of State with extended reportage of internal Irish affairs. Cornwallis' customary coolness continued for the duration of his term, which ended in the late spring of 1801. Governmental criteria in Ireland were entirely different from those applied to the mainland, and thus Irish records bear little resemblance to their British counterparts, notably the

75 Three JPs, Roscrea, to Asgill, 9 April 1801; the 'many small robberies . . . Committed' in Justice Hall's Newry jurisdiction, were so numerous that 'I do not recollect them'; to Campbell, 13 April 1801, National Archives of Ireland, State of the Country Papers, I, 1020/41; 620/59/81.

76 Wells, *Insurrection: The British Experience*, Chs. 9 and 10.

77 The principal exception occurred when reporting the initial attempts to procure extra foodstuffs in 1799; these would 'tranquillize the minds of the people which were getting into a state of irritation, and to prevent the disaffected from converting this unavoidable calamity into an instrument to promote their plans of mischief'. Cornwallis to Portland, 11 November 1799, Public Record Office, Home Office Papers 100/89, ff. 270–77.

many details of the moral economy's violent implementation supplied by local magistrates to the Home Office.[78] Cornwallis and his military commanders had much more serious phenomena to confront than orthodox food rioting, which given the gravity of his main concerns was of insufficient moment to warrant reportage to Whitehall. Thus the apparent paucity of the evidence of subsistence disturbances is at least in part the product of the nature of governmental communications.

This critical contrast between Ireland and the mainland is also revealed notably by governmental attitudes to the fact that every movement of the French navy which might presage an invasion attempt, together with such intelligence as the United Irishmen were still capable of transmitting down their interpersonal networks, generated adrenalin-driven excitement throughout Ireland. But militant rebel 'responses' to invasion possibilities after 1799, like that in the spring of 1801, were largely confined to Munster. Rumours flew that nationalists 'should very shortly want their pikes' to rise in support of the French. Populist rallies secretly convened in parts of Co. Limerick and emissaries were encountered by post-riders who were too frightened to relay intelligence to local postmasters, important sources for the transfer of provincial information to Dublin Castle. This invasion scare was in fact yet another feint. The French fleet eventually sailed for the West Indies, but the apparent preparations for an invasion, notably arms raids, continued into 1802, despite the peace preliminaries signed in October 1801.[79]

In the following May, the new Lord Lieutenant, Hardwicke, reported that 'the Country in general, with exception of a very few districts in the Counties of Tipperary and Limerick, is perfectly quiet'. Munster disturbances increased over the early part of the 1802–03 winter. Many arms raids, intimidatory attacks on the residences of yeomanry officers, pike manufacture, distributions of notices predicting a rising and something approaching a localized *jacquerie* in January, still during the peace, were taken seriously. William Wickham, currently Chief Secretary, but the accomplished master of political intelligence collation, intrigue and covert operations, hastened to the scene to investigate personally. He concluded that 'As banditti the numbers engaged in disturbances are formidable, as rebels they are nothing', 'a ridiculous farce'. As a Clonmel resident wrote of the Special Commission trials of the leaders of this

78 Cornwallis to Portland, 20 July and 18 September 1799, 4 February, 17 March, 17 June, 28 July, 13 October and 3 December 1800; Cooke to King, 10 March 1800, Littlehales to Cooke, 16 April 1800, Marsden to Cooke, and King, 28 April and 26 June 1800, Public Record Office, Home Office Papers 100/87, ff. 65–66, 196–97; 100/93, ff. 188–90; 100/94, ff. 122–23, 177–78, 256–60; 100/95, f. 190; 100/96, ff. 38, 46, 297.

79 M. Elliott, *Partners in Revolution: The United Irishmen and France* (Yale, Yale University Press, 1982), pp. 276–77. R. Foster, Cork, to the Rev. Foster Archer, Dublin, 28 May 1801; Postmaster, Limerick, to Lees, 23 April 1801; Colonel Ross, Limerick, to Abbot, 24 December 1801, National Archives of Ireland, 620/59/82; 620/60/23; State of the Country Papers, II, 467.

rising, the evidence revealed little 'of a rebellious or political tendency', and comprised:

> nothing more than a revival of the old Whiteboy Spirit that for fifty years past has for
> different and frequent periods prevailed most furiously in this quarter of Ireland . . .
> less do I think there is anything of religious bigotry or jealousy.

There were elements of complacency in this analysis. Populist regulation of the Irish agrarian economy was not simply sectarian and the intensification of capitalism was rapidly elevating class as an alternative, indeed confrontational, critical ingredient of social polarizations. Wickham was more incisive, intoning to Prime Minister Addington that 'If the French come in our present state the Lord have Mercy upon us'. However, he could see no strategic rationale, only contradiction:

> from the system now adopted by them of flogging the poor Labourers who come to
> seek Work from other Counties, and the lower order of Farmers; the first of whom
> they would have been anxious to secure as friends, and without the latter as leaders it
> would be impossible for them, to act in any kind of combined insurrection extending
> beyond their own immediate district.

Moreover, in his estimation, the policy of the local gentry 'to separate the farmers' from their social inferiors 'and unite them to the Gentlemen' was perfectly timed. 'The moment is favourable as the farmers, for the first Time . . . are becoming rich.' That wealth derived in part from inflated prices of farm products since the declaration of war in February 1793, but it also reflected considerably enhanced profits by surplus-producing farmers during the shortages in 1795–96 and famine in 1799–1801.[80]

IX

The evidence from the 1799–1801 famine, together with events in the southwest extending to 1803, facilitate a number of conclusions. First, sufficient evidence emerges from the famine years of both populist moral-economic precepts and commensurate mass mobilizations. Second, the principal contrasts between Irish and English responses to hunger include the *apparent* relative paucity in the former of the classic *taxation populaire* form in urban locations, though price-fixing was not absent in Ireland. Indeed, it was a central component of rural reactions. Another contrast derives from the seeming

---

80 Hardwicke to R. Pole-Carew, 7 May 1802, Cornwall County Record Office, Carew Mss. CC/L/34.
  Wickham to Addington, 18 December 1802, 12 and 25 January and 12 September 1803, Hampshire
  County Record Office, 38M49/1/45/6, 7, 27, 29. Statement, Volunteer Colonel Bouchier, Kilrush,
  7 January 1803. General Morrison, Limerick, to Wickham, 6 January 1803, with enclosures,
  including address 'To my dear Countrymen'. Redesdale to Addington, 19 January 1803, Devon
  County Record Office, Addington Papers re. Ireland 1803 (uncatalogued, 1978). T. Prendergast,
  Clonmel, to Marsden, 14 January 1803, British Library, Add. Mss. 35737, ff. 262–63.

dominance of movements to stop provisions being transported from regions already deprived of adequate supplies, and this phenomenon is common to both rural districts, market towns and ports, both large and small, inland and coastal. Third, the injection of moral-economic values into the litany of objectives enforced by traditional rural regulation of agrarian economies by secret societies is an important facet in its own right which has little by way of English parallels, with the possible exception of the motivation of some countryside arsonists. Fourth, in some parts of Ireland, especially the south-west, there was a conjunction between politically-motivated rebels and agrarian regulators, which came to a climax in early 1803. But this must not obscure the speed by which the likes of Captain Slasher adopted moral-economic precepts, prohibiting sales of produce for distant markets and setting maximum prices to be observed in the localities.

The conflict between market and moral economies is unmistakable in Ireland over 1799–1801. If government did intervene with substitute foods at this time, and commit funds to subsidizing charities, it also vehemently supported free-market economics in internal trade. Comtemporary claims that all provision traders made fortunes through extorting high prices from consumers require critical evaluation. But there seems little doubt that dearth inflated profits. The principal beneficiaries were the farmers who produced corn and potato surpluses, the merchants and indeed the millers, who organized distribution and processing of cereals. In that scenario, Irish moral-economic criteria, both commercial and landed, aimed to protect poor consumers from the worst effects. In so doing, moral-economic forms both acted as a form of brake on intensifying unrestricted capitalism and accelerated capital formation in times of famine. Some successes were registered in the countryside, with the intimidation of farmers and the millers and merchants on whom they depended, as the intensity of enforcement achieved the proportions of a blockade in some districts, notably in the south-west as the crisis intensified in the spring of 1801.[81] Similar successes were chalked up in the towns, even if acknowledgements of the crowd's powers were concealed in eulogistic statements exemplified by the Mayor of Limerick's public address praising the city's 'corn merchants' after their subjection to violent protests, specifically:

> for the handsome manner in which you came forward, and continued to supply Oatmeal to the Markets during the late trying season, which not only enabled me to give Provision to the Poor at Half the Price it brought in other parts of this Kingdom—but also to preserve the Peace . . . of this City.[82]

81 D. O'Leary, Cork, to Lord Shannon, 24 February 1801, National Archives of Ireland, State of the Country Papers, II, 441.
82 Sir C. Knight, Limerick, to Cooke, enclosing press cutting, dated 24 November 1800; cf. Chairman of Cork Relief Committee, to Cooke, 11 March 1801, National Archives of Ireland, 620/9/103/7; OP, 100/3/3. *Cork Advertiser*, 20 April 1801.

Finally, the famine of 1810–12 occurred after free trade in foodstuffs was established throughout the United Kingdom. Unprecedented volumes of cereals were shipped from Ireland to the mainland, attracted by the equally unprecedented prices in the latter's markets. This ruthless exploitation of market opportunities galvanized many more recorded incidents of food rioting, including price-fixing, and even more importantly populist blockading of communication centres and arteries.[83] Moreover, at this period, serious nationalist organization and their capacity to conspire had virtually ended and the United Irishmen's alliance with the French for military aid had evaporated.[84] Evidence from 1810–12 powerfully reinforces that deriving from 1799–1801, and indicates the applicability of Thompson's moral-economic model to Ireland.

The principal rider to the relevance of the moral-economic model concerns the scale of robbery, especially of foodstuffs, which observer after observer attributed to desperation and which clearly climaxed over the 1800–01 winter and the following spring. No doubt some of the victims were selected following their infringement of moral-economically driven directives, though there were other dimensions, as articulated by the acting judge advocate late in 1800, as he prepared prosecution cases against leaders of 'flogging parties':

> The distress arising from the high price of provisions and competition for land, the payment of tithes, giving information, disobeying the orders of Committees, and in many instances private picques, have been revenged, by flogging, burning, murder and confiscating the property of the Offender.[85]

Many, if certainly not all, of the victims were drawn from the more affluent sector of rural communities, or they would not have possessed the often considerable volumes of foodstuffs and beasts which were seized. As many of these victims were Catholics, sectarianism cannot have legitimated such incidents, which correspond to the class-warfare analysis proffered by Chief Secretary Wickham in 1802–03. Even more ironically, the emergence of the principally proletarian Caravats spawned opposition in the form of a predominantly capitalist middle-class secret society, the Shanavests, who appear to have been nationalist and included past United Irishmen members.[86] This manifestation also fits Wickham's perceptions, and perhaps proved fatal to the rejuvenation of unified insurrectionary nationalism during the remainder of the war against France.

83 R. Wells, 'Commercial moral-economic models and Ireland: some observations' (forthcoming).
84 Elliott, *Partners in Revolution*, Ch. 10.
85 Ormsby, Limerick, to Littlehales, 18 October 1800, National Archives of Ireland, 620/9/103/7.
86 P. E. W. Roberts, 'Caravets and Shanavests: whiteboyism and faction fighting in East Munster, 1802–1811' in S. Clark and J. S. Donnelly Jr. (eds), *Irish Peasants and Political Unrest 1780–1914* (Manchester, Manchester University Press, 1983), pp. 66–68, 91–93.

INDEX

Acland, James 113
Addington, Henry 191
Albert, W. 64
America 2, 43, 149, 169
Anderson, B. L., 3
Assize of Bread 11, 15, 16, 39–41, 99–100, 143
Association Movement 71, 84

Bacon, Edward 127
bakers 32, 33, 35, 40, 42, 98, 99–100, 101, 102, 103–04, 113, 122, 126, 128, 140, 147, 157, 158, 167, 175
Barnard Castle (Durham) 49
Best, John 148
Best, William 148
Bick, William 67
Bignell, Richard 110
Birmingham 11, 94, 153
Bohstedt, J. 3, 18, 91, 92, 112, 114, 137
Bossom, Charles 148
Brewer, J. 22, 80
Brickdale, John 98, 109
Bristol 9, 11, 19, 21, 22, 29, 72, 87, 91–114, 115, 122
    Company of Bakers 100–01
    Society of Merchant Venturers 92–93, 99, 101–02
Brown, Henry 149
Burke, P. 57, 58, 67
Burrows, Thomas 150
butchers 19, 106, 108, 130, 145, 152, 154
Bute, Earl of 23, 69, 77, 83
Butskellism 2
Byng, Admiral 22

Captain Slasher 19, 183–85, 189, 192
Carmarthen (Carmarthenshire) 44
carnival 57–61
Carter, James 148
Chandos, Duke of 63
Charles, John 6
Chatham, Earl of 30, 121
Cider Tax 7–8, 17, 20, 23, 69–90

Clapham, J. 15, 40
Clare, Lord 99
Clark, P. 138
Clements, John 97–98
clothiers 14, 134
Clover, John 124, 127, 131
Coates, Robert Trotman 161
Cocks, Reginald 168
Codrington, Sir William 85
Coleridge, S. T. 108
Coles, Isaac 53
Collet, John 15
Colston, Edward 93
Cooke, John 154, 155, 159–60, 161, 162
Cornewall, Velters 89
Cornwall 69, 71
    Padstow 102
Cornwallis, Lord 10, 19, 167, 169, 170–72, 180, 183, 186, 189
Coventry 150
Cox, Thomas 53
Coynham, Lord 174
Cutland, William 153

Dallaway, William 18
Danzig 102
Dashwood, Sir Francis 69, 73–75
Davis, J. 125
dealers 7, 9–10, 12–15, 16, 19, 22, 29, 31–32, 33, 34, 41–42, 43, 66, 70, 75, 86, 104, 105, 109, 110, 112, 116, 124, 125, 131, 139–40, 150, 157, 167, 172, 175, 176–79, 181, 192
Defoe, Daniel 116
de la Fuente, J. 43–44
Denmead, William 53
Derrick, John 53
Devon 28, 38, 69, 72, 73, 91, 109
    Bideford 38
    Cullompton 161
    Exeter 77, 80, 83, 87
    Honiton 88
    Plymouth 71
    South Hams 72

Dillon, Colonel 188
Ditton, J. 125
Dorset 121
Dowdeswell, William 7, 70, 74–75, 85
Drinkwater, John 131, 132
Dudley (Staffordshire) 153
Duff, General 178, 181, 189
Dundas, General 186
Durbin, Stephen 51, 56–58
Durell, Dr 153, 156, 160
Dyke, William 37

Eden, Sir F. M. 8
Elwin, Robert 132
Essex 121

Faringdon (Berkshire) 39–40, 42
farmers 7, 10, 13, 16–17, 20, 21–22, 30,
     32, 33, 35, 36–38, 42, 50–51, 53, 54,
     59, 65, 66, 71, 73, 74, 86, 89, 111,
     112, 155, 159, 165, 167, 174, 175,
     176, 178, 183–85, 192
Faulkner, Samuel 149
Fisher, Reuben 182
fishmongers 19, 106, 108
food riots 17–23, 42, 94, 113
     1753: 18, 27, 94, 97–98, 99
     1757: 35, 99, 146–49, 154
     1766: 14, 17–21, 23, 33, 40, 82, 89, 94,
        99–100, 109, 120–28, 146–49, 154
     1795: 14, 19, 37, 43, 44, 94, 100–04,
        107–08, 110, 152–53, 156–57
     1800–01: 14, 43, 94, 104–05, 107–08,
        110, 153–56, 157–62

Gage, William 108
Gambia 44–45
gentry 16, 22, 39, 52, 54, 61, 63–64, 70,
     74, 76, 85, 89, 103, 113, 118, 129,
     130, 174, 180, 183
Gilmour, I. 112
Gloucestershire 9, 14, 18, 22, 29, 33, 65,
     66, 69, 71, 72, 82, 85, 94, 102
   Cheltenham 12, 77, 82
   Cirencester 23, 29
   Dursley 48
   Forest of Dean 60, 87
   Gloucester 17, 29, 33, 36–37, 38, 48, 67
   Kingswood 18, 20, 48–56, 63, 96, 97,
        98, 99, 105

Lechlade 66, 72
Ross 48
Stonehouse 48
Stow 42
Stroud 48
Stroudwater 77
Tetbury 29, 36, 37
Tewkesbury 16, 29, 30, 33, 34, 37, 41,
     48, 99
Upton on Severn 36
Glynn, Stephen 118
Goodlake, Thomas 39
Gould, Sir Henry 126
Gray, Susannah 153
Green, John 148, 149
Grenville, George 85

Hall, John 127, 131
Hamburg 104
Hampshire 121
Hancock, Alderman 127
Hardwicke, Lord 7, 62–64, 74, 83, 85
Hardwicke, Lord Lieutenant of Ireland
     190
Harrison, G. 28
Harvey, Robert 130, 137
Hearne, Thomas 143
Herefordshire 48, 63, 69, 72, 73, 87
   Hereford 94, 99
   Ledbury 48, 63, 86
   Wilton 29
Hewitt, John 31
Hont, I. 3
Hoppit, J. 8, 26
Houghton, Samuel 132
Howkins, A. 60
Hughes, David 158–59
Hunt, Henry 34–35, 37–38

Ignatieff, M. 3
Ireland 10, 163–93
   Aghern 180
   Antrim 173
   Ballina 179
   Ballinabay 174
   Baltimore 162, 182
   Belfast 165
   Carlow 188
   Carmavy 173
   Carrick-on-Shannon 186

Carrick-on-Suir 182
Castlebar 186
Clonakilty 182
Clonmel 177, 178, 184, 190
Clonmore 186
Connacht 163, 164, 176, 185
Cork 166, 168, 169, 171, 177, 178, 180, 181, 182, 187, 188
Derry 188
Donegal 167
Down 166
Drogheda 168, 169, 173, 175, 176, 177, 180, 181
Dublin 163, 166, 167, 168, 170, 171, 173, 174, 175, 176, 177, 180, 182, 186, 188
Ennis 180
Enniscorthy 179
Galway 174, 188
Kerry 164, 182, 184
Kilcock 187
Kildare 186
Killaloe 176, 182, 183
Killybegs 166
Kinsale 166
Lanesborough 178
Leitrim 178
Lisburn 173
Listowel 169
Limerick 166, 180, 181, 182, 183, 190, 192
Longford 178
Louth 182
Meath 164, 187
Mosstown 187
Mountmelick 187
Munster 19, 183, 185, 189, 190
Navan 174
North Leinster 169
Portarlington 174
rebellion of 1798 163, 179, 189
Roscommon 188
Ross 179
Slane 167, 173, 175
Strangford 166
Tipperary 179, 182, 183, 186, 190
Ulster 169, 173
Waterford 176, 178, 188
Wexford 164

Wicklow 188
Ives, Clement 130

Jack-a-Lent 20, 23, 51, 59–60
Jackson, Cyril 161
Jebb & Co. 10, 167, 175–77, 181
Jenkins, J. 100
John the Painter 93
Johnson, Dr 6–7
Jonassen, F. B. 59
Jones, Thomas 154
Joule, Francis 153

Keily, John 187–88
Kerridge, E. 4
Killala, Bishop of 176
King, John 156
King, P. 125
Knighton of Mosstown 187
Kula, W. 27, 31

labourers 8, 54, 62, 65, 71, 73, 74, 86, 89, 91, 124, 134, 140, 159, 165, 169, 176, 183, 184, 191
landholders 10, 21, 32, 33, 35
Langford, P. 46, 62
Latham, A. J. H. 3
Lay, Charles 128
Linebaugh, P. 26
Liverpool 95, 153
Lloyd, W. F. 142
local authorities 11, 14, 16, 17, 33, 34, 35, 61, 92–93, 116–19, 127, 141, 149–50, 157–58, 160, 177
London 9, 16, 17, 34, 38, 72, 75, 81, 83, 116, 122, 138, 141, 146, 149, 153, 163, 178, 180
Long, David 127, 131
Lubbock, Richard 126

Macfarlane, A. 4
magistrates 16, 34, 39–40, 41, 43, 62, 97, 99, 100, 101, 102, 106–07, 120, 122, 123, 126, 156, 160, 161, 171, 180, 182–83, 187, 189, 190
Maidstone (Kent) 27
Malcolmson, R. 48
Malinowski, B. 43–44
maltsters 35–36, 131, 140
Manchester 91, 114, 134

markets 1–24, 27–45, 71, 80, 92, 94, 95, 96, 100–05, 109–12, 116–17, 122, 124–25, 127, 128, 134, 137, 138–41, 142–45, 146, 149–52, 154–58, 160–62, 163, 166–67, 170, 174–79, 181, 182, 192–93
Marlborough, Duke of 161
Marsh, William 153
Marshall, William 43, 72, 73
McFlynn, F. 68
M'Comas, Andrew 185–86
Medick, H. 8
Merricks, L. 60
Middlesex 131
Milford Haven (Pembrokeshire) 104
military 19, 95, 97, 98, 105–06, 107–08, 124, 179, 182, 186–87, 189–90
millers 27, 35, 36, 66, 103, 123, 140, 172, 175, 192
miners 18, 20, 29, 48–56, 63, 87, 93, 96, 97, 98, 99, 105–06, 107
Money, William 19, 123, 131, 133
Monmouthshire 40
  Monmouth 83, 87, 94, 103
moral economy 4, 9, 17–18, 20, 26, 33, 36, 39, 115, 117, 124–25, 127, 133–34, 137, 142, 156, 163, 185, 192–93
Morris, William 149

Neeson, J. M. 47
Newbury (Berkshire) 95
Newcastle, Duke of 61–65, 83
Nobbs, Henry 128
Noble, John 103, 105
Norfolk 72, 118, 121, 127
  Kings Lynn 122
  Norwich 19, 20–21, 115–35
  Thetford 127
  Wells 121
  Yarmouth 103, 121
Nottingham 112

Ogle, O. 151
O'Gorman, F. 27, 79
Outhwaite, R. B. 143
Oxfordshire 144, 151
  Abingdon 139, 154, 158
  Banbury 29, 150, 154
  Burford 147
  Chipping Norton 149

Deddington 153
Hanney, East 139
Hanney, West 139
Oxford 9, 11, 112, 137–62
Thame 139
Witney 155
Oxford University 11, 141–45, 154–55, 159, 161–62
  Vice-Chancellor 140, 142–43, 147, 148, 150, 153, 155–56, 159–60

Panting, Sarah 148
Parliament 10, 17, 23, 84, 121
  lobbying of 85, 113
  Members of 75, 85, 101, 104
  petitions to 32
Parr, Elizabeth 127
Patteson, John 125, 126
Pearson, G. 125
Perren, R. 6, 7
Perryman, Thomas 53
Peshall, Sir John 143
Pettit, T. 55, 56
Phipps, Job 93
Pierce, Ruth 13
Pitt, John 14, 15, 21, 85
Pollock, John 174
Poole, James 125
Portland, Duke of 103, 106, 155, 156, 158, 160–61
press 21, 42, 81–83, 86, 109–11, 123, 168, 177–78, 181–82
Prior, Mary 141
Prowse, Thomas 67

Randall, A. 125, 134
Roach, John 53
Rockingham, Earl of 121
Rogers, N. 117
Romney, Lord 27
Rooke, James 106–07
Root, H. L. 3–4

Scotland 60
Scott, J. 55, 59
Seal, G. 55, 56
Seed, J. 115
shops 5, 51, 98, 109, 129
Shropshire 43
  Shrewsbury 29, 71, 76

skimmington 60–61
Slack, P. 138
Smith, Adam 1, 3, 4, 10
Smith, Joseph 103
Somerset 23, 29, 50–61, 65, 66, 67, 69,
    72, 85, 94, 111, 112, 113
    Bath 41, 61, 66, 76, 83, 85, 95, 101,
        103, 104
    Bedminster 49, 51, 56
    Bridgwater 94
    Castle Cary 99
    colliers 52–53, 56
    Forest of Braydon 60
    Frome 99
    Glastonbury 42
    Ilminster 83
    Keynsham 101
    Nailsea 51
    Taunton 27, 30, 53, 99, 107, 111
    Wellington 13, 41
    Yeovil 88
Soons, Susan 128
Staffordshire 151
Stevenson, J. 18
Suffolk 121
Surrey 31

Taunton, T. H. 161
Taunton, W. E. 152, 156, 157, 160, 161,
    162
Tawney, Edward 150
textile workers 20, 29, 54, 72, 93, 129,
    130, 168
Thompson, E. P. 9, 18, 21, 24, 55, 64, 68,
    79–80, 137, 142, 145, 161, 179, 180,
    193
Torrington, Viscount 147

tradesmen 18, 97, 98, 103, 111, 126, 139,
    159, 169
turnpikes 6–7, 23, 46–68, 120

United Irishmen (UI) 189–93

Wales 99, 112
Walker, Thomas 152, 157, 161
Walpole, Sir Robert 78
Walters, James 102
Warwickshire 151
weights and measures 8–9, 16, 25–45, 101,
    143
Wesley, John 62
Wickham, William 190–91, 193
Wilkes, John 70, 84
Wilkites 79
Williams, D. E. 3, 18, 120
Willoughby, Sir Christopher 155
Wiltshire 9, 14, 18, 29, 72, 134
    Bradford upon Avon 66
    Devizes 13, 29, 33, 99
    Fisherton 12
    Potterne 13
    Salisbury 12, 22, 33, 37, 53
    Warminster 29, 33, 36
Winchester bushel 8, 17, 26, 28–45
Winter, Justice 180
Wolverhampton 30
Wood, Anthony 138, 142
Woodland, P. 71, 84, 89
Worcestershire 33, 69, 71, 72, 86
    Evesham 94
    Worcester 29, 48, 75, 76, 77, 94, 99
Wyvill, Christopher 84

Yonge, Sir George 88
Yorkshire, West Riding 60
Young, Arthur 126, 143